ISSUE 7

THE
POINT

FALL 2013

TABLE *of* CONTENTS

letter from the editors

essays

symposium: what is marriage for?

reviews

THE EDITORS
Jon Baskin
Jonny Thakkar
Etay Zwick

DESIGN
Marie Otsuka
Etay Zwick

COVER ART
Chicago Lake Front, South Side
Special Collections Research Center,
University of Chicago Library

ART EDITOR
Claire Rabkin

ASSISTANT EDITORS
Charles Comey
Emilie Shumway

EDITORIAL CONSULTANT
Gregory Freeman

COPY EDITORS
John Colin Bradley
J. Michael Eugenio
Lindsay Knight

EDITORIAL BOARD
Danielle Allen
Thomas Bartscherer
J. C. Gabel
Jonathan Lear
Mark Lilla
Martha Nussbaum
Geof Oppenheimer
Robert Pippin
Douglas Seibold
Tom Stern
Ralph Ubl

ADDRESS
The Point
732 S. Financial Place, #704
Chicago, IL 60605

PRINTER
McNaughton & Gunn Inc.
Saline, Michigan

DISTRIBUTOR
Publishers Group West (PGW)

WEBSITE
www.thepointmag.com

LETTER FROM THE EDITORS:
ON SECURITY

The N.S.A. has built an infrastructure that allows it to intercept almost everything. With this capability, the vast majority of human communications are automatically ingested without targeting. If I wanted to see your e-mails or your wife's phone, all I have to do is use intercepts. I can get your e-mails, passwords, phone records, credit cards. I don't want to live in a society that does these sorts of things. ... I do not want to live in a world where everything I do and say is recorded. That is not something I am willing to support or live under.

EDWARD SNOWDEN, N.S.A. WHISTLEBLOWER

He knew in advance what O'Brien would say: that the Party did not seek power for its own ends but only for the good of the majority. ... The terrible thing, thought Winston, the terrible thing was that when O'Brien said this he would believe him. You could see it in his face. O'Brien knew everything. A thousand times better than Winston, he knew what the world was really like.

GEORGE ORWELL, *1984*

I think it's important for everybody to understand, and I think the American people understand, that there are some trade-offs involved. You know, I came in with a healthy skepticism about these programs. My team evaluated them. We scrubbed them thoroughly. We actually expanded some of the oversight, increased some of the safeguards. But my assessment and my team's assessment was that they help us prevent terrorist attacks. And the modest encroachments on privacy that are involved in getting phone numbers or duration without a name attached and not looking at content—that on, you know, net, it was worth us doing. That's—some other folks may have a different assessment of that. But I think it's important to recognize that you can't have a hundred percent security and also then have a hundred percent privacy and zero inconvenience.

PRESIDENT OBAMA

He shall spurn Fate, scorn Death, and bear
His hopes 'bove Wisdom, Grace, and Fear.
And you all know, Security
Is mortals' chiefest Enemy.

WILLIAM SHAKESPEARE, *MACBETH*

There is a massive apparatus within the United States government that with complete secrecy has been building this enormous structure that has only one goal, and that is to destroy privacy and anonymity, not just in the United States but around the world. That is not hyperbole. That is their objective.

GLENN GREENWALD, COLUMNIST

If there is something comforting—religious, if you want—about paranoia, there is still also anti-paranoia, where nothing is connected to anything, a condition not many of us can bear for long. ... Either They have put [Slothrop] here for a reason, or he's just here. He isn't sure that he wouldn't, actually, rather have that reason.

THOMAS PYNCHON, *GRAVITY'S RAINBOW*

We have now arrived at the principal object of the Laws: the care of security. This inestimable good is the distinctive mark of civilization: it is entirely the work of the laws. Without law there is no security; consequently no abundance, nor even certain subsistence. And the only equality which can exist in such a condition, is the equality of misery.

JEREMY BENTHAM, *PRINCIPLES OF THE CIVIL CODE*

For the laws of nature (as justice, equity, modesty, mercy, and, in sum, doing to others as we would be done to) of themselves, without the terror of some power, to cause them to be observed, are contrary to our natural passions, that carry us to partiality, pride, revenge and the like.

THOMAS HOBBES, *LEVIATHAN*

In the last analysis, "love of thy neighbor" is always something secondary, partly conventional and arbitrary—illusory in relation to *fear of the neighbor*. After the structure of society is fixed on the whole and seems secure against external dangers, it is this fear of the neighbor that again creates new perspectives of moral valuation. ... Here, too, fear again is the mother of morals.

FRIEDRICH NIETZSCHE, *BEYOND GOOD AND EVIL*

A person who is not engaged in an unlawful activity and who is attacked in any other place where he or she has a right to be has no duty to retreat and has the right to stand his or her ground and meet force with force, including deadly force if he or she reasonably believes it is necessary to do so to prevent death or great bodily harm to himself or herself or another or to prevent the commission of a forcible felony.

EXCERPT FROM FLORIDA'S STAND YOUR GROUND LAW

Be peaceful, be courteous, obey the law, respect everyone; but if someone puts his hand on you, send him to the cemetery.

MALCOLM X, "MESSAGE TO THE GRASS ROOTS"

You can stand your ground if you're white, and you can use a gun to do it. But if you stand your ground with your fists and you're black, you're dead. In the state of Florida, the season on African-Americans now runs year round. Come one, come all. And bring a handgun. ... One man accosted another and when it became a fist fight, one man—and one man only—had a firearm. The rest is racial rationalization and dishonorable commentary.

DAVID SIMON, CREATOR OF *THE WIRE*

Thus grew up a double system of justice, which erred on the white side by undue leniency and the practical immunity of red-handed criminals, and erred on the black side by undue severity, injustice, and lack of discrimination. ... When, now, the real Negro criminal appeared, and instead of petty stealing and vagrancy we began to have highway robbery, burglary, murder, and rape, there was a curious effect on both sides [of] the color-line: the Negroes refused to believe the evidence of white witnesses or the fairness of white juries, so that the greatest deterrent to crime, the public opinion of one's own social caste, was lost, and the criminal was looked upon as crucified rather than hanged. On the other hand, the whites, used to being careless as to the guilt or innocence of accused Negroes, were swept in moments of passion beyond law, reason, and decency. Such a situation is bound to increase crime, and has increased it.

W. E. B. DU BOIS, *THE SOULS OF BLACK FOLK*

In the case of the American Negro, from the moment you are born every stick and stone, every face, is white. Since you have not yet seen a mirror, you suppose you are, too. It comes as a great shock around the age of 5, 6, or 7 to discover that the flag to which you have pledged allegiance, along with everybody else, has not pledged allegiance to you. It comes as a great shock to see Gary Cooper killing off the Indians, and although you are rooting for Gary Cooper, that the Indians are you.

JAMES BALDWIN, "THE AMERICAN DREAM AND THE AMERICAN NEGRO"

The injustice inherent in the killing of Trayvon Martin by George Zimmerman was not authored by a jury given a weak case. The jury's performance may be the least disturbing aspect of this entire affair. The injustice was authored by a country which has taken as its policy, for the lionshare of its history, to erect a pariah class. The killing of Trayvon Martin by George Zimmerman is not an error in programming. It is the correct result of forces we set in motion years ago and have done very little to arrest.

TA-NEHISI COATES, "TRAYVON MARTIN AND THE IRONY OF AMERICAN JUSTICE"

Listen, I'm going to be honest with you. This is a practice that I engage in every time I am stopped by law enforcement and I've taught this to my son, who is now 33, as part of my duty as a father to ensure that he knows the kind of world in which he's growing up. I take my hat off and my sunglasses off, I put them on the passenger's side. I roll down my window, I take my hands and stick them outside the window and on the door of the driver's side because I want that officer to be as relaxed as he can be when he approaches my vehicle. And I do that because I live in America.

LEVAR BURTON, ACTOR

There are very few African American men in this country who haven't had the experience of being followed when they were shopping in a department store. That includes me. There are very few African American men who haven't had the experience of walking across the street and hearing the locks click on the doors of cars. That happens to me.

PRESIDENT OBAMA

The issue of "law and order" has recently become prominent ... [but] instead of seeking to understand its origin, many radicals—along with most of the liberals—interpret the need for order as incipient fascism. They argue that productive workers are so strongly committed to the existing industrial system that they will gladly opt for fascism to preserve it. ... [T]his view confuse[s] a commitment to order and economic security with a commitment to capitalism as such.

CHRISTOPHER LASCH, THE WORLD OF NATIONS

When we finally achieve the full right of participation in American life, what we make of it will depend upon our sense of cultural values, and our creative use of freedom, not upon our racial identification. I see no reason why the heritage of world culture—which represents a continuum—should be confused with the notion of race. Japan erected a highly efficient modern technology upon a religious culture which viewed the Emperor as a god. The Germany which produced Beethoven and Hegel and Mann turned its science and technology to the monstrous task of genocide; one hopes that when what are known as the "Negro" societies are in full possession of the world's knowledge and in control of their destinies, they will bring to an end all those savageries which for centuries have been committed in the name of race. From what we are now witnessing in certain parts of the world today, however, there is no guarantee that simply being non-white offers any guarantee of this. The demands of state policy are apt to be more influential than morality. I would like to see a qualified Negro as President of the United States. But I suspect that even if this were today possible, the necessities of the office would shape his actions far more than his racial identity.

RALPH ELLISON, SHADOW AND ACT

What constitutes the bulwark of our own liberty and independence? It is not our frowning battlements, our bristling sea coasts, the guns of our war steamers, or the strength of our gallant and disciplined army. These are not our reliance against a resumption of tyranny in our fair land. All of them may be turned against our liberties, without making us stronger or weaker for the struggle. Our reliance is in the love of liberty which God has planted in our bosoms.

ABRAHAM LINCOLN

The thirst for liberty does not seem to be natural to man. Most people want security in this world, not liberty. Liberty puts them on their own, and so exposes them to the natural consequences of their congenital stupidity and incompetence. Historically, it has always been forced upon the masses from above.

H. L. MENCKEN, *MINORITY REPORT*

The friction among men, the inevitable antagonism, which is a mark of even the largest societies and political bodies, is used by Nature as a means to establish a condition of quiet and security. Through war, through the taxing and never-ending accumulation of armament, through the want which any state, even in peacetime, must suffer internally, Nature forces them to make at first inadequate and tentative attempts; finally, after devastations, revolutions, and even complete exhaustion, she brings them to that which reason could have told them at the beginning and with far less sad experience, to wit, to step from the lawless condition of savages into a league of nations.

IMMANUEL KANT, "IDEA FOR A UNIVERSAL HISTORY WITH A COSMOPOLITAN PURPOSE"

"They seem to have things under control," I said.
"Who?"
"Whoever's in charge out there."
"Who's in charge?"
"Never mind."

DON DELILLO, *WHITE NOISE*

Our laws are not generally known; they are kept secret by the small group of nobles who rule us. We are convinced that these ancient laws are scrupulously administered. Nevertheless, it is an extremely painful thing to be ruled by laws that one does not know.

FRANZ KAFKA, "THE PROBLEM OF OUR LAWS"

essays

Alex Arnell, *Maggie with Polkadots*, 2012

*ressentiment

NO SUCH THING?

MARGARET THATCHER AND THE END OF SOCIETY

by Jonny Thakkar

WHEN MARGARET THATCHER died on April 8th of this year, my Facebook friends reacted with glee. Several posted a Glenn Greenwald article saying we should feel free to speak ill of the dead. Others rejoiced in a campaign to take "Ding Dong The Witch Is Dead" to number one in the UK charts (it made #2). Being both an expatriate and an academic, I often look upon British news with a certain degree of befuddled bemusement; questions such as whether Cornish pasties count as hot foods for tax purposes seem to lose their urgency when one spends one's life across the Atlantic reading Plato. But Thatcher's death was hard to ignore, and my friends' posts pricked something in me. Greenwald was right that it can be dangerous to allow political figures to become sanctified—as he observed, the bizarre fascination of American neoconservatives with Winston Churchill seems to have shaped their post-9/11 hysteria—and that insight would certainly have been worth sharing in the pages of the *Telegraph* or the *Mail*. But were *Guardian* readers, or any of my friends for that matter, seriously in any danger of idealizing Thatcher? It didn't seem likely. In left-wing circles Thatcher enjoys a level of prestige somewhere above Hitler but below Mussolini. What people like us needed to hear, it seemed to me, was precisely the opposite of what Greenwald said: that we should *refrain* from dancing on Thatcher's grave. From the perspective of a Plato or a Socrates, the first law of living well is to examine your own beliefs and way of life at every opportunity. By allowing a full human being to finally come into view, the passing of a once-hated political figure can occasion just such an examination. Interpreting an opponent's actions charitably can be hard, painful even. But it permits political life to disclose itself as the essentially tragic space that it really is, a space in which pursuing one value most often entails suppressing another. And in that light self-aggrandizement and demonization come to look like two

13

sides of the same coin, both symptoms of our anxiety in the face of this troubling complexity. To sympathize with the other is, in the end, to sympathize with ourselves.

WHY DID WE hate Thatcher so much, my friends and I? She was eminently detestable, there's no denying that. She gutted local democracy while claiming to be against big government; she fought inflation by deliberately running up unemployment; she labeled miners resisting the destruction of their livelihood "the enemy within"; she even managed to call Nelson Mandela a terrorist. And then there was her general bearing, which bespoke the strained snobbery of a lower-middle-class girl who had acquired a place at the top table and an accent to go with it and who now looked down her nose at those who hadn't. For Brits ashamed of their class structures, as all should be, Thatcher's whole manner was traumatic. She seemed to relish class warfare and to embody it. Even if she tried her damnedest to replace a system based on birth and schooling with one based on individual achievement, her apparent contempt for life's losers was if anything more galling than the old prejudices, and not only because the two systems seemed to map onto one another rather too neatly. The following story is most likely apocryphal but it's no surprise it stuck: at a private fundraiser in the Eighties, Thatcher is said to have declared that "a man who, beyond the age of 26, finds himself on a bus can count himself a failure." Mitt Romney had nothing on that.

We had reason to hate her, right enough. But whence the intensity of our feelings for Thatcher? Whence the ongoing passion, more than 23 years after she was forced from office?

Some of it is personal, it has to be said. The most compelling reflection I found on Thatcher's death came from Russell Brand, surprisingly, writing in the *Huffington Post*. Brand certainly came to bury Thatcher, not to praise her—"Her death must be sad for the handful of people she was nice to and the rich people who got richer under her stewardship. It isn't sad for anyone else"—but what really drove the piece were his ruminations on growing up during her reign. His description of Thatcher's voice, "a bellicose yawn, somehow both boring and boring—I could ignore the content but the intent drilled its way in," captured the feeling of listening to her better than anything else I read, and the memoir was sprinkled with comic gold:

As I scan the statements of my memory bank for early deposits (it'd be a kid's memory bank at a neurological Nat West where you're encouraged to become a greedy little capitalist with an escalating family of porcelain pigs) I see her in her hairy helmet, condescending on Nationwide, eviscerating eunuch MPs and baffled BBC fuddy duddies with her General Zodd stare and coldly condemning the IRA...

But there's a serious point in there too. In raging against Thatcher, our generation is, among other things, raging against the forces that shaped us—but rage as we might, they did still shape us, and they continue to do so. Brand himself is a case in point, as he well knows: he can lament the neoliberal erosion of the "unseen bond" of community all he wants, but at the end of the day he's not exactly Mother Teresa. He admits to feeling nostalgia for the Thatcher years, bound up as they are with his childhood, yet "what is more troubling," he owns, "is my inability to ascertain where my own selfishness ends and [Thatcher's] neoliberal inculcation begins."

Might something similar be true for all of us who grew up in the neoliberal era? If so, might not our loathing of Thatcher—or its positive correlate, our longing for the primordial community she supposedly shattered—be rooted in anxieties about our own moral stature? It certainly rings true of me; I am, undeniably, one of Thatcher's *inheritors*. The bequest began in an oddly symbolic way: when I was seven or so, the other kids used to call me Thatcher on account of the similarity in our surnames (better that, admittedly, than a subsequent sobriquet that began with "f" and rhymed with "sucker"). Later on, in the complacent, pre-post-imperial environment of an elite boarding school, I came to rebel against the whole of Torydom; by blood I'm half-Indian and a quarter Irish and as a thirteen year-old I was sure that gave me the nobility of the oppressed. But it's hard to maintain your victim status when you're on your way "up" to Oxford, and although many do seem to pull it off I wasn't equal to the challenge. As I gradually realized that I was and probably always would be on the winning side of Thatcher's great divide, I came to feel complicit in the cruelty of her supposed meritocracy. Privilege may not have been a gift that I ever asked for, but it was a gift I would receive nonetheless. Just as my younger self used to bristle at the accusation that I was spoiled, unanswerable as it was, so my eyes still water at Billy Bragg's reproach to Thatcher and her plummy progeny: "Just because you're going forwards / Doesn't mean I'm going backwards / Just because you're better than me / Doesn't mean I'm lazy."

THE CONDITION OF being unable to respond, of being lost for words, or arguments, is perhaps especially traumatic in politics, where self-identification and self-justification are almost the same thing. So traumatic, in fact, that we tend to hide it from ourselves—but in others we can see it clearly.

I recently engaged in a deal with a right-wing American friend whereby each of us had to subscribe to a magazine from "the other side"; for me he chose *First Things*, a journal of Catholic thought devoted to something like "keeping religion in the public square." The magazine is basically pretty good, if somewhat predictable, and it's been well worth reading for an atheist like myself—but if there's one thing in God's creation the writers simply refuse to contemplate, it's how their opponents understand themselves. They consistently portray liberals as wanting to drive religion out of the public realm in order to undermine practice and belief and make way for some kind of hedonistic utopia. This may be true of some liberals. But in America the best and most influential arguments for religiously neutral public discourse have come from so-called "political liberals," like John Rawls, who actually take themselves to be *defending* religion. Only by remaining as neutral as possible with respect to religion, so the argument goes, can the state accord individual conscience, and hence religious belief, the respect it deserves. *First Things* writers never really take that argument on; they simply ignore it and bash the hedonists instead.

Let's assume, though, for the sake of argument, that political liberalism does in fact end up contributing to the secularization of public life; maybe citizens are more likely to maintain their faith if a religious worldview is taken for granted on public radio and so on. To someone like Rawls that will no doubt seem like an unfortunate side effect of his theory; to *First Things*, it will seem to have been the goal all along. Of course, the fact that you never intended something doesn't always excuse you for doing it—it just changes the nature of the culpability. Every point of view has its blind spots, and their location is always revealing; even if a general can never exactly foresee collateral damage, the rate of civilian casualties always says something about his priorities. But this is where it gets complicated. For what if you hate the side effects but have no alternative to the way of thinking that produces them?

It would be easier if your opponents were in power, especially if they didn't seem to care all that much about the collateral damage. That way you could blame them without having to account for your own position. If your own side were on top it would be much tougher, psychologically speaking. You would then be the ones producing the side effects you despise, and in principle you would have to be ashamed of yourselves. In practice, however, there is always one get-out: you can simply deny that you *are* in power.

The *First Things* crew have this technique down to a tee. If they're honest, they probably agree with the vast majority of what political liberalism has to say about toleration, devoted as they are to the image of America as a haven from religious oppression—had the 2012 election resulted in Mormonism being preached from the presidential pulpit, they would have been as horrified as the rest of us. What allows them to have their cake and eat it too is their ability to attribute the side effects of the liberal system of thought—their own system of thought—to godless elites who surreptitiously commandeered the country sometime during the Sixties, the Depression or the Civil War. This is quite a feat of self-delusion, and it must take its toll on the psyche: to sustain such a fantasy, after all, you have to both demonize and aggrandize your opponents, and do so continually, in the face of reality, without end.

What does any of this have to do with Thatcher? Well, one of the greatest mysteries of the last three decades has been why leftist parties, so quick to criticize neoliberal policies in opposition, have consistently pursued them once in power. Since 1979, when Thatcher was first elected, almost all Western governments, left and right, have, to greater or lesser degrees, privatized public services and utilities while lowering taxes on corporate and individual incomes; inequality has risen inexorably; and the common perception is that citizens have become more consumerist and individualistic. In coming to terms with the failure of their elected representatives to arrest these trends, leftists have tended to cry corruption or cowardice; but the phenomena in question are too universal to be explained by personal vice alone. Either politics in general is just a cynical masquerade conducted by the rich and for the rich—a tempting explanation, to be sure—or there is something about the contemporary situation that makes it virtually impossible to resist neoliberalism. There must be various factors at work, but one of them is surely the absence of a compelling counter-ideal to neoliberalism in recent leftist thought. In the last three decades intellectuals and activists have mostly directed their attention towards foreign policy, climate change or identity politics rather than economic questions; when they have engaged directly with neoliberalism, it has typically been to offer what should technically be called *conservative* complaints, seeking to slow or reverse change rather than to suggest any new direction or ideal. And this, it seems to me, is because with respect to what we take to be our signature issue, economic equality, we have found ourselves in a similar position to *First Things*.

Economists of all stripes agree that the underlying cause of growing inequality in Western societies is the integration of the global economy, which has simultaneously increased the earning power of the highly educated while decreasing that of the rest. At the top end, HSBC can proclaim itself the world's

Chris Beckett, *I Still Hate Margaret Thatcher*, 2013

local bank; at the bottom end, unskilled labor cannot compete abroad. Even if neoliberal tax cuts and privatizations have exacerbated the problem, they are by no means its source. This leaves leftist politicians, most of whom understand these facts perfectly well, in the depressing position of having to hold neoliberals to account for crimes against equality while having no idea how to avoid such crimes themselves. In such circumstances the only way to keep your hands clean is to stay out of politics altogether; that allows you to blame the whole thing on the political and financial elites who are *really in charge*, as per Occupy Wall Street. But the position of disdainful superiority is itself unstable. If millionaires on Wall Street are immoral for not wanting to give more of their wealth to the unemployed of Detroit, how can any of us justify not giving more of our own riches—for such they surely are—to the starving of Africa? And although globalization may produce rising inequality within Western societies as a side effect, wouldn't protectionism harm the poor in the developing world? Insofar as economic inequality is the left's principal field of battle in contemporary political life, the fact is that it has no real response to neoliberalism. Idealists without an ideal, moralists without morals, to be on the left today is frequently to be both helpless and hypocritical. Faced with such a predicament, hating Thatcher is the easy part.

Plato was very attuned to this kind of situation. One of the recurring themes of his dialogues is how angry people get when they realize their inconsistencies, or rather in the moments just before the fact of their inconsistency rises to the surface of their consciousness, as their self-image, their sense of what is due to them, begins to be squeezed by the pressures of reality. But Plato thought such humiliation was the precondition for arriving at wisdom, and I think he was right.

"THERE IS NO such thing as society," Thatcher infamously remarked.
Coming across this statement for the first time it feels like you've discovered the secret memo that explains everything, as if Thatcher were a Bond villain who just couldn't resist explaining her entire evil scheme before enacting it. A common way of summing up Thatcher's legacy, exemplified in Pankaj Mishra's pronouncement that the London rioters of 2011 were "Thatcher's grandchildren," is that her policies and attitudes rendered Britons more individualistic and self-seeking. Russell Brand, who considers himself one of Thatcher's *children*, remembers being implicitly taught "that it is good to be selfish, that other people's pain is not your problem, that pain is in fact a weakness and suffering is

deserved and shameful." And the evidence that both Mishra and Brand adduce for the idea that Thatcher wanted to impart such a lesson, the shorthand for it, is that she said "there is no such thing as society." The phrase is weirdly enigmatic, in and of itself; it rings of Yoda. Brand glosses it as "we are alone on our journey through life, solitary atoms of consciousness," as if Thatcher believed friendship or community impossible, and something of that interpretation is manifest in the way the phrase gets used as a trump card against neoliberalism from pubs to parliament. When David Cameron decided to name his political philosophy "Big Society" conservatism, for instance, no one doubted that he wanted to signal a move away from Thatcherism. "There is no such thing as society" has become a political Chernobyl.

Yet the phrase contains an important insight, I believe—one that might actually guide today's left. When you go back and look at the 1987 interview in which the phrase was uttered, it's obvious that Thatcher had no intention of glorifying selfishness.

> I think we have been through a period when too many people have been given to understand that when they have a problem it is government's job to cope with it. "I have a problem, I'll get a grant. I'm homeless, the government must house me." They are casting their problems on society. And you know, there is no such thing as society. There are individual men and women and there are families. And no governments can do anything except through people, and people must look to themselves first. It is our duty to look after ourselves and then, also, to look after our neighbors.

> There is no such thing as society. There is a living tapestry of men and women and people and the beauty of that tapestry and the quality of our lives will depend upon how much each of us is prepared to take responsibility for ourselves and how much each of us is prepared to turn round and help by our own efforts those who are unfortunate.

Once we've stripped away the ugly layer of contempt in which Thatcher encloses her remarks—"I'm homeless, the government must house me"—something rather surprising emerges. For the central idea here, it seems to me, is not that there can never be any community between humans, nor that nothing can ever merit the name "society," but that community and society don't simply exist out there regardless of what we do; each of us, rich and poor, has to take responsibility for producing them. "There is no such thing as society" is a peculiar way of saying that, for sure, but then great rhetoric is often counterintuitive.

Plato is not a name one associates with Thatcher, to put it mildly, but he would have agreed with her on that point: there is no such thing as society—at least not at present. He thought of true society as an ideal, a goal, an aspiration; something that can be achieved but never assumed. Among the many topics addressed in the *Republic*, his masterpiece, is the question of what a true society would be like. To answer that question, he suggests that we need to think about why societies come into existence.

> A society comes to exist ... because none of us is individually self-sufficient, but each has many needs he cannot satisfy. ... Because we have many needs, and because one of us calls on another out of need, and on a third out of a different need, we gather many into a single settlement as partners and helpers. And we call such a shared settlement a society.

The origin of society, then, its "real creator," is our need. Society comes into existence because we cannot satisfy our needs on our own; to do so, we have to contribute our laboring energies to the collective enterprise that is society. What society *is*, at the most fundamental level, is a cooperative scheme born of individual weakness. And the form of that scheme will determine not only the type of society we have but also the degree to which it counts as a genuine society at all.

But what are our needs, exactly? Thatcher seems to picture individuals as relatively self-sufficient. To succeed, in her view, is "to look after ourselves and then, also, to look after our neighbors," which presupposes that we can separate looking after ourselves from looking after our neighbors. Plato, by contrast, views us as *fundamentally* social creatures, relying on each other for even our most basic needs. He is clearly right that we need to share to survive. The more complex society becomes, the less likely we are to see this. But when you think about a simple society, like the one Plato has us imagine, it becomes obvious: if we each had to make our own shoes, clothes and houses we would have little time to do the farming. We depend absolutely on the division of labor.

Where Plato becomes radical, though, is in his view that we depend on the division of labor not only for our continued existence but also for our ultimate happiness. Nowadays we tend to think of our life prospects as relatively independent of one another, and that's what Thatcher assumes as well. But Plato thinks we sink or swim together. No one can be happy if his desires are not sound, his capacities developed and his opportunities felicitous; and our desires, capacities and opportunities are shaped by the people and institutions around us. In a bad society we can always hide ourselves away, but this will never shield us completely. In Book VI of the *Republic*, Socrates advises us to avoid political life in an unjust society, "like someone who takes refuge under a little wall from a storm of dust or hail driven by the wind." In Book VIII, however, he returns to this quietist, depicting him as a tragically impotent father, incapable of teaching his son to live well in the face of outside influences. We are all, in some sense, each other's parents. The ultimate goal of our social cooperation is therefore to create an environment in which virtue, and hence the possibility of happiness, can be reliably fostered. That would be a true society.

On Plato's view, then, society is a collective project aimed at securing the good life. It is as if we find ourselves thrust together with no option but to work as a team, at least if we are to survive and to prosper. But if the team is to function properly, each of us needs to *play for the team*. This is less a matter of fuzzy altruism—Socrates emphasizes that "if [citizens] share things with one another ... they do so because each believes that this is better for himself"—than of having the discipline to carry out a particular role. Think of soccer. Defenders need to stick to their positions, and not wander around in search of excitement. If each player simply follows the ball (as often happens in pick-up games) there really *is* no team. Likewise with society: if everyone does his own job, and the jobs combine appropriately so that each contributes to the collective good, there will be a functioning society. If not, there will be no such thing.

CONTINENTAL EUROPEANS TEND to drop the "neo" in "neoliberalism"—to them it is simply "liberalism." And from a Platonic perspective that's just about right. Where economic life is concerned, the contemporary political scene is split between *left-liberals* and *right-liberals*. What they have in common is an unwillingness to say anything about the goals of work. Provided they commit no crimes, how citizens choose to spend their laboring energies is seen as a private matter. What then comes up for debate is what to do with the proceeds: whether to force citizens to contribute to public goods such as infrastructure and education, for instance, or to improve the welfare of the poorest. In the Platonic view, however, all such debates are secondary to the question economic liberals invariably suppress: What do we actually do with our work?

If not all "societies" are real societies on Plato's account, then not all "jobs" are real jobs either. A hermit has work to do, but no job. Jobs exist only where there is a division of labor: you peel the carrots, I'll peel the potatoes. A division of labor in turn presupposes a collective enterprise, like an evening meal, towards which the various jobs aim, and in terms of which we understand what counts as a genuine job. For Plato, as we have seen, the goal of a society's labor is first to maintain that society in existence, and then to enable each citizen to lead the best life he can. And these goals determine what counts as a real job. Just as checking your email plays no part in preparing dinner, so blackmail doesn't contribute to a good society. Real jobs, by contrast, are *crafts*, skilled activities directed towards producing particular social goods; medicine, for example, is the craft that restores sick bodies to health. In a genuine society, Plato thinks, everyone—shoemakers and shepherds, soldiers and statesmen—will be a craftsman in this sense. But the statesman's craft is peculiar, since he is the one who regulates the other crafts to make sure they are really directed towards the social good. To return to the team analogy, the statesman is like a soccer manager, deciding which functions need to be carried out in a given situation: sometimes even the goalkeeper has to join the attack. The job of the statesman, then, is to decide what counts as a real job. He is a "philosopher-king."

Talk of "philosopher-kings" sounds far-fetched and utopian to the contemporary ear—yet Plato's vision of society as a team of craftsmen regulated by a master craftsman passed, partly through the influence of his pupil Aristotle, into the basic legal structures of medieval Europe. The idea of labor as teamwork aiming at the common good, rather than at one's own immediate gain, complemented the thought of the Christian Fathers: Christ had despised the rich; for Paul avarice was "the root of all evil"; and Augustine had seen lust for possessions as one of the three principal sins of fallen man. The medieval Church therefore held up an ideal—often flouted in practice, but an ideal nonetheless—of economic activity as subordinate to moral purposes. William of Auxerre, a thirteenth-century monk, was typical, for example, in arguing that private property was to be suspended in times of need, or that a contract resulting from unequal bargaining power was necessarily invalid. The central doctrine was perhaps that of the "just price," propounded in the second half of the thirteenth century by Albert the Great and Thomas Aquinas. Albert and Thomas argued that one ought always to sell an article for its true worth (understood primarily in terms of the labor required to produce it) rather than for the highest price the market will bear. If one village were struck by a crop failure, for example, the next village should not seek to profit by raising the price of their wheat. As Aquinas put it,

> if someone would be greatly helped by something belonging to someone else, and the seller not similarly harmed by losing it, the seller must not raise the price, because the benefit that goes to the buyer comes not from the seller, but from the buyer's needy condition: no one ought to sell something that doesn't belong to him.

Given human fallenness, however, this doctrine had to be inculcated by law and habit rather than mere preaching. It was therefore up to public officials to determine prices, wrote Henry of Langenstein in 1483, since "to leave the prices of goods at the discretion of the sellers is to give rein to the cupidity which goads almost all of them to seek excessive gain."

When put into practice, then, Plato's economic thought quickly led to what we would now call *socialism*. The label seems perverse at first, since we tend to think of socialism as aiming at equality, whereas the largesse of the medieval Church was legendary and monks proved only too happy to sustain the feudal hierarchies at whose summit they naturally imagined themselves seated. But what else to call the price controls, limits on private property and so on that were instituted in the Middle Ages? Better to think of socialism as having a core sense beyond its more recent egalitarian incarnation—Plato's vision of society as an ideal, not a given, something that has to be continually created by citizens working towards the common good. With Plato, in other words, we can put the social back into socialism.

TODAY'S ECONOMISTS WOULD probably dismiss medieval strictures on price and property as primitive misunderstandings, much as they now view twentieth-century command economies with more contempt than alarm—the first chapter of the most widely used textbook, Hal Varian's *Intermediate Microeconomics*, consists of a simple demonstration of why an economy with price controls will necessarily allocate goods and services inefficiently. But the sophistication of contemporary economics, unquestionable though it is, risks blinding us to the fact that its medieval ancestor was barely concerned with efficiency at all. It was a branch of ethics. Citizens had a *duty* to work for the common good, and it was taken for granted that the purpose of economic regulation was to ensure this duty was performed. If the ethics-first approach to economics has come to seem absurd to us today—if right- and left-liberalism seem like the only live possibilities—then that represents an intellectual revolution. And much of the credit must go to one man: Adam Smith.

Most institutions try to socialize us out of egoism; even competitive sports attempt to engender—or at least enforce—values and habits that place the survival of institutions above individual success. Smith argued that the economy should be an exception to this rule, a self-standing sphere with rules and norms that contradict those of society at large. Bernard Mandeville, a Dutch doctor living in London in the early eighteenth century, had argued in his *Fable of the Bees* that a sufficiently artful politician could transform private vices, like the desire for luxury, into public benefits. Smith took up this line of thinking but freed it from its moralistic premise and its reliance on individual dexterity. Replacing "vice" with "interest," he argued that given appropriate institutional frameworks the general welfare would be best served if everyone pursued his own private interest in economic matters.

> By directing domestic industry in such a manner as its produce may be of the greatest value, [a businessman] intends only his own gain, and he is in this, as in many other cases, led by an invisible hand to promote an end which was no part of his intention. Nor is it always the worse for the society that it was no part of it. By pursuing his own interest he frequently promotes that of the society more effectually than when he really intends to promote it. I have never known much good done by those who affected to trade for the public good.

To pursue one's own interest in economic affairs is not only acceptable, on Smith's view, but noble. Whereas those who try to work for the public good end up being ineffectual, in a competitive marketplace those who serve themselves will inevitably end up serving others. If people want a given good, there will be an incentive to produce it; if they don't, there won't. "It is not from the benevolence of the butcher, the brewer, or the baker, that we expect our dinner, but from their regard to their own self-interest," Smith writes. "We address ourselves, not to their humanity but to their self-love, and never talk to them of our own necessities but of their own advantages." Self-love or self-interest, greed or avarice—call it what you will, the invisible hand promises to wash it clean.

Smith does not think we should always act selfishly, of course, or even that we do. If there is to be any kind of stable social order we must forbear from harming others; this is what Smith calls justice. More than that, we all have a natural interest in the plight of the badly off; this is what he calls charity. But what shapes today's economic thinking is not these nuances but Smith's central proposition, which is that in a competitive marketplace egoistic economic agents will raise productivity and thereby create a "universal opulence which extends itself to the lowest ranks of the people." Whatever our highest ends are, from alleviating misery to building opera houses in the jungle, wealth can only serve them. And if the opulence should turn out to be less than universal, well, we can always redistribute—whether through private philanthropy, as right-liberals recommend, or the state, as do left-liberals.

This way of thinking forms the unspoken background of Thatcher's "there is no such thing as society" interview. It's a vision of small shopkeepers like

Thatcher's father, living in small market towns like Grantham, where she was raised, pulling themselves up by their bootstraps and encouraging others to do the same. "It is our duty to look after ourselves and then, also, to look after our neighbors." There's no room for large-scale capitalists or global corporations in this idealized marketplace of butchers and brewers and bakers, as liberals would happily point out. But there's also no place for the idea of work in Plato's sense—and that is an objection that tends to pass liberals by completely.

I MAGINE A DEBATE between Smith and Plato today; ignore the anachronism, if you can. Plato would argue that the tradesmen Smith mentions in his famous example are not butchers, brewers or bakers at all, but what he calls "moneymakers"—they are guided by profit, not product. As such, he would claim, they will never create a genuine society.

In Book I of the *Republic*, Socrates insists that strictly speaking a doctor (and by extension any craftsman) must be distinguished from a moneymaker. Doctors do make money, of course, but Plato's point is that anything that counts as one activity will be governed by a single organizing principle, something that gives unity to all the sub-activities, and that for a true doctor this will be healing the sick. The true doctor still earns money, but since this is not the goal in reference to which he makes his professional decisions he should not be called a moneymaker; it is incidental to his activity that he earns money, whereas it is essential to it that he treats the sick. Imagine, on the other hand, a "doctor" who treats the sick with one thing in mind: earning money. Plato would say that this man *masquerades* as a doctor.

Smith would see no problem with that. After all, both doctors and "doctors" heal the sick. In a system where the incentives are correctly aligned, such as a competitive marketplace with perfect information, it should make no difference to a patient whether or not he is treated by a true doctor. But Plato might ask what happens if the incentives come apart. Imagine, for example, a country—let's call it America—where psychiatrists find they can make more money prescribing drugs than offering talking cures.* Some psychiatrists believe that drugs are more effective than talk; imagine one who doesn't. This doctor really believes the best treatment he can give involves personal contact for sessions of 45 minutes or more, but knows he can earn almost twice as much by

---

* See, e.g., "Talk Doesn't Pay, So Psychiatry Turns Instead To Drug Therapy," *New York Times*, March 5, 2011.

scheduling three 15-minute sessions for dispensing medication. All other things being equal, a true doctor will make a decision based on his patient's needs; a moneymaker will simply prescribe drugs. And since similar decisions are made every day in countless hospitals and clinics, it will matter a great deal whether a society has doctors or "doctors."

Since society is itself created and sustained only by the work its members perform on its behalf, like a team in which everyone has a role to play, Plato would also, as we have seen, distinguish between a society and a "society." If every citizen carries out his social work to the best of his ability, there will be a real society. But if each worker is a moneymaker who performs his role only incidentally, when the incentives happen to be correctly aligned, then society will be nothing but an incidental byproduct of moneymaking. It will be a "society" rather than a true society. So what?—Smith might once again ask—we each get to do what we want, productivity is raised to unprecedented levels, and as a "collateral benefit" we produce something that to all intents and purposes looks like a society! Would you really rather live in the Middle Ages, toothache and all?

Wealth without virtue may indeed be pointless, as Socrates says in the *Apology*, but this rejoinder is unlikely to carry much weight in contemporary debate, however justified it might be in the abstract. As Deirdre McCloskey observes in *Bourgeois Dignity*, living standards have shot up since moneymaking began to be perceived as a respectable activity: in 1800 the global average income was just $3 a day (in today's money); now it is $30, and in Norway it is as high as $137. Smith was right about productivity, essentially, and it's hard to see many of us choosing to swap its benefits for the rigors of virtue. As Thatcher used to enjoy repeating when pushed to defend neoliberalism, "There Is No Alternative."

Checkmate? Not necessarily. For even if Plato were forced to accept that labor should be allocated via the market and its price signals rather than conscious reflection on society's needs, he might still ask how we as individuals are to understand our roles in this system. Consider this reformulation of Smith's argument by Thatcher's intellectual hero, Friedrich Hayek:

> Profit is the signal which tells us what we must do in order to serve people whom we do not know. By pursuing profit, we are as altruistic as we can possibly be, because we extend our concern to people who are beyond our range of personal conception.

This is polemical of course—neither Smith nor his followers need say anything so extreme. But what it brings to the fore is the first-personal dimension of our debate. Should we respond to price signals *in order to serve others*? Or should we simply seek profit full stop? Do we consider ourselves as craftsmen or as moneymakers? Sometimes it is obvious that pursuing profit won't benefit others. The social function of financiers, we are sometimes told, is to ensure the efficient allocation of capital across society so as to spur economic growth. But suppose that for some reason or other the financial system actually rewards speculation that does *not* fulfill this function, speculation that actually *lowers* economic growth in the long run, and imagine—if you can—that our men of finance just happen to be moneymakers at heart...

PLATO THOUGHT HE could rely on a class of philosopher-kings whose craft would be to ensure that each part of society carried out a genuine job. But in *The Road to Serfdom*—a book that shaped Thatcher's ideology from her days as an undergraduate at Oxford—Hayek pointed out that a decentralized market economy will allocate social resources far more effectively than a team of experts ever could, since the price system instantaneously collates information about local conditions and needs. Besides, Hayek and other liberals argued, citizens tend to disagree about what is good for society or the individual, and hardly anyone still believes, as Plato did, that there is expert knowledge to be had about such matters. The basic tenet of social liberalism, that the state should not impose a vision of the good on individuals, is justified both in theory and in practice. Being able to shape your own course in life is a prerequisite for that life to be worth living; and experience shows that a society that does not respect individual freedoms will end in oppression. There is no way around liberalism.

The temptation is for socialists to repress the fact of liberalism, to blame elites for refusing to give economic life more ethical direction, and to cocoon themselves in hermetic discussions that pretend a top-down approach were still possible—to become, in short, the mirror image of the Catholics at *First Things*. Such escapism might well have its pleasures, but it also has its pains, not least psychically. And in any case there is no need: for economic Platonism is in fact compatible with social liberalism.

Socialists cannot force citizens to be craftsmen, true. Nor can they dictate a vision of the good life. But the state can legitimately encourage citizens to work according to their *own* conceptions of the good life. Just as it is a citizenly duty to look after the physical environment, throwing away litter, placing items in the right receptacles and so on, a duty that is promulgated but not enforced by the state, so it should be considered a citizenly duty to look after the social environment: to play one's part in producing the kind of institutions and goods that enable us all to flourish—not least our children, whom no parent, no matter how privileged he be as an individual, can isolate from society's influence. Granted, we may have different understandings of what would constitute a good environment and what would count as a contribution towards it. But within the framework of a liberal state, where no one forces anyone else to pursue a given way of life, we can live with that. This is socialism from the ground up.

The state must provide more than moral support, however, if such socialism is to become a reality. Imagine a stereotypical movie scene with an idealized worker—a fireman, say—nobly ignoring his own well-being for the sake of the common good and steadfastly refusing all congratulations: "I'm just doing my job," he says. Now imagine a real-life patient protesting to his psychiatrist that no, something really important has come up in the last few days and he just has to talk it over; the psychiatrist responds that he only has fifteen minutes to review the prescription; the patient gets angry and starts shouting; the psychiatrist tries to calm him down by saying, "Look, I'm just doing my job, alright?" What the phrase typically means in real life, in other words, is: "Leave me alone—it's not up to me." The psychiatrist might actually want to be a true doctor, yet be constrained to be a "doctor" by the insurers who pay his wage and the bankers who hold his student debt. To turn "doctors" into doctors will therefore require more than a change in their personal priorities; it will require changing the priorities of their institutions.

And this brings us back to the question that socialism has always raised, from the Middle Ages to the twentieth century, namely ownership. Businesses tend to serve the interests of those who own them, whether shareholders, workers or communities. To make institutions serve people rather than profit, we will therefore have to think about alternative forms of ownership: scholars like Erik Olin Wright and John Roemer have shown that social ownership can come in many forms, and these should be studied with an open mind.* What is vital, however, as we renew our assault on the neoliberal dogma of private ownership, is to remember that the ultimate goal is not to strengthen the central state or even simply to benefit the poor, but rather to free workers to use their own initiative to serve the common good as they see it.

---

* See Erik Olin Wright's contribution to *The Point*'s Issue 5 symposium on the left, "Toward A Social Socialism."

WHEN I THINK of Thatcher and the rage she induces in me and my friends, I can't help feeling that at the end of the day it's all quite simple: she won. In the face of her onslaught our arguments about equality feel abstract and phony. We know that we don't want too much inequality, but how much is too much? And what are we going to do about it? G. A. Cohen pointed out that if you really believe in redistribution, you don't have to wait for the right government to get elected—you can start giving your money away this minute. His book was entitled *If You're An Egalitarian, How Come You're So Rich?* but the principle applies to most of us, especially when you start thinking on an international scale. However just the idea of worldwide redistribution may be in theory, few of us are principled enough to really countenance it. And we know that. Our accusations and our insults therefore sound shrill and frail. Lacking an ideal towards which to work, we are impotent and reactive—we can reject but we cannot affirm.

Nowhere is this more evident than in the matter of career decisions. We—my circle, at any rate—tend to despise those who take the "easy option" of corporate labor. As opposed to what, though? It seems to me that to earn a free pass from today's moralizers all you need to do is not sell out. It's considered absolutely fine, for instance, to while away your twenties in grad school playing video games, watching reality TV and occasionally turning your thoughts to the writings of some obscure author. A life like that actually gives you some kind of moral purchase vis-à-vis a banker or a lawyer—at least you're not increasing inequality. Even if we ignore the fact that a disdain for materialism has often been a marker of class distinction, it's clear that there's something fundamentally warped about this ethic. It tells us what is bad, but as to the good it is silent.

If leftists are to look neoliberals in the face with confidence rather than bitterness, we need an ideal that can orient us. Is Platonic socialism too distant to serve? I don't see why it should be. It gives us an overarching logic for resisting the march towards privatization, for one thing, above and beyond outrage at the corruption and incompetence that inevitably accompany such schemes; and it gives new focus to campaigns against personal debt. More than that, though, it gives us something to live by as individuals. For one way to bring about an ideal is to act as if it already existed. And in a service economy you can very easily ask yourself what service your work actually performs. Does it count as a *job* in the Platonic sense, a contribution to the collective enterprise of society as you see it? To be a craftsman you don't have to be a saint, running a soup kitchen or helping little old ladies with their shopping. But it might be hard, for example, to combine tutoring rich kids for their SATs with holding others in contempt for selling out, as so many twenty-somethings try to. For Platonic socialism demands that you provide some account of how your work might help constitute a healthy social environment. You can always refuse that demand, of course, but you thereby accept Thatcher's bequest, however implicitly, and take your place in the neoliberal family alongside the bankers and the rest.

If, on the other hand, you do try to direct your labors towards producing a slice, no matter how small, of the common good, to make your product the best it can be while charging only as much as you consider fair—if you do all this you may end up contributing to the creation of a genuine society. Yet your work need not be in vain even if that larger goal remains unmet. "The highest reward for a man's toil is not what he gets for it but what he becomes by it," John Ruskin is supposed to have said, and Plato would certainly have agreed. In any case, however, society, like a team, is not an all or nothing proposition: every little helps. We may never produce a true society, sure. But what we can certainly produce is some such thing—and from where we stand right now, that will do just fine.

PERILOUS AESTHETICS

PHOTOJOURNALISM AFTER INSTAGRAM

by Barrett Swanson

THE FIRST PHOTO: a fireman, a woman, and a child wait on the top-floor landing of a fire escape. Smoke purls from the windows behind them. As the gallant-eyed fireman reaches for the approaching rescue ladder, the woman and girl hug one another, their faces wounded by fear. In the second photograph, the fire escape has buckled and detached from the building. The fireman dangles from the ladder while the woman clutches onto his legs, in the postural arrangement of trapeze swingers. The little girl is not anywhere in view. We see in the third photo that the fireman is safely on the ladder, but the woman and little girl are floating, halfway into their fall, arms and legs gravity-splayed. The woman's expression is eerily serene, as if already resigned to her fate. The final photograph (above) shows the woman and girl suspended in mid-air, like Degas ballerinas; the girl faces the camera with her arms out-stretched, her pajama bottoms inflated with the wind of her fall. The woman plummets headfirst, a hideous, limb-tangled descent into oblivion. The woman, a nineteen-year-old named Diana Bryant, died on impact, but her two-year-old goddaughter, Tiare Jones, landed on Bryant's body and lived.

Originally published in 1975 in the *Boston Herald* and taken by Stanley Forman, who thought he was merely documenting some gawk-worthy scenes from a heroic rescue, the photographs are so expertly composed and nakedly harrowing that they resemble film stills from a Hollywood blockbuster. And despite its disquieting content, Forman's work, known simply as "Fire Escape Collapse," was reprinted in over four hundred U.S. newspapers. The response was uniformly negative, as most readers thought the photos were opprobrious and obscene, on par with the tawdry muckraking and bone-jostling sensationalism most often disseminated by such journalistically dubious organs as the *National Enquirer* or the *New York Post*. Readers argued that Bryant's privacy had been invaded, that publishing these photos was just a strategy to boost paper sales. One reader wrote the *Chicago Sun Times*: "I shall try to hide my disappointment that Miss Bryant wasn't wearing a skirt when she fell to her death. You could have some award-winning photographs of her underpants as her skirt bellowed over her head, you voyeurs."

In her essay "The Boston Photographs" (1978), Nora Ephron—the warmhearted screenwriter of some of our most saccharine romantic comedies (*Sleepless in Seattle*, *You've Got Mail*)—submits a decidedly chilly argument in favor of Forman's images, one that stands in crisp disagreement with the public opinion. Ephron attributes reader outrage to the simple fact that Bryant died. Had Bryant lived, people would have instead marveled at the aesthetic excellence of Forman's work. This is why she thinks publishers shouldn't be leery of printing photographs of death, since such squeamishness is "merely puritanical." In the end, newspapers were justified in printing "Fire Escape Collapse," but not because the photos documented a newsworthy event, evinced something characteristic of slum life, or portrayed the dangers of fire escapes. Rather, they warranted publication because they were "great pictures, breathtaking pictures of something that happened." To Ephron's mind, it is a photograph's aesthetic excellence—and not the newsworthiness of its content—that merits its publication.

It turns out that Ephron wasn't alone in this belief. "Fire Escape Collapse" won the 1976 Pulitzer Prize for Spot News Photography and was later dubbed the World Press Photo of the Year.

I teach "Intro to Critical Thinking" at a small college in Wisconsin, and every semester I assign "The Boston Photographs" in an attempt to generate the sort of life-altering discussions that Robin Williams inspired in *The Dead Poets Society*. While I'm embarrassed to admit it, I construct most of my daily lessons with the hope that my students will be so roused by the exercise that they'll climb onto their desks, lock eyes with me, and recite Whitman's "Oh, Captain, My Captain" with vim and vigor. It's at this fulsome display of student approval that I always imagine myself smiling coyly and giving a little bow before exiting the room. It hasn't happened yet.

All but a few of my students are between the ages of eighteen and twenty-two, meaning most of them uttered their first words and shed their Huggies around the same time they learned to point and click. Bright and self-assured, albeit still emotionally swaddled by their helicopter parents, they happily attest to the fact that many, if not all, of their formative years were spent gazing at pixelated screens, which perhaps explains why during my lectures they oftentimes possess the bovine impassivity of cinema audiences. And yet what worries me most about these digital natives is how readily they accept Ephron's formulation as true—obvious, even. When I ask them to write an essay about Ephron's argument, the students overwhelmingly defend "The Boston Photographs," and while most of them resort to specious logic and gooey clichés ("a picture is worth a thousand words"), the better ones posit a more interesting idea—one that evolves Ephron's argument from a claim about aesthetic admiration (they should be published because they are "breathtaking photos") to one about the telos of photojournalism. The top students posit that "Fire Escape Collapse" warrants print because it precipitates an emotional response in the viewer. Consequently, the aesthetic excellence of a photo—i.e., its capacity to achieve artfulness or beauty—is permitted, necessary even, because it helps to garner viewer pathos.

It's discomfiting to think a photograph of death could be "beautiful" or "artful," but as Susan Sontag points out in *Regarding the Pain of Others*, even the most troubling images can strike us as astonishing—perhaps even as excellent:

> That a gory battlescape could be beautiful—in the sublime or awesome or tragic register of the beautiful—is a commonplace about images of war made by artists. The idea does not sit well when applied to images taken by cameras: to find beauty in war photographs seems heartless. But the landscape of devastation is still a landscape. There is beauty in ruins. To acknowledge the beauty of the photographs of the World Trade Center ruins in the months following the attack seemed frivolous, sacrilegious. The most people dared say was that the photographs were "surreal," a hectic euphemism behind which the disgraced notion of beauty cowered. But they *were* beautiful...

Indeed much of the vitriol elicited by Richard Drew's "The Falling Man," an AP photo published on September 12th, 2001 in newspapers around the country, was due to the fact that it possessed obvious aesthetic attributes—its sense of symmetry and scale, the way the tower perfectly frames the falling person. The photograph freezes in still frame a single millisecond from an unfathomable horror and repackages it as an icon of either American bravery or desperation, depending upon your interpretation.

Images like Forman's "Fire Escape Collapse" and Drew's "The Falling Man" achieve what we might call an *accidental aesthetic brilliance*, since there was no way those photographers could have purposely stylized these photographs to achieve their most striking attributes. Rather, the images were captured with high-powered cameras that can document multiple frames per second, and were later selected by an editor for their special aesthetic appeal. But such newsroom decisions, coupled with the advent of digital technologies, have spurred an increasing trend among photojournalists to intentionally aestheticize reality in order to create "great photos," a tendency that would be sanctioned by my students' argument that beauty helps to elicit viewer emotion. But at what point does the aesthetic excellence of the photograph eclipse the depicted event, or, worse, distract the viewer from inquiring into what happened?

T HE IMPORTANCE OF this question becomes most acute when what we're talking about are carefully stylized photographs that stagger the border between journalism and art. For instance, on December 16th, 2012, the *New York Times Magazine* ran a photo-essay entitled "The Color of War," which featured Richard Mosse's photographs of the conflict in the Congo.* The *Times* notes that for the past two years Mosse has been "documenting what he calls 'The Hobbesian state of war,'" and that he uses infrared technology to "reveal camouflaged troops and buildings, as well as produce the pink tints in these pictures." The chosen subject of the two-page-spread is a gravel road that vanishes into a steroidally fertile forest.

Flanking the road are lines of M23 rebels, who appear to be patrolling the Virunga National Park. The infrared film presents these men as faceless silhouettes, some of whom stand at nervy attention while others slouch at ease. The soldiers' roadside arrangement and the oneiric color-palette make the photo an arresting aesthetic achievement. While the road is a drab gray, the approximate color of a dead tooth, the infrared filter has stained the trees a Seussian pink, as if the surrounding flora had been treated with food coloring. A small-print caption offers the reader a few bits of supposedly relevant trivia:

---

* The entirety of Mosse's project can be found in his book, *Infra*, a project that was co-commissioned and co-published by the Pulitzer Center on Crisis Reporting, which, as its website states, "promotes in-depth engagement with global affairs through its sponsorship of quality international journalism across all media platforms and an innovative program of outreach and education."

Number of persons displaced by current conflict around Goma, Demo-cratic Republic of Congo: 130,000. Estimated death toll related to violence in Congo, 1998-2008: 5.4 million. D.R.C.'s percentage of the world's re-serve of coltan (used to make cellphones): 64. Year Kodak Aerochrome III Infrared film was discontinued: 2009.

Mosse's work is, I'm sure, meant to be disruptive. And yet when I first viewed "The Color of War" I felt that his eye-poppingly gorgeous images were ethically and emotionally disorienting in ways that I couldn't for a second believe he had intended. Perhaps the caption, which suggests that the year Kodak discontinued Aerochrome film is just as important as these other appalling statistics, offered a hint as to what was bothering me. What exactly was I looking at?

Here's something that's weird but true: a photograph is unlike almost every other art form because it isn't merely a representation of the world; it is a record of the world. Such is the form's indexical ontology. When we look at a photo-graph of a tree, we see the physical reality—the miraculous interplay of physics and light—that transpired at the exact instant the photographer activated the camera. Unlike a painting of a tree, which is a stylized representation of the object, infused with the artist's sensibility (and, probably, his or her tree-related feelings), a photograph records and ratifies the existence of the actual tree. While the precision of a photographic index depends on a number of factors—the camera in question, whether the photographer used a filter, the extent to which the photo was treated during darkroom emulsification or digital processing—a photograph still serves as a reliable document of reality.*

Of course, the history of photographic manipulation has made the claim to indexicality shaky at best. Even before the digital revolution, manipulation was accomplished with gouache paints, kneaded erasers, charcoals and airbrushes.

---

* Whether a photograph should be considered a representation, an index, or both has been the nidus of much dispute among art critics and theorists since the early 1970s. Because it's difficult to discern what, exactly, about a photograph is deliberate and intentional (and what, on the other hand, is a mere accident of physics and light), some critics like Walter Benn Michaels and Michael Fried argue that the only way for photography to transcend its indexical status and become rep-resentation—in other words, art—is if a photographer stages the photograph so that it contains only his or her intentions. For instance, Jeff Wall, the Canadian art-photographer, stages his pictures (and surfeits them with blatant indications of that staging) as a way to control his pictorial environment. For similar reasons, Thomas Demand takes photographs of life-size paper sculptures of actual places, which he himself made. The sedulous effort to purge the photographs of natural accidents allows these artists to avoid those pesky problems of indexicality. Photojournalism is necessarily stuck with the blurry status of being both representation and record, and thus, for critics like Michaels and Fried, wouldn't attain the status of art photography. Since photojournal-ists are charged with presenting images of actual events, they are forbidden from carrying out the kinds of staging necessary to avoid the problems of indexicality.

Pre-exposure effects—executed in the dark room—were just as crude: splicing and rearranging negatives, double-exposing photos or scratching out subjects. (Pertinent bit of trivia: in the early 1860s, a photographer grafted Abraham Lincoln's head onto John C. Calhoun's body to create a now-canonical portrait.) In the last thirty years, a whole nomenclature of digital technologies has made the photograph's status as an index all but obsolete. In the early 1980s, photographers doctored their pictures with Quantel Computers' Paintbox and Scitex imaging stations, but by the end of the decade Adobe had sent both of those primitive editing programs into commercial oblivion. Now, programs like Photoshop, Paint Shop Pro, Corel Photopaint and Pixelmator can be used to finesse images to such an extent that it can be nearly impossible to ascertain the faithfulness of the image.

And yet, even though we are on some level aware of these manipulations, we still tend to trust what we see in photographs, perhaps because it's hard to repudiate that dusty, old photographic dictum: "The camera never lies." This might explain why, despite mammoth advancements in digital technology, photographs remain the most unquestioned and effective of documentary technologies (just think of how vastly different our response would have been to the Abu Ghraib scandal if all we'd had were field reports).

Such assumptions are most problematic in the realm of photojournalism. Newspapers and periodicals claim to transmit objective information about contemporary events, and we instinctually trust the camera's verisimilitude, expecting in good faith to approach a newspaper photograph as an authentic document of something that happened. And photojournalists are acutely conscious of that public trust. Here's Howard Chapnick—founder of the worldwide picture agency Black Star and the author of *Truth Needs No Ally: Inside Photojournalism*—warning photojournalists about the perils of manipulation: "Credibility. Responsibility. These words give us the right to call photography a profession rather than a business. Not maintaining that credibility will diminish our journalistic impact and self-respect, and the importance of photography as communication." And Chapnick isn't some harebrained purist. These kinds of journalistic standards have been codified in the National Press Photographers Association's (NPPA) Code of Ethics, which cautions photojournalists against manipulating images "in any way that can mislead viewers or misrepresent subjects."

So here's a question: Are Mosse's photographs misleading? Is the submerged concern I felt upon first viewing them now bubbling up to the surface as a realization of Chapnick's worry? Certainly Mosse's series doesn't lead the viewer to believe that something stood in front of his camera that in fact never did; in that sense, his work is not a classic case of photographic deceit. But maybe there is more than one way to fail to "communicate," as Chapnick puts it, the truth of the photographed subject. Perhaps Mosse's infrareds actually enact a more insidious manipulation, where the aesthetic enhancements ensorcel the viewer with a fever-dream landscape quite distant from the real horror taking place in the D.R.C. While adding or excising objects from photographs are blatant misrepresentations of events and obvious threats to the profession, this isn't the only way a photographer can be unfaithful to his subject.

HERE IS A portrait of a father holding his young son. The family stands on a patio, looking out on the rubble that their East Coast town has become. There's a stony grimness to the father's expression, the kind of vacant resignation seen in the faces of those who have weathered baffling disasters. The New York Giants insignia is stitched to the left breast of his bright blue jacket. His hair is cupreous and newscaster-swooped. Barnacled to his side is a boy of Gerber-level cuteness. The child is coy, turned away from the camera, about to burrow his face into his father's neck. But what is most beguiling to me about this photograph is not the family's stoic grief. Instead, what preoc-cupied me upon initial viewing was a question: Is this really a photograph? Its lines are gauzy, like they might have been brushstroked with acrylics. The father and son are seemingly unaware of the camera, a nod to Diderot's thematics of absorption. Meanwhile, the oily tactility of the photo's pixilation—a digital craquelure created by the Instagram filter—resembles the lacquered surface of a Rembrandt. And the mise-en-scène invokes a Madonna with child.

The photograph comes from Radcliffe Roye's Hurricane Sandy series, images that were published on the *New Yorker*'s website in November 2012. No one would deny that Roye—a Brooklyn-based photojournalist with self-proclaimed "painterly abilities"—has a gift for yoking austere subjects to lurid colors in a way that furnishes seismic artistic effects. His website states that he's "inspired by the raw and gritty lives of grass-roots people, especially those of his homeland of Jamaica. [He] strives to tell the stories of their victories and ills by bringing their voices to matte fibre paper."

For me, Roye's aesthetic ingenuity flatly contradicts his role as a photojournalist, and the "painterly" qualities of his work end up undermining, rather than intensifying, the communication of the family's plight. And I submit that there's something unsettling, if not soul-sickening, about seeing a family that has been ravaged by disaster and has lost everything, and then thinking: "Wow, this is a beautiful photograph." But this is exactly the kind of moral hazard that is involved in aestheticized photojournalism, which interprets someone else's tragedy as beautiful. It calls to mind the way eighteenth-century aristocrats collected Baroque paintings of beggars and peasants to chronicle the exotic lifestyle of the lower class. In his essay, "Notes on the Photographic Image," the French philosopher Jacques Ranciére argues that the very beauty of these paintings (see right: Bartolomé Esteban Murillo's *Beggar Boys Eating Grapes and Melon*) aimed to elevate their subjects out of their poverty, giving them the same artistic status as Olympian gods. As a result, the paintings presented the "common aesthetic neutralization of the social hierarchy," blinding the viewer to the very real suffering of the working poor and exonerating him of any part he may have played in causing it. In this case, the viewer feels absolved because Murillo's painting makes poverty look like a beautiful life.

This might begin to explain what's wrong with the argument that the aestheticization of photojournalism is permissible whenever it helps to garner viewer pathos. The problem is that there exists a vital difference between an aesthetics that communicate and an aesthetics that *reimagine* a harrowing reality. Roye beautifies his subjects in such a way that it becomes distressingly easy for me to fool myself into thinking that these Hurricane Sandy victims aren't in immediate need. And so the beauty of the photograph, as Sontag puts it, "drains attention from the sobering subject and turns it toward the medium itself, thereby compromising the picture's status as a document."

Please be apprised that I'm not so Pollyannaish as to suggest that every piece of photojournalism should inspire us to stop whatever we are doing, haul ass to our cars, and burn custom rubber to the nearest disaster site in order to lend an altruistic hand. As far as I can tell, photojournalists generally have a less sexy job, and that is to offer an enfranchised public faithful records of what's happening in our world. Their role is to provide a context for public awareness and civic accountability, something that is indispensable to the health of a democratic society. All of which might explain what's so concerning about Roye's photos, because when we are seduced into seeing hurricane survivors as objects of aesthetic appraisal, it can numb our sense of responsibility—as citizens, as human beings—to these tragedies.

This concern takes on a new dimension when we click through the entirety of Roye's Hurricane Sandy series. In shot after shot—of storm-incinerated towns, survivors toting rescued dogs, a ship pushed onto land by ravaging winds—reality has been stylized with gorgeous palettes and a sense of staged arrangement. The skies alone in these photos are utterly lovely, enough to make you swoon. Roye's low ceiling of cumulous clouds is flecked with a sooty granularity and softly infused with impressionistic lavenders and blues, recalling the sullen London sky in Monet's *Houses of Parliament*. What's more, these scenes of devastation and ruin, distilled through the Instagram filter, are given color schemes that are themselves so mesmeric and captivating that the feeling I get is primarily of wishing I had been there, the ludicrousness of which highlights yet another peril posed by the aesthetics of reimagination.

It's not just that the aesthetics in these photos are so captivating that they divert our attention away from the subject and place it on the prettiness of the medium—though they do—but also that they seem designed to evoke an emotion or state of mind that is either starkly antithetical or wholly irrelevant to the set of feelings we would otherwise associate with their content. In these cases, the photographers reimagine their subjects to the point where we are no longer prompted to countenance the very real suffering of those depicted, or to consider the geopolitical forces that might have created such suffering in the first place.

And this might go some way toward explaining why my students tend to use vapid abstractions ("gorgeous," "pretty," "cool") to describe Richard Mosse's Congo. One student, upon first viewing, submitted an especially trenchant comparison between Mosse's D.R.C. and the Technicolor of Oz. And it's true: Mosse's photos transport us to a netherworld of beauty that makes us feel as if we have been beguiled by a pleasant and whimsical dream.

It seems important to recognize that Mosse's intention wasn't to pacify our moral anxieties or perform an aesthetic legerdemain. In his interview with the *Liverpool Daily News*, Mosse opines: "I was looking for new forms to represent a very old and tired war which no one really cares about anymore." In other words, these lurid landscapes are meant to estrange us from our usual response to the surfeit of Congo-related news coverage, to wake us from our perceptive slumber. Which suggests that, in the end, our choice is between his kind of photograph and not thinking about the events in the Congo at all.

Three things immediately come to mind: first, my students' responses to these photos suggest that Mosse's effort to estrange us from the stolid response we usually have to journalism actually has the opposite effect and ends up simply estranging us from the conflicts his photos purportedly "document." What's most distressing is that while I silently click through this photo-essay up on the classroom projector, measuring my students' reactions, none of them know nor ask what these are photographs of. This montage of Mosse's work arouses only a chorus of dead descriptors and a spirited discussion of what kind of filter was used here—i.e. Instagram or Hipstomatic—which lasts a good five minutes before I step in and settle the score, explaining that it's infrared film. When I do offer a compendium on just some of the horrors that have recently occurred in the Congo—horrors that (it's worth mentioning) my students claim to know nothing about—they report feeling a little queasy about having been duped into a psychological state of whimsy and color-drunk hebetude.

Second, the very fact that the journalistic response to Mosse's *Infra* series has been humid with praise for the glitzy prettiness of the photos themselves (*ABC News*: "Beautifully violent"; *Time Out Paris*: "His radical approach colors images from the war in the eastern Congo a bright candyfloss shade"; *Irish Times*: the work throws "us into an hallucinogenic, surreal world that in some respects recalls Francis Ford Coppola's film *Apocalypse Now*"), as opposed to focusing on how the photos help convey the exigencies of the Congolese situation, would seem to announce the failure of Mosse's objective to spur viewer engagement via gross aestheticization.

And, finally, Mosse's claim that our culture's image saturation compels photojournalists to beautify tableaux from the ugly flux of real life only contributes to the ever-increasing tendency to snow over the border between news and entertainment, suggesting that our capacity for apprehending and empathizing with the world's glories and horrors can only be sustained when such events are presented with a pixelated finish.

D ON'T GET ME wrong: beauty, in and of itself, does not deactivate a photograph's communicative function. There is, of course, a lot of aesthetically excellent photojournalism that succeeds in transmitting states of mind that are pertinent to its subjects. These photos utilize what we might call an aesthetics of communication.

For instance, have a look at "Nicaragua 1979" by Dutch photographer Koen Wessing.* The photograph is a black-and-white shot of a rubble-strewn urban intersection, populated only by Catholic nuns and Nicaraguan soldiers,

---

* This is a photograph that Roland Barthes pretty much drools over (though for a very different reason than I do) in his seminal meditation on photography, *Camera Lucida*.

though the two demographics don't much interact. It stands as a salient photojournalistic achievement precisely because its aesthetic virtues—the gorgeous depth-of-field, the symmetry of soldiers on either side of the passing nuns—distract me in no way from comprehending what took place at that hour of that year in that part of the world. In fact, the aesthetics actually go far in helping me understand the socio-political climate of the Sandinista revolution, insofar as they describe the causal malice the Catholic Church directed at the Somoza dynasty. What's more is that this hackle-raising juxtaposition of the guns and the nuns, this visual dissonance between the secular and the spiritual, helps convey the pathos of a country reduced to mayhem by war: everything here shrinks to a death toll and the promise of paradise that comes after. In short, this is a photograph that communicates—rather than reimagines—the reality it depicts.

The same holds true for Richard Drew's "The Falling Man," even though this is a bit of photojournalism that is, for me, very difficult to look at. Rather than reincarnate the tragedy as an artistic dreamscape, the aesthetics of "The Falling Man" actually convey the horror of that day. What is both strange and upsetting is that the man, as he free-falls between the Twin Towers, looks relaxed, almost insouciant. He is in the approximate posture of someone leaning James Deanishly against a brick wall or on the hood of a car to have a smoke—an attitude that somehow seems to embody the relative comfort enjoyed by Americans before the events of that morning. Except this is a photo of man falling upside down. It's the photo's enjambment of this calm, carefree posture and the inevitability of the man's death that produces an emotion that seems kindred to the total panic, the psychic terror, the doom and confusion, the plain old little-kid fear I felt that day. This photo captures the before and the after, and in this way it eulogizes our swift and unwanted entry into a new era, a vexed and violent decade punctuated by mayhem and war. The seeming impossibility that a photograph like this even exists mirrors in some way the impossibility of planes colliding with buildings and people jumping to their deaths and the tallest buildings in New York collapsing into plumes of rubble one September morning.

Whatever other relative differences exist between Drew's "The Falling Man" and something like Mosse's "The Color of War," we must acknowledge that there is a serious variance in how their aesthetics set out to affect us. Drew's communicate. Mosse's reimagine. Drew brings us reality, and Mosse leaves it behind.

I T'S THIS DISTINCTION between the aesthetics of communication and the aesthetics of reimagination that can account for the weird antipathy that Mosse's and Roye's works enkindle in me. Mosse's Pepto-Bismol pink and Roye's digital acrylics announce that these photojournalists privilege their own aesthetic visions over the realities they claim to document. And this is especially incensing when the subject of the photograph is suffering and when the seriousness of that suffering gets obscured by the photo's gorgeous distortions. Such instances of photojournalistic reimagination demonstrate the potential conflict between the deliberate effort to make "great photos, breathtaking photos," as Ephron calls them, and the communicative function that makes photojournalism a necessary and worthwhile profession in the first place.

But maybe we, as a culture, don't have the time or the energy to make such distinctions anymore. Consider the public's wildly different reactions to Drew's and Mosse's respective photographs. In his essay, "The Falling Man," Tom Junod notes how, within days of publishing Drew's photo, "[p]apers all over the country, from the *Fort Worth Star-Telegram* to the *Memphis Commercial Appeal* to the *Denver Post*, were forced to defend themselves against charges that they exploited a man's death, stripped him of his dignity, invaded his privacy, turned tragedy into leering pornography." And yet, only a decade or so later, Mosse's work gets roundly acclaimed as "gorgeous" and "appropriate." Why is this so? It cannot simply be that Drew's image is more horrifying, or because his work shows someone dying and Mosse's photos don't. In fact, if you click through Mosse's work on the *New York Times* website, you'll eventually find an image of a dead F.A.D.R.C. soldier lying on a desolate road that curves through dense stretches of Candyland forest. The soldier is splayed out on the gravel, as if he fell from a terrible height.

Perhaps it is because the people in Mosse's photos live halfway around the world and so their suffering seems proportionately remote? Or maybe we have become inured to this type of aestheticization? Maybe the abrupt ubiquity of Instagram and other digital stylizing devices has allowed us to constantly re-imagine our own lives to the point where something that happened only moments ago can get tinted with the patina of history, aged with the waterstains of nostalgia, or deported to the landscape of a pastel fantasia. But I've been trying to suggest that there's something more urgent and concerning going on here, a conflict between two modes of presentation. One approach clears the way for reality to come to us. The other claims to fetch us from the basement of our complacency but actually just takes us by the hand and leads us to a glass window so beautifully stained that we can no longer see out of it. The difference, here, is moral before it is artistic. After all, it's disturbingly easy to interpret suffering. To look at it, though, to simply bear witness, is more difficult—for it is then that we risk coming away hurt or humbled or changed.

Erwin Wurm, *Adorno as Oliver Hardy in the* Bohemian
Girl *(1936) and the burden of desperation,* 2006
acrylic, 70 x 143 x 65 cm

THE LONELY INTELLECTUAL

DAVID SHIELDS'S REAL PROBLEM

by Justin Evans

The child's imperfection is, first, not to know what is horrifying, and then by the same token to shrink from something else in horror.

SØREN KIERKEGAARD

I SOMETIMES GET MORE pleasure from learning a thing's name than from learning about the thing itself. When, a few years ago, my then girl-friend offered me a potato pancake, I wasn't impressed, even though she told me about the history behind it. When she called it a latke, on the other hand, I was thrilled. The same thing happened when I found, in my college's listings, the course title "Literature and Phenomenology." I had no idea what the lat-ter was, but—*phenomenology*—it had to be fascinating. This effect is heightened when it comes to the particularly useless or obscure. Take the jargon of rhetoric: anacoluthon, antanaclasis, asyndeton. Soraismus. Lovely. Now, I'm not praising myself. People like me are a less enthusiastic, less entertaining—"Did you say I'm self-righteous? I think you mean comminatory"—version of that guy who makes six to ten puns per day. Such close attention to the sound of language can come at the expense of attention to its meaning. I'm not proud of my tendency to ignore this fact.

I went to college in the late Nineties, which made the problem worse; back then new ideas could be expressed only in new and fun-sounding words or phrases (Rhizome. Ideological sublime). I hadn't learned to write in the margins of my books, so if you flick through my copy of, say, *The Foucault Reader*, I won't be embarrassed by over-enthusiastic exclamation marks or all-caps scribblings of YES! But I know what caught my ear because I marked passages in pen, sometimes quite insistently. And my love of big, complicated sounds (*Captatio benevolentiae!*) must have led to a love of big, complicated ideas; I obviously enjoyed the sound of "polymorphous techniques of power," and at some point may even have come to understand what it meant.

I didn't end up taking "Literature and Phenomenology" (there was required reading over the summer) but I did take almost every other course featuring a post-Nietzschean thinker: "Sartre and de Beauvoir," was an easy choice, as was "Deleuze and Foucault." I had to check the listings to ensure that "Philosophy of Language" would include Nietzsche, Heidegger and Foucault. "Aesthetics" started with Kant but got to Bataille and the twentieth century in the third week; "Feminist Philosophy" included Irigaray, Kristeva and Cixous.

I know now that these thinkers can't really all be lumped together, but at the time what mattered was that they offered me immediate access to big, important questions about the human condition. To do anything interesting in biology, I would have had to go through four years of lab work, then at least three more years in graduate school as I started to understand the complexities of genetic systems. To do something in philosophy, I had to read endless articles in *Mind*, define a position I had in common with others, then work with them to clarify that position in opposition to very slightly different positions. But men and women like Sartre, Foucault and Irigaray invited me to start thinking right now. I'd been putting it off for eighteen years. The time had come.

So I burrowed into those big problems: What is truth? Does it even exist? How do we justify life after God's death? What is "literature"? How do we undermine the author function? How can we reject the book, that "encyclopedic protection of theology and of logocentrism against the disruption of writing ... and ... against difference in general" (Derrida)? My high school teachers and parents, far from being able to answer, couldn't even have asked these questions. I was engaged in (anti-) metaphysical, existential battles, and these words and ideas gave me a kind of power I'd never experienced. They made me brave. They also gave me an urgent, relentless mission to disenchant.

And I was courageous in that mission. Where others saw cause for joy, I saw the inevitability of death. Where others saw a freedom, I saw a compulsion: you believe you're free when you watch televised sport, but I know you're just part of a power matrix that crushes the third world. Where they found meaning, I recognized an illusion that I had to tear aside to reveal the meaningless of human existence. So when a friend and I started a reading group, and others wanted to talk about the themes in a Peter Carey short story, I wanted to talk about how all narrative is necessarily oppressive, since it assumes life to be a linear movement and a totality, and literature (e.g., Peter Carey) that doesn't undermine that assumption is, *ipso facto*, complicit in it. Improbably, I believed I'd won the argument.

This is the kind of excitement and fervor that's really possible only for adolescents, but I still feel a quiver when I open a reader of existentialism or contemporary critical theory. I look back on it calmly, but in many instances, I still think I was right.

In many ways, I am David Shields's ideal reader.

T HIS IS NOT to say that Shields and I are alike or even all that similar. Shields was born in 1956, attended Brown University, then got an MFA at the University of Iowa. An extremely successful writer, he has published two traditional novels, a novel in stories and a series of mixed-genre non-fiction. Shields has won the PEN/Revson Award and been a finalist for the National Book Critics Circle and PEN USA Awards. His works are often on best books of the year lists. He has a prestigious position at the University of Washington, and a daughter. I have written one essay for *The Point* before this one, and have a dog.

But Shields didn't really break out with his novels or writings on sport. If his name means anything to you, it's probably because you've heard about the project he has undertaken in his two most recent books, *Reality Hunger* (2010) and *How Literature Saved My Life* (2013). Combining quotations, narrative, memoir and argument, the books have been compared to mix-tapes or mash-ups; Shields himself calls them "collages." But these comparisons hardly do justice to the scope of their ambition. Shields's recent work gives us a manifesto for, and a model of, a new form of writing. That form is characterized by a "deliberate unartiness: 'raw' material ... randomness, openness to accident and serendipity; artistic risk ... reader/viewer participation," and, most infamously, "a blurring (to the point of invisibility) of any distinction between fiction and nonfiction."

Reality Hunger consists of hundreds of numbered sections, *How Literature Saved My Life* scores of titled ones. Many of the books' aphorisms are written by other people, whom Shields quotes without attribution. That has led to some backlash, and Shields has responded with a theoretical defense of plagiarism,* but the real question is whether it works, and Shields's strings of quotation are often effective, allowing him to move fluidly between ideas, arguments and great thinkers—as at the start of *Reality Hunger*'s chapter "U: Alone":

---

* From an interview published by the *Los Angeles Review of Books*: "Malcolm Gladwell talks about this, you know—all of journalism is this hugely self-generating plagiarism machine whereby ideas are endlessly stolen, but god forbid if you use the actual language. There's plagiarism and then there's *plagiarism*. It's almost as if plagiarism is litigated at the micro level because at the macro level it's so pervasive as to be ubiquitous."

524

Democracy turns man's imagination away from externals to concentrate on himself alone. ... Here, and here alone, are the true springs of poetry among them, and those poets, I believe, who do not draw inspiration from these springs will lose their hold over the audience they intend to charm.

525

Not only does democracy make every man forget his ancestors ... it throws him back forever upon himself alone and threatens in the end to confine him entirely within the solitude of his own heart.

The appendix (which, Shields says, lawyers forced him to add) tells you these quotes are from Alexis de Tocqueville, but you don't have to know that to understand their connection to what follows —"It is almost impossible to know someone else completely. We radiate feelings to others, but ultimately we are alone." That's from Laszlo Kardis. Contrasts like these, between an early-nineteenth-century French theorist of American democracy and a twentieth-century Hungarian author and editor, allow Shields to build his argument, as Luc Sante put it, "forcefully and passionately, but not like a debate-team captain, more like a clever if overmatched boxer, endlessly bobbing and weaving."

Much of the commentary about *Reality Hunger* and *How Literature Saved My Life* has focused on the form of Shields's recent writing, and on his demand for new forms; relatively little has been said about the logic behind that demand. In some sense, Shields is heir to the modernists, who thought that new literary forms were needed to deal with the technological, social and economic transformations of the early twentieth century. "On or about December 1910 human character changed," as Virginia Woolf announced in "Modern Fiction." The older forms of literature were tied to the world of horses and buggies, aristocracy and the riches of empire. Those ties could not be undone, so new literary forms were needed to express the experience of the new world: trains, the bourgeoisie and the democratized masses. Shields argues that our society has witnessed transformations on a similar scale, and that a similarly radical new form of writing is needed to deal with them.

In Shields's memorable phrasing, inhabitants of the twenty-first century have become "obsessed with real events because we experience hardly any." This is our reality hunger—we hunger for the *feeling* that we are experiencing something real. The works that will be best able to satisfy that hunger are those that "foreground ... the question of how the writer solves being alive," the familiar project of European existentialists from Kierkegaard to Nietzsche to Thomas Bernhard. These thinkers didn't pretend to any certain, objective knowledge;

instead they tried to come to terms with the experiences of modern men and women. It turns out that modern experiences are not pleasant, so they also tended toward pessimism, an attitude Shields happily embraces: "Death is my copilot ... *love equals death, art equals death, life equals death* ... all literature and all philosophy have come from this." Shields's pessimism is bolstered by contemporary advances in cognitive science and genetics, which he says are the ultimate explanations of the human condition: we are animals, determined by our brains, and our genes before them.

Today's inheritors of existentialism must address two features of this condition above all. First, we are "existentially alone on the planet." Though awash in images and media, we're isolated from other *people*. And second, we no longer experience strong or authentic emotions; "the endemic disease of our time [is] the absence of feeling." But, according to Shields, neither contemporary fiction nor traditional non-fiction have managed to address these issues:

> Living as we perforce do in a manufactured and artificial world, we yearn for the "real," semblances of the real. We want to pose something nonfictional against all the fabrication—autobiographical frissons or framed or filmed or caught moments that, in their seeming unrehearsedness, possess at least the possibility of breaking through the clutter. More invention, more fabrication, aren't going to do this. I doubt very much that I'm the only person that's finding it more and more difficult to want to read or write novels.*

While conventional novels give us "bubble wrap, nostalgia, retreat"—just another manufactured fiction in a fictional world—most non-fiction is confined by the outdated conventions of reportage and fact-checking. Neither are able to convey what it "feels like to be alive right now."

By contrast, the new non-fiction Shields calls for promises unmediated reality, raw nerve endings and naked feeling. On the one hand, it expresses how it feels to live with reality hunger; on the other, it helps us deal with that hunger by offering us "larger and larger chunks" of the reality we crave. The leading works of the new genre, like Dave Eggers's A *Heartbreaking Work of Staggering Genius*, make us feel like we are in contact with another "real" person—in some cases the artist, in others the "real" subject of the (quasi-documentary) work. This helps us to "feel as if, to the degree anyone can know anyone else, [we] know

---

* In *Reality Hunger* Shields tells the story of how, in trying to write his fourth novel in the mid-Nineties, he suddenly realized he "simply could not commit the requisite resources to character and scene and plot."

someone—[we]'ve gotten to this other person." We see this, Shields says, in Joe Frank's radio shows; the quasi-home movie *Open Water*; pseudo-documentaries like *Borat*; autobiographical dramatizations like *The Eminem Show* and *Curb Your Enthusiasm*; and the "tossed off" poetry of Billy Collins.

Yet Shields remains a pessimist, who believes that "language never fails to fail us." Literature cannot fully or finally solve our isolation or make us feel authentic emotions. The task for good art now is therefore to address the loneliness and unfeelingness of modern existence, without lying about the fact that it must always fail to resolve it. In the end, "nothing can assuage human loneliness." But the new non-fiction will at least succeed in failing better.

S HIELDS'S RECENT BOOKS have elated critics and reviewers. "The ideas he raises are so important, his interests are so compelling," wrote *Bookforum*'s Jan Attenberg, "that I raved about this book the whole time I was reading it and have regularly quoted it to friends in the weeks since." Other commentators have praised Shields, in less personal terms, for "challeng[ing] our most basic literary assumptions" (Andrew Albanese), and for offering the most "effective description (and example) of the aesthetic concerns of the internet age" (Edward King). Shields "succinctly addresses matters that have been in the air ... waiting for someone to link them together," wrote Luc Sante, in a *New York Times* review that compared the book to the *Surrealist Manifesto*.

The project certainly sounds exciting. Shields focuses on the problems of loneliness and *ennui* that have worried many recent readers and writers, and he proposes a radical overhaul of literary form to address them. Meanwhile, he brings together dozens of men and women, from the ancient world to the present, who have thought and written about similar problems. Because his work is so broad and ambitious, it's easy to complain that Shields misuses some of his sources. But he is not doing academic research, and part of the charm of his project is the way he makes such a wide range of figures speak directly to contemporary concerns.

Still, as I read *Reality Hunger* and *How Literature Saved My Life*, I began to wonder if they really delivered in the way Shields said they did. The use of different voices is meant to allow Shields to set up a dialogue, but a dialogue requires not just different voices but differing arguments. Whereas in *Reality Hunger* and *HLSML* it often sounds as if Kafka, Kierkegaard, Sacha Baron Cohen, Alexis de Tocqueville and Ben Lerner are all saying the same things—all saying, that is, what Shields is saying. If all the voices in a dialogue agree, no participant takes anything from any of the others, and we can all stay right where we started—alone, disconnected. The more I read, the more it seemed that Shields was, far from using his form to find a way out of the isolation that, he insists, is our greatest problem, simply assimilating every other voice to his own.

The problem was perhaps clearest when I got to Shields's use of a thinker who has become more important to me than the existentialists and post-Nietzscheans I spent so much time on in college: Theodor Adorno. If you're familiar with Adorno, you can see why Shields finds him inspiring. He wrote in an aphoristic style ("An element of exaggeration is essential to thought"; "The whole is the false"), alternated registers at will, produced unconventional, highly self-reflexive texts, and frequently crossed over into other genres altogether. The numbered sections and personal spirit of his *Minima Moralia*—which, Adorno wrote, begins in "the narrowest private sphere" of the émigré intellectual's experience, but develops into "philosophy, without ever pretending to be complete or definitive"—could have served as a model for Shields's recent books.

But considering what he wrote *about*, and why, few thinkers are less appropriate to Shields's purposes. Shields is obsessed with the big problems that obsessed me when I was in college: death, meaninglessness, loneliness, metaphysical uncertainty. But Adorno argued that such big problems are just ways of (at best) ignoring actual problems or (at worst) contributing to them. When people discuss "the human condition" or "human nature," Adorno felt, they tend to mistake currently "existing" empirical facts for "existence" as a whole. (It's as if I, a resident of Los Angeles, said that the human condition involves being a Lakers fan.) Whereas the real problems, the hard problems, are not part of some inescapable condition. They're historically specific injustices, and they're our fault.

Adorno first comes up in *Reality Hunger* where Shields quotes his discussion of the essay in "Essay as Form":

> The usual reproach against the essay, that it is fragmentary and random, itself assumes the givenness of totality and suggests that man is in control of this totality. The desire of the essay, though, is not to filter the eternal out of the transitory; it wants, rather, to make the transitory eternal.

This is followed by lines from the experimental fiction writer David Markson's *Reader's Block*: "Nonlinear. Discontinuous. Collage-like. An assemblage. As is already more than self-evident." Both of the quotes are used to describe, and perhaps admire, the form of Shields's own project—fragmented, aphoristic, non-linear.

But Adorno didn't praise fragmentation in itself. For Adorno, the fragmentary nature of the essay is useful because (and this is what the quote actually *says*) it allows us to combat the problem of "givenness," which is an attitude we take when we assume that something is natural and inescapable. An example of that attitude can be found when people say things like "we just have to get out of the way and let the free market work." And I don't choose that example innocently. When Adorno said that "man is not in control of this totality," he meant capitalism. To vastly oversimplify, that's a social system in which humans (workers) are used as a means to economic ends (e.g., continual growth), rather than one in which economic practices (e.g., increased productivity) are used as means to our ends (e.g., reducing the length of time we have to work to pay for food/clothing/shelter). Accepting that this system is natural and inescapable is quite a depressing way to go about our lives, and the essay's fragmented form helps us to avoid doing so. The essay, Adorno thinks, has the potential to combine (universalist/eternal) philosophy and (individualist/transitory) literature. In doing so, it stands against our bad society, without pretending that the bad doesn't exist or that the individual is a unique and special snowflake floating free of it.

Adorno comes up again in the *Reality Hunger* chapter on "contradiction":

> A successful work is not one that resolves objective contradictions in a spurious harmony, but one that expresses the idea of harmony negatively by embodying the contradictions, pure and uncompromised, in its innermost structure.

This is preceded by Philip Lopate's advice to the essayist to "develop a dialogue between the parts of yourself that in a way corresponds to the conflict in fiction." It's followed by the poet Robert Hass, who says that "there's nothing and everything going on." In the first case, Shields's reader is encouraged to understand Adorno's "contradiction" to refer to a clash within her personality; in the second, to an overarching metaphysical principle that nothing coheres.

But that's not what Adorno meant at all. Most of us have some idea of what a good piece of art looks like, and it usually includes something like consistency. A country song about the inevitability of death that starts off slowly, then speeds up to black metal pace for no obvious reason and stops halfway through a line ("It is the familiar place that the road leads toward/ Forever dying and stripped of ..." what? Pants? Dignity? The ball?*), won't make it onto many playl-

---

* Stripped of all but nothing and fed to nothing. This is obviously not a country song at all, but a track by *Altar of Plagues*, "Feather and Bone," off the album *Mammal*. A great album, with, as this line suggests, more or less the same philosophy as David Shields.

ists. But Adorno thought that we shouldn't overstress consistency. Given that we don't, at present, live in a harmonious world—i.e., the interests of individuals are not in harmony with the processes of the economy; or, society is contradictory—it seems reasonable to say that consistent, harmonious art works are, in some sense, lies.

So should we just reject the "idea of harmony"? Adorno said not. The idea that a good work of art "embodies the contradictions, pure and uncompromised, in its innermost structure" doesn't mean that it should contain contradiction as a general principle. True, good art doesn't blithely lie about the continuing existence of disharmony by creating, as most pop music does, a naïvely harmonious tune. But nor does good art simply mirror our disharmonious society by creating irrationally dissonant works, as Shields seems sometimes to recommend. That's just bad art, like my country cover of a metal song.

In between these two bad options, the best works of modern art express the broken relationship between individual and world by embodying the specific contradiction of our society: economic ends have taken precedence over human ones. So Adorno's preference was for works constructed with painstaking care; such works (e.g., Beckett, Berg), perhaps despite themselves, hold onto the idea, the final goal, of social harmony. No matter how depressing their content, the forms of *Endgame* and *Wozzeck* are utopian. They're internally inconsistent, but not in a capricious or random way; rather, their contradictions are an image of our own. They're also moving and effective, incredible artistic achievements—and that achievement in itself is an imperfect image of what we *could* do, if our interests and our society matched up. Whether such works should take the form of fiction or non-fiction is an irrelevant and even an uninteresting question, from this perspective. Adorno's continual plea was: don't replicate the world by acting the way the world acts, because then you'll just be a part of a bad society; but don't lie about it, either, because change will only come when we understand the problem, and the responsibility we bear for it.

But Shields uses Adorno to suggest almost the exact opposite. In *Reality Hunger* and *How Literature Saved My Life*, he takes disharmony as a natural given of the human condition that cannot be overcome, and suggests that good art should strive simply to reproduce it. Adorno would see such art as irrational and nihilistic—and, despite some press to the contrary, these were the two characteristics he was most desperate to avoid. In fact Adorno, far from seeing art as quenching our "reality hunger," embraced the fact that art gets between us and society, scorning the promise of direct, "immediate" contact. The real problems, Adorno argued, are not the human condition, death, or metaphysical disharmonies, but the specific injustices of our time: [Insert your favorite example here, there's no shortage, economic, environmental, political, etc. ... My current favor-

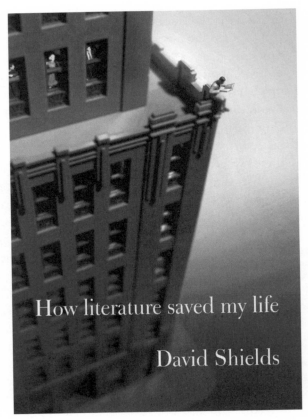

Chip Kidd, cover art, 2013

ites are rising ocean levels and the combination of record high corporate profits with wages that have remained stagnant since the 1970s]. Talk about the human condition will do nothing to solve the problem you inserted in the brackets; nor is that problem something we must accept as a metaphysical necessity.

Of course Shields doesn't have to understand the ins and outs of all the philosophies from which he quotes. But his use of Adorno points to a larger problem. Recall his motto, "death is my copilot ... all literature and all philosophy have come from this," and its quick slide from death is *my* copilot, to the claim that *all* literature and philosophies are copiloted by death. Shields's work is, in fact, informed by his own discomfort with the idea, and fact, of death. But the leap from *my* philosophy to *all* philosophy should give you pause, particularly given how often he makes the same move ("*I* feel so remote from things ... *we're* existentially alone on the planet").

Many writers have taken their own experiences to be evidence for the experiences of all human beings; many have, like Shields, tried "to convey what it feels like for *one* human being to be alive, and by implication, *all* human beings." But although Shields claims throughout his writing that what he wants is access to another consciousness, he ends up isolating himself—capable of hearing what Adorno has to say *for* him, but not what he has to say *to* him. He is like a man who builds a prison around himself and then complains about the guards. Shields and his friends, he tells us, can only communicate to one another that "life is shit. We are shit." But maybe Shields and his friends don't constitute the whole world.

WHEN HE WAS at Brown, Shields (he notes it with appropriate irony) "actually scratched into the concrete wall above my carrel, 'I shall dethrone Shakespeare.'" At Iowa, he grew out of this hope because he was surrounded by instructors who helped him realize that he should write what he knows. This, the first commandment of American fiction, has been attributed to Twain and Hemingway, among others. It's a truism, in a sense—you can't write anything you don't know—but the directive is often used to justify writing that is childish and self-indulgent. The novelist Nathan Englander suggests, plausibly enough, that "write what you know" is really a statement about emotions: write what you feel. And this is more or less where Shields lands with his paraphrase: instead of trying to be a genius, "you write out of your own experience."

But, judging from his recent writing, Shields hasn't outgrown his ambition to be a genius; he's just decided that he can achieve it by writing what he feels, a commitment that conveniently saves him the trouble of ever having to learn anything new.* And the result is predictable: in the absence of concrete knowledge, he moves straight from his own intensely personal experience ("I feel so alone...") to the universal conclusions that "life equals death"; "language never fails to fail us"; "the endemic disease of our time is the absence of feeling"; or—a flashback to my Peter Carey reading group—"fiction teaches the reader that life is a coherent, fathomable whole that concludes in neatly wrapped-up revelation. Life, though ... flies at us in bright splinters." What fiction does that? Whose life?

Two of the most disturbing (in a bad way) passages in Shields's recent books show, perhaps even more lucidly than his appropriation of Adorno, the potential excesses of his approach. At the age of thirty, Shields encountered Milan Kundera's claim that it's not hard to write "about the intersection of personal and political lives ... when you go to the grocery store and the cannon of a Soviet tank is wedged into the back window." He theorized that the American version of that tank is the fictional nature of American life, "the ubiquity of the camera, the immense power of the camera lens on our lives, on my life, on the way I think about life." Similarly, in *Reality Hunger*, Shields informs us that the point of Brian Fawcett's *Cambodia: A Book for People Who Find Television Too Slow* is to show how "wall-to-wall media represent as thorough a raid on individual memory as the Khmer Rouge."

A bit of context: after the reformist Prague Spring of 1968 (Kundera took part, and was later expelled from the Party), Czechoslovakia was invaded and occupied by the U.S.S.R.; between 1948 and 1989, hundreds of thousands of people were imprisoned for their political beliefs. The Khmer Rouge took power in Cambodia in 1975. Between one and three million Cambodians, around twenty percent of the population, were executed, died in labor camps, or died in famines that were more or less caused by Khmer Rouge policies—in four years.

What kind of a person, I wonder, responds to Kundera's revealing statement by immediately wondering how oppressed *he* is, or compares "wall-to-wall media" to the Cambodian genocide?† Such a person would have to take for

---

* I wonder what Shields must think of, say, *War and Peace, Beloved, Gilead* or *The Recognitions*, not to mention Shakespeare's plays or Borges's essays? None of them were written from the author's own experience in any but the most trivial sense: they needed research on, among other things, international war, American history, theology, art history and domestic politics. The "write out of your experience" approach suggests, to the contrary, that the writer sits down before a blank computer screen and starts to pour his or her feelings out onto the screen.

† For the sake of comparison, imagine reading a book called *The Holocaust: A Book for People Who Find Television Too Slow*, and thinking to yourself, "Yes, that's right. All these iPads do make me feel like I'm in Auschwitz."

granted all of the assumptions of the post-boomer, post-avant-garde American public intellectual, including: there is something deep within me that I'm inherently unable to express; life has been drained of meaning; the human animal never gets what it wants; anything we put into language is inevitably distorted; we're all terrified of and obsessed with death; all "truth" is "relative"; ~~the Internet Blogs MySpace Texting Facebook Smart Phones Twitter Cloud Computing Tumblr Vine Reddit~~ Instagram ~~have~~ has fundamentally changed the world, which is why nobody reads anymore; we want to connect with reality, but can't, and that's tragic; our time is uniquely chaotic and everything has to change in order to adjust to that chaos. Someone sufficiently immersed in this intellectual culture might well note that he, like the victims of the Khmer Rouge, is suffering (for all the reasons listed above), and that his suffering is as deep as the suffering of others. Someone immersed in this culture might be incapable of understanding anyone other than himself, might believe in the importance of theorizing about the effects of choosing to watch lots of television, and be unable to distinguish between that theorizing on the one hand, and, on the other, brutal and/or genocidal military repression. Thankfully, our language does not fail to provide a word for this kind of person: an adolescent. Unless he's an adult; in that case, we call him a narcissist.

T HE BIG SUCCÈS *de scandale* of the late 1970s, (similarly controversial to *Reality Hunger*), was Christopher Lasch's *The Culture of Narcissism*. Today people still read the book as a cry against American egoism, which makes sense given what happened to the country in the following years. But Lasch wasn't worried that his contemporaries were too selfish. He was worried that otherwise normal Americans displayed the character traits of clinical narcissists. They found it difficult to connect with the world, because they didn't recognize their own boundaries: "The point of the story is not that Narcissus falls in love with himself but, since he fails to recognize his own reflection, that *he lacks any conception of the difference between himself and his surroundings.*" The narcissist simply doesn't understand that there are people who don't have his experiences and understanding of the world, or that there is a world that is not a part of himself. The "cure," so to speak, is a "recognition of our need for and dependence on people who[m we recognize] ... as independent beings with desires of their own. More broadly, it lies in acceptance of our limits." Understanding our own limits allows us to live with and for others—we recognize that we need them, and, in fact, come to find comfort in this fact. If we're fortunate, we discover, with others, "a world in which we can find pleasure and meaning."

Clinical cases aside, this describes what happens, or should happen, when (particularly middle-class) people grow up. We leave home and have to find ways to live without the rules and customs that the family unit provides. Like many teenagers, I rebelled. I wanted to be my own man, so I had to cut through all the filters that other people—parents, teachers, even friends—set up around me, to go beyond everything upon which I had, until then, depended: hence my mission to disenchant. But doing that is scary, so, like most teenagers, I also looked for certainty, things I could fall back on, anchors in culture (anarchism, post-structuralism, punk) and in what I took to be my personality (straight-edge, dying my hair black—not a good idea—wearing mismatched socks). Like most teenagers, I incessantly joined or identified with parties, teams and groups, while also trying to abolish the rules and customs that allow groups to function. Now, thank god, much of this is behind me: I find pleasure and meaning in the fact that I depend on other beings who are radically different from me. My wife, for instance. Sometimes my dog.

Like all memoirists, David Shields has been attacked for being self-obsessed. But he's not self-obsessed: he's a narcissist. Shields is unable to recognize the difference between his experience of the world—as an extremely privileged, intelligent, highly educated American—and the experiences of others. So he assimilates everyone else's experiences to his own. At the same time, he wants to make grand proclamations about the human condition, which leads him to the wild and abstract language of existentialism and post-structuralism. (As a lonely ambivalent review suggested, his works "might be mistaken for the notebook of a naïve undergraduate after a first encounter with Postmodernism 101.") But the worst of it is that Shields is just one instance of a group of American intellectuals—particularly prevalent in the arts—that live as narcissists. Having never grown up, they congratulate one another for gossiping about the endlessly important topics of sex, loneliness, death, and the fact that life is shit.

Not surprisingly, these literati have come out strongly in favor of Shields's work. Jonathan Lethem was "astonished, intoxicated, ecstatic, overwhelmed" by *Reality Hunger*. Chuck Klosterman thought it "might be the most intense, thought-accelerating book of the last ten years." Wayne Koestenbaum described it as "the book our sick-at-heart moment needs—like a sock in the jaw or an electric jolt in the solar plexus—to wake it up." Sam Tanenhaus explained that the book "tells us that everybody is doing everything wrong," while for Jonathan Safran Foer *Reality Hunger* was "more than thought provoking"—it was beautiful. And the attention to his ideas apparently extends beyond flattery, at least as Shields tells it: "I see my work endlessly inscribed and reinscribed in other people's work. ... Sometimes the bigger ideas behind a work, to me, that come from my work are not credited, and sometimes a tiny line's credited."

No doubt, there's something very attractive about the conversation Shields has with his friends. I know I once appreciated being able to talk about the human condition before I knew anything about the conditions under which most people actually live. Moreover, short of joining a revolutionary movement—there are almost none—it can feel as if there's very little you or I can do on our own to improve the world immediately. I try not to use A/C; like everyone else, I obsess about what I eat; I've stopped using plastic bags. But as my father never tires of pointing out, e.g., "studies have shown" that plastic bags contribute only (say) 0.01 percent of a nation's trash—meaningless. It can be charming to read, every now and then, a book which claims to have identified the one big problem and a way of solving it, thus relieving us of helplessness, or, even better, to have shown that the one big problem is insoluble, thus relieving us of further guilt. But, pleasure aside, you only need to deal with one hundred small, real problems like plastic bags and you'll effect a one percent reduction in trash, which is hardly insignificant. If we're extraordinarily lucky, we might be able to survive with a fifty percent reduction, which means dealing with 5,000 such problems, one at a time.

As it happens, I borrowed *How Literature Saved My Life* from the Los Angeles Public Library. A previous reader had left a Post-it in the book. S/he'd written on it something that sounds like a thought David Shields would quote: "In a universe so indifferent to our fate—how best to endure—to go on." My first thought was that the universe isn't indifferent to our fate, any more than my desk is indifferent to my fate: the universe is not the kind of thing that could be interested or indifferent. My second thought was that I have a family and friends, none of whom are indifferent to my fate.

My third thought was to look up the sponsor of the post-it, Kaletra. It's a brand of AIDS medication.

There really are some people for whom life is a daily struggle. I'm pretty sure that the point and meaning of life is to ensure that as few as possible have to exist in that way. And that's only possible if we stop assuming that we all do.

Derek Paul Boyle, *rorschach test (ink on cardboard)*, 2011

LOOKING BACK

CHRISTOPHER LASCH AND THE ROLE OF THE SOCIAL CRITIC

by Michael J. Kramer

I N COWBOY HAT and roller skate boots, Olivia Newton-John glided toward the viewer from the cover of the July 9, 1979 issue of *People* magazine. Below her, a headline announced that Americans had gone mad for roller skating. *People* went so far as to suggest that the fad, taken up by Cher, the Village People, JFK Jr., Andy Warhol, Newton-John and other celebrities might inspire citizens to forgo cars and, *voilà*, solve the energy crisis plaguing the country. Inside the issue, however, a more pessimistic voice could be found. *People* featured an interview with the historian and social critic Christopher Lasch. Though the cover story promised a future where fitness fads solve political problems, Lasch presented a more dour message about the crises facing Americans in the 1970s: "I have no easy solutions," he grumbled.

Lasch's appearance in *People* stemmed from the surprising success of his book, *The Culture of Narcissism*. Despite—or perhaps because of—its pessimistic tone and grim analysis of contemporary American culture, *Narcissism* had cracked the bestseller list in the spring of 1979, going so far as to attract the attention of President Jimmy Carter, who met with Lasch and a group of intellectuals while preparing his ill-fated "Crisis of Confidence" speech. America's economy was mired in "stagflation," while its international standing had waned after the Vietnam War. A kind of desperation and apathy dominated the country's mood. But Lasch saw this desperation as signaling not a momentary shift, but rather the decay of certain ideals:

> Bourgeois society seems everywhere to have used up its store of constructive ideas. It has lost both the capacity and the will to confront the difficulties that threaten to overwhelm it. ... This book ... describes a way of life that is dying—the culture of competitive individualism, which in its decadence has carried the logic of individualism to the extreme of a war

of all against all, the pursuit of happiness to the dead end of a narcissistic preoccupation with the self.

Many at the time missed the point of Lasch's dark, brooding analysis, which applied psychoanalytic theory to the broader cultural setting of American life, arguing not so much that Americans had grown self-involved during the so-called "Me Decade" as that the modern institutions of what he called the "therapeutic state" and of consumer capitalism had infantilized them. The term "narcissism" meant more than simply self-involvement for Lasch: it indicated a frail sense of self, weak ties to one's community and feelings of despair. The result, Lasch suggested, was a population of clinical narcissists, oscillating between outsized fantasies of their own grandiosity—dreaming of their own celebrity—and recurring anxieties about even getting by.

What set Lasch apart from most critics of American selfishness was that he did not blame individuals, or "culture," for the emergence of narcissism; he blamed larger structures of power. The welfare state, together with consumerist society, had penetrated to the core of American lives, stripping them of both inner resources and immediate spaces of control in their families and communities. The state's "helping professions" (social workers, therapists, child-rearing "experts," etc.) offered social assistance, but in the bargain they undermined the role of parents and local communities. The market offered new products and opportunities for pleasure, but it "simultaneously [made man] acutely unhappy with his lot." Both the state and the market promoted themselves as offering freedom through abundance and progress, but in fact "eroded everyday competence, in one area after another":

> Having surrendered most of his technical skills to the corporation, [the American individual] can no longer provide for his material needs. As the family loses not only its productive functions but many of its reproductive functions as well, men and women no longer manage even to raise their children without the help of certified experts.

The Culture of Narcissism solidified Lasch's reputation as a leading anti-modernist critic of an America that seemed to have lost its balance as it roller-skated into oblivion. Mistrusting America's affluence and growing technological achievements, Lasch even critiqued the anti-authoritarian liberation struggles of the 1960s, which belonged for him to the same modernist cult of progress that, failing to recognize necessary limits, would destroy all in its path. The counter-culture's myth of exaggerated self-realization was but the flipside of the retreat into basic self-preservation. Detached by state and market from connections to a more sustaining sense of purpose or obligation, Americans inhabited a culture that left them rootless.

But Lasch should not be remembered merely as a grumbling reactionary. What he feared was "liberation," not "modernity"—dismissing anti-modernist nostalgia as the fantasy of progress in reverse. For most of his life (he died of cancer in 1994), he remained committed to a more egalitarian society and clung to the hope that change might still occur. As he said toward the end of a career that had turned, beginning with *Narcissism*, increasingly dark and pessimistic: he still had faith even though he lacked optimism. It was a statement that flummoxed many interviewers, but it is key to understanding Lasch's complex vision of American culture—and of the role of the social critic within it.

SOCIAL CRITICISM *for* SOCIAL CRISIS

WHAT SHOULD WE expect from social criticism? When should we say that the social critic has actually served his society? Today's most popular social critics are barely critical at all, often offering platitudes of flat worlds, creative classes, long tails and disruptive technologies. Meanwhile, a robust world of blogs and small magazines is split between desolate cynicism and simplistic earnestness. The pages and websites of venues such as *Harper's*, the *Baffler*, *n+1*, *Jacobin* and the *New Inquiry* are filled with piercing, often quite funny, critiques by the likes of Thomas Frank and others; but these works often end up calling for a return to vanished modes of political and cultural life or, worse still, celebrating the subversive pleasures of sardonic hopelessness itself. Meanwhile, in publications such as the *Believer*, a new sincerity glows, insisting that in place of critique we "just say yes" (as *Believer* founder Dave Eggers insisted we do in a notorious 2000 interview). Both camps would do well by reading Lasch's first book—*The New Radicalism in America*—his diagnosis of how twentieth-century intellectuals had mistaken their own cultural rebellions for political activism.

In our own era, continuous commentary on the political maneuverings around DOMA, health care and immigration has sometimes obscured a massive failure to engage with the issues of poverty, mass incarceration, growing wealth disparity, corporatization, endless war, ecological catastrophe and the striking abandonment of the concept of the common good. Lasch set a useful bar for commenting on matters of political strategy without abandoning either larger social analysis or cultural critique. Although best known for his later works, it was during the 1960s that Lasch wrote most widely and actively—about everything from the war in Vietnam to the American family, from the New Left and the counterculture to the fate of the working classes in the so-called postindustrial economy. Throughout these essays, he insisted that deep inquiry and careful analysis could go along with smart action, and that shallow cultural rebellion need not replace sustained ideological and political struggle.

Lasch's social criticism from the Sixties provides a model, imperfect but worthy, of using the firm ground of American social values to make a stand, of finding a way forward without insisting on the chimera of progress. Particularly for those who are sympathetic to yet dissatisfied with the left in America, there is much to be learned from Lasch's ability to criticize liberalism and progressivism, to fuse historically-informed analysis with explorations of political strategy, and to uncover a countertradition to the worst aspects of modern American life.

BEYOND LEFT and RIGHT

WITH THE ANTI-WAR movement growing, civil rights struggles widening and Lyndon B. Johnson's Great Society taking shape, the 1960s seemed destined to extend the intellectual dominance of American liberalism. It was at this moment that Lasch emerged as one of America's most astute critics of liberalism. For Lasch, modern liberalism's great flaw was its contempt for limits. Forever urging Americans to move forward, modern liberalism (in whatever guise it took) failed to root them in a meaningful context in which tradition could mingle with transformation. The liberal left's obsession with liberation even worked against its ideal of social equality, playing "into the hands of the corporations, which find it all too easy to exploit a radicalism that equates liberation with hedonistic self-indulgence and freedom from family ties."

To Lasch's mind, even what passed for conservatism in post-Sixties America—Ronald Reagan's New Right, as well as the rise of neoconservatism—fell under the umbrella of liberalism broadly construed. These movements were but shrill reactions to the radical upheavals of the 1960s left (this was especially true of neoconservatism, which was founded mostly by defected left-wing intellectuals). They emphasized a faux-traditionalism whose veneration of the past barely masked support for the expansion of corporate capitalism. Rather than preserving the values of localism, community, family and self-reliance that it so sanctimoniously endorsed, the right in fact swept them into the nostalgized dustbin of history. Yet the right had "managed to present itself, infuriatingly, as a form of cultural populism, even though its own ... economic program ... seeks only to perpetuate the existing distribution of wealth and power."

All of Lasch's work focused to some degree on reformulating American intellectual life outside the frame of liberalism, but in his essays of the late Sixties and early Seventies, he began to articulate a new kind of radicalism, one that resisted both the empty nostalgia found on the post-Sixties right as well as the fixation on progress and liberation found on the battered post-Sixties left. Although he was committed to Marxist economic analysis as a necessary starting point for social critique, Lasch emphasized the need to engage with "a long tradition of conservative criticism of modern culture" frequently dismissed by Marxists as retrograde. Indeed, the ideals of transformation and conservation might mingle in productive ways, as they had in the tradition of socialist social criticism dating back at least to William Morris and John Ruskin.

In his breakthrough 1965 book, *The New Radicalism in America*, Lasch criticized liberal intellectuals of the early twentieth century for conflating their own need to break free of middle-class bourgeois mores with the wider need to create a more just and democratic society in the United States. But the problem for social critics on the left went even deeper. The challenge, which remains familiar today, was to find some way of articulating leftist ideals without seeming to abandon the everyday concerns of ordinary Americans or condescend to them from the heights of technocratic expertise:

> Faced with the embarrassing gap between Leftist ideology and "existing popular consciousness" ... the American Left has had to choose, in effect, between two equally futile and self-defeating strategies: either to wait helplessly for the revolution, while fulminating against "capitalism," or to try to gain its objectives by outflanking public opinion, giving up the hope of creating a popular constituency for social reform, and relying instead on the courts, the mass media, and the administrative bureaucracy.

To help Americans construct a "new culture," Lasch thought, social critics would do well to resuscitate a conservative-minded emphasis on self-reliance, autonomy, community spirit, directness, commitment and a sense of limits. Lasch distinguished his case from the "so-called cultural revolution identified with one wing of the new left." That revolution may have had "many promising possibilities," but "in its present form it [did] not represent an alternative social vision capable of attracting large masses to its support." Radicals were wrong to overthrow all tradition even if much of it was fraught with inequality.

MICHAEL KRAMER

A SOCIALISM SUITABLE *for* AMERICA

THROUGHOUT HIS CAREER, Lasch sought a form of radicalism that neither relied on personal liberation nor implied rigid submission to outmoded ideologies. In *The Agony of the American Left*, he framed the problem this way: "The almost overwhelming difficulties confronting the radical movement in America are suggested, more clearly perhaps than by anything else, by the vagueness and imprecision of the term 'socialism.'" In Lasch's time as in our own, the term "socialism" is often reduced to a belief in so-called "big government." For Lasch, however, the term could mean much more. Most of all, it served to emphasize a commitment to developing political and cultural mechanisms that gave people control over their lives. Social criticism's role was to elucidate why socialism was essential to the political and psychic survival of Americans, and also to demonstrate how much more consistent it was with American ideals than many in the country assumed.

In his historical surveys of radicalism in early-twentieth-century America, Lasch argued that the divergent traditions of populism and socialism intersected to produce "the beginnings of a mass movement against the dehumanizing effects of the new industrial order." At its peak in 1912, the Socialist Party boasted 118,000 members; the largest of the socialist newspapers, the *Appeal to Reason* of Girard, Kansas, enjoyed a weekly circulation of 761,747. The party's strength lay in "its ability to combine a commitment to thorough-going social transformation with 'constructive' political action, in the party's terminology—that is, responsiveness to the needs of its constituents." If socialism in American began to die out in the aftermath of World War I, it was not because there was no need or sympathy for it among the American populace, but rather because an influx of ideology "drawn from European experience and tied organizationally to the fluctuating political requirements of the Soviet Union" divided the movement and alienated segments of its leadership from their constituents. Lasch called for a revival of early American socialism's broad-based radicalism. Especially for those advocating for fundamental change in America, it was imperative to learn from those "impressive and partially successful attempts to create a mass-based, indigenous radicalism among disaffected groups—socialism among the working-class poor and among middle-class intellectuals, black nationalism in the Negro ghetto."

By mining the ideals and values of this older tradition, Lasch believed that the social critic could do more to advance the cause of socialism than economic and political analysis could do on their own. Culture mattered here as much as redistributive politics. The task was to nurture a radicalism that intersected with the time-honored values still lingering in the hearts and minds of Americans both radical and conservative. But this would require drawing heavily on "older values which the ruling classes were in the process of gradually discarding":

> In our own time, the ruling class has broken the last ties to its own cultural traditions and has imposed on society a technological anticulture charac-terized by its ruthless disregard of the past. The agent of the new anticul-ture is the bulldozer, which destroys familiar landmarks, liquidates entire communities, and breaks down every form of continuity. ... "Revolution" today may represent, among other things, the only hope of preserving what is worth preserving from the past.

What traditions of community, localism, self-reliance, work and limitation might conjoin with liberal values to address the modern economic, political and cul-tural situation? The social critic, Lasch thought, should work to help Americans understand why they felt so enraged at—and so helpless to change—the world around them. This meant resisting easy answers, including the easy answer that often went by the name of "revolution." The work of revolution was always, in part, the work of preservation. The social critic's role thus required him not so much to reject the past as to sift through it and pick out which materials might be of continued use.

"The MANY-FACETED CRISIS of WORK"

MOST OF ALL, in a culture rapidly moving away from older notions of craftsmanship and professional responsibility, the social critic had to find a way of rehabilitating the nobility and satisfaction of independent work. Yet this recovery had to avoid the temptation to retreat into fantastical escapism or to trumpet individual "choice" in a "free" marketplace. The hard and urgent project was to create institutional contexts in which individuals could make professional choices that actually mattered.

If Lasch were around today, he would undoubtedly see Occupy Wall Street as a source of both optimism and despair—as many of us have. One of his interests would be the movement's vacillation between two conflicting visions of work. Its populist ninety-nine-versus-one-percent rhetoric, as well as its emphasis on debt and widespread unemployment, seem to point to a society in which good and meaningful work might be available for all. Yet in the carnivalesque at-

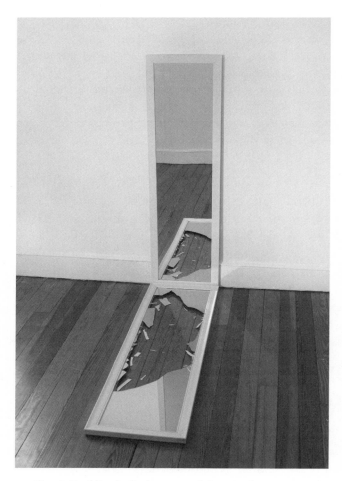

Derek Paul Boyle, *broken mirror below another mirror*, 2012

mosphere of the protests, with their drum circles and festive feel, there was also a sense that all work was oppressive, that a revolution would entail liberation from work entirely. Forty years ago, Lasch had already criticized the tendency for certain radicals to "define personal liberation ... as freedom from work, discipline and from authority in general":

> The trouble with this definition of the "cultural revolution" is that it tends to divert attention from work to leisure, thereby reinforcing one of the strongest and most dangerous tendencies of advanced capitalist society—the attempt to compensate for the meaninglessness of work by holding out the possibility of spiritual fulfillment through consumption. Contrary to a widespread cliché of popular sociology, "the challenge of leisure" is not the most important issue in advanced society. The most important issue remains work—the loss of autonomy on the job, the collapse of high standards of workmanship, the pervasive demoralization that results from the mass production of goods that are widely recognized as intrinsically worthless by those who produce them, and the general crisis of a culture historically oriented around the dignity of labor.

Counterculturalists, Lasch believed, tended to picture "utopia as generalized leisure, thereby reaffirming, instead of contradicting, the vision of industrial society itself." Yet, Lasch contended, "centuries of experience ... have taught us that work is one of the deepest of man's needs." The task confronting the left was therefore not to overthrow the work ethic—which was already under attack from within capitalist society—but to invest it with new meaning.

In the late Sixties and early Seventies, such concerns informed Lasch's criticism of a militant student movement that increasingly saw itself at the cutting edge of revolution. Suspended in an extended adolescence during a time when access to higher education rapidly expanded in the United States, university students became "temporary members of a leisure class." This meant that they experienced life at a distance from the immediate pressures of the industrial system—or, as one analyst whom Lasch admired called it, the "super-industrial" system of a society increasingly concentrated on finance, information and symbolic analysis rather than on straightforward factory production. In their temporary identities as students, young Americans were in no position to satisfy the need for a more durable vision of social change.

At the same time, Lasch might have looked with some suspicion on the Fox News-style criticism that the Occupy movement represents merely the rumblings of a temporary leisure class, suspended in a world of hedonism while they wait for "real life" to begin. For this criticism relies on an opposition that Lasch believed was rapidly evaporating even in his own time. College students in the 1970s, he argued, were already experiencing the alienations that lay in their future. Although the need "for large numbers of trained technicians and professionals [had] led to an unprecedented expansion of higher education," he noted, "in the course of its expansion, the university [had] come more and more to be operated on industrial lines." Because they were positioned as "prospective workers," students tended to "experience the many-faceted crisis of work" in their education itself. The modern system of higher education—large classes, instrumentalized versions of the liberal arts, a sense that their education was neither transformative nor practical—brought them face-to-face with "not only their enforced leisure but also the knowledge that they are being trained for meaningless work."

At this level, Lasch believed that there was a "possibility that the university and university politics might come to play an important role in the development of a new kind of 'working-class' consciousness." Perhaps students, especially those who had grown dispirited with the demise of the New Left in 1969 and the thinness of countercultural "lifestyle" as a mode of revolt, might connect to the working-class not via some formulaic model from Marxist-Leninist theory, but rather as part of a broader movement of professionals witnessing the deskilling of their jobs right alongside the traditional proletariat. "The industrial system's need for the carefully controlled production of knowledge means that increasing numbers of intellectual workers will face declining autonomy, regimentation, and loss of status," Lasch wrote. "Their common subordination to bureaucratic control may overcome the many barriers between the professional and technical strata and the new working class, bringing into being a new labor movement."

Lasch was hesitantly hopeful. He noticed former New Left activists joining the workforce, and "rediscovering the importance of institutional ties." Instead of denouncing all professional organizations as "purely imprisoning," these new workers were growing more interested in the kinds of solidarity they might discover in the workplace, as sites of potential "ferment," "fellowship" and "support for the creative use of one's talents." To Lasch, a "revolt against narrow professionalism and professional irresponsibility" was key to the unleashing of radicalism in America. But it had to be a "revolt not against the professions but within the professions." One had to, in the language of our own times, occupy institutions of work in order to infuse them with new values. "What seems to be needed," he mused,

> is a fusion of community politics and trade union politics—two dissident traditions that have increasingly grown apart. The product of this fusion would not be simply a new unionism or a new kind of community organizing but a new form of politics altogether, centered on the factory—and on

the research and development laboratory, the intellectual assembly line, the professions, the media—but always heedful of work in its larger social implications.

Today, as many students sink into crushing debt as the price for credentials that increasingly do not even guarantee professional employment, Lasch's observations about the relationship between student life and work seem all the more applicable. His insights—about the connections between an alienating education and future work, and about the import of workspaces for building solidarity—offer new directions for the ninety-nine percent. Lasch's reflections on student-worker dynamics indicate that the contemporary effort to delineate between the large, quite diverse group of have-nots and the increasingly small group of elites, must focus not only on the ability to own a home or participate in the consumer market, but also on the draining of meaning from work at all levels.

The NEW LEFT and ORDINARY AMERICANS

HIS RECONCEPTUALIZATION OF the left-right divide, as well as his focus on the topic of work, led Lasch to develop a far greater sensitivity to the anxieties and concerns of Americans who were unsympathetic to the more militant calls for social change in the late Sixties and early Seventies. Lasch did not simply ignore or explain away the reactionary dimensions of the petit bourgeois or the emerging New Right in America at that time (as, say, Thomas Frank did in *What's the Matter with Kansas?*)—he grappled with them. And he did so in ways that are useful for considering the potential intersections between right and left, and the social critic and society, today.

Consider the rhetoric around an issue like the environment. In the late Sixties and early Seventies, Lasch was already encouraging social critics to address what he saw as the decoupling of ecological issues from everyday economic ones. Today, the importance of "green jobs" is occasionally remarked upon by Democratic politicians, but by and large the need to "grow the economy," as the odd phrase goes, is placed in opposition to environmental matters—as if the common man is being asked to sacrifice his job for the sake of benefits that are unsure and which anyway he is unlikely to enjoy. Rarely do liberals emphasize that our exploitation of the natural world will inevitably hinder the growth of the economy. Lasch saw this lack of clarity as an opportunity for social criticism. "One of the major tasks confronting the left," he wrote, "is to show how the urban crisis and the more general 'environmental crisis' originate in capitalist production":

Agitation around ecological issues, if these issues were properly explained, would help to create a common consciousness of deprivation among students, workers, and members of the "new middle class" by showing that the industrial system victimizes *everybody*—except the very rich, who can provide themselves with means of escape from the environmental devastation that their own policies have brought about. Pollution, noise, congestion, violence, crime, the physical and moral destruction of the city in the interests of developers, the ravaging of the landscape, suburban sprawl, and the deterioration of the schools have created widespread fear, resentment, and anger in the working and middle classes; but this anger, instead of venting itself against the corporations, too often finds secondary targets—the blacks, liberals, radical students, "bureaucracy," "government interference." The left then misinterprets the symptoms of popular resentment as incorrigible racism, devotion to the status quo, and proto-fascism, and writes off the working class and new middle class as reactionary. Instead, the left should be trying to demonstrate that the deterioration of the environment and the collapse of public service, which people experience most acutely in their capacity as consumers and citizens, must be attributed not to the blacks or to the state but to the corporations and to a system of production that has outlived its economic and social utility.

This kind of forceful language was required, Lasch felt, to shift the debate over ecological catastrophe away from the sphere of consumption, in which by buying "greener" we might save ourselves and the world, and back to the processes of production, where the exploitation and expropriation actually occurs. Recoupling this delinked aspect of environmental degradation and capitalist expropriation is not only a better way of understanding the problems that Americans face; it might turn the environment into a source of common cause and solidarity.

Lasch's perspective might also inspire better thinking today about the connections between the climate crisis and the economic crisis. These are concurrent phenomena, of course, but they are rarely explored as interlinked political problems. How might the critique of America's reliance on fossil fuels be linked to widening economic inequalities? Is there something pernicious in the very concept of "growth"? Celebrated by Republican and Democrat politicians alike, rarely questioned as an ideal by mainstream economists, and even utilized as the primary language of personal development and happiness in what Lasch later bemoaned as America's "culture of narcissism," perhaps the perpetual demand for "growth" comes with its own costs—to our environment, our traditions, and even our psychological well-being. In place of the moralistic tone of much radical environmentalism, emphasizing the limitations of the ideal of limitless forward motion might open up opportunities for a different, more inclusive, brand of radicalism. But this would also require moving beyond portrayals of working-class Americans as either Archie Bunker reactionaries or, the mere flip side of this image, as militant trade unionists marching in solidarity toward the Marxist future, hand in hand with their radical brethren from the academy. It means taking seriously the populist perspective of Americans suspicious of all larger forces—legal, political, cultural and economic—sweeping through their lives, upending their sense of autonomy and control.

IS THIS WHAT WE WANT?

LASCH'S WRITING REMAINED passionate and cogent to the end, but he grew more bitter and, at times, more brittle in his attacks on the modern liberal narrative of ever-increasing individual rights and collective progress. Gone was the balance between hope and despair, typical of his Sixties and early-Seventies criticism. Moreover, Lasch himself seemed at times to abandon his commitment to taking seriously the ideas and values of ordinary Americans, ironically in favor of the seemingly endless task of chastising other social critics for failing to take seriously the ideas and values of ordinary Americans. The move toward lambasting professional elites at the end of his career seemed oddly to reproduce the very "new radicalism" that he had so cogently critiqued in *The New Radicalism in America*, with Lasch rather narcissistically projecting his isolation from other intellectuals into a fantasy of "anti-intellectualism" among the lower classes.

Yet there remains even in Lasch's late books, and especially in his final book, *True and Only Heaven*, hints and portents of what a truly engaged and "radical" social criticism might look like. A test for this criticism would be its ability to provide a vision of the good life that rejected a progressive fantasy of abundance without sliding into nostalgia for yesteryear. Already in the early Seventies, Lasch had begun to explore how Americans could be made to wake from the dream of perpetual progress:

> It is only therefore when we find ourselves imprisoned in our private cars, marvelously mobile but unable to go anywhere because the highways are choked with traffic; when we find ourselves surrounded by modern conveniences but unable to breathe the air; provided with unprecedented leisure to fish in polluted rivers and swim at polluted beaches; provided with the means to prolong life beyond the point where it offers any pleasure; equipped with the power to create human life, which will simultaneously

destroy the meaning of life—it is only, in short, when we are confronted with the contradictions of individualism and private enterprise in their most immediate, unmistakable, and by now familiar form that we are forced to reconsider our exaltation of the individual over the life of the community, and to submit technological innovations to a question we have so far been careful not to ask: Is this what we want?

By connecting the big questions of liberal progress and perfectibility to an even larger, more pressing question—"Is this what we want?"—Lasch challenged his readers to search for a way out of the impasse where the only two options seemed to be a crackpot realism that insisted on technological degradation as a necessary corollary of progress, and a glazed-over utopian drive for perfection. As was so often the case, Lasch looked to the past—and to the populist past—for help articulating such a path. In place of the idea of history as linear progress, he argued for "concepts like nemesis, fate, fortune, or providence." Instead of "luxury for all," he endorsed "competence, as [American populists] would have called it—a piece of earth, a small shop, a useful calling." Competence, Lasch believed, "was a more reasonable as well as a more worthy ambition" than consumerism or perfectionism, embodying "a humbler set of expectations" in addition to "a more strenuous and morally demanding definition of the good life."

Populism, Lasch acknowledged, was becoming "increasingly defensive" and had always expressed "some of the worst impulses in the American character: anti-intellectualism, xenophobia, racism." The movement had, nevertheless, also offered what Lasch called the "only serious attempt to answer the great question of twentieth-century politics: What was to replace proprietorship as the material foundation of civic virtue?" To be sure, the Tea Party—currently our most prominent representative of plebeian radicalism—repeats the quasi-fascistic characteristics that Lasch admits have always played a part in American populism. Yet lurking below the Tea Party's reactionary surface are other energies and ideologies, other politics: most of all a desire to hang on to something real, material, immediate and autonomous in a world that feels as if it is sucking life itself up into the "cloud" of expertise, wealth and the disembodied forces of finance. It is easy to dismiss the rage that distorts those impulses as simple prejudice (at our black president, for instance); it is harder, but perhaps also more hopeful, to see it as indicative of the frustrations many Americans feel with what Lasch called "the exhaustion of the progressive tradition."

For social critics, the task now requires recalibrating away from cynical glibness or faux-naïve sincerity, to something more than a "wistful hope against hope that things will somehow work out for the best" or its opposite: a forsaking of hope altogether. Lasch urged us to seek out and recover "a more vigorous form of hope, which trusts life without denying its tragic character." At its best,

Lasch's criticism gestures toward a form of social inquiry that he was himself able to pursue only sporadically. So bitter on account of the contempt with which other elites seemed to hold the ideals of America's middle class, Lasch never got around to fully imagining a world that took those ideals seriously. That work remains.

Jonathan Dalton, *Driftwood*, 2011
32" x 24"
jonathandalton.ie

PREY

WRITING ABOUT THE DEAD

by Katharine Smyth

WHEN I WAS in my mid-twenties, an aspiring writer casting about for material, I made a date with my friend Laura to visit the cadaver she was dissecting for anatomy class. Her professor had invited his first-year medical students to share the rite of passage with a friend or family member, and Laura—who hated anatomy class—had chosen me. "I would never inflict this on anyone else," she said, "but I thought you might like to write about it." Implicit in her assumption was the notion, both perverse and correct, that a writer seeking a story will readily, even gladly, undertake the kinds of encounters most others go to great lengths to avoid. And while I had no prior affinity for the subject of human dissection, I was indeed intrigued by Laura's morbid observations: how cutting into the cadaver's chest for the first time made her feel guilty, as though she were desecrating the body and causing the woman pain. How, when she put the plastic bag back over the woman's head, she could not dispel the feeling she was suffocating her, "killing her further." How she loathed the smell of formaldehyde, which, after two and a half hours in the lab, seeped into her hair and skin, seeming to embalm *her*. And how, afterward, upon first seeing her boyfriend's undressed body, there was a moment in which he too had seemed a corpse. "He walked into the bathroom fully clothed," she said, "and when he came out again, he was naked. And for an instant he was only a body, and his penis, which was unexcited, hanging there, was just dead flesh, a dead thing."

I wanted to hear more about Laura's experience, but I noticed that my own attitude toward the visit was one of cynicism. Not only was I treating the cadaver as a mere curiosity, but there was a hint of self-satisfaction in my conviction that its sight would not affect me—I think it derived from a leftover tomboyish belief that invulnerability is always preferable to fear. I envisioned the piece I would write (the organs gleaming like gemstones), as though the visit itself were a formality. Yet such irreverence troubled me. The notion of going to see a cadaver with the prior knowledge I would write about it struck me as manipulative. If I described the lab scene to a trusting reader, but while *in* the lab had thought only of its literary potential, must a truthful rendering of that scene thus include admission of my mindset? And what of the poor cadaver, whose former occupant had decided to bequeath her body to the medical school, but had likely not foreseen an outcome such as this? Finally I wondered about the repercussions of undergoing certain "significant" experiences simply because they might provide fodder for one's stories. In *Holy the Firm*, Annie Dillard asks her students which of them want to be writers, and then she tells them what the decision must mean: "You can't be anything else. You must go at your life with a broadax..." The line had long appealed to me—Dillard's vision of the artist, whom she later describes as a kind of sacrificial flame, is flattering, particularly if, as she asserts, "the world without light is wasteland and chaos, and a life without sacrifice is abomination." But until I visited Laura's cadaver, I had always assumed it was one's past one must attack. It had never occurred to me that one must "go at" one's present and future as well.

Several days before my trip to the lab, my friend Sarah and I shared a cab uptown; we were on our way to a black-tie birthday party. "Guess what I'm doing on Friday," I said. "I'm going to see Laura's cadaver."

"Do you think you'll be able to handle it?" she asked. I said I thought that I would.

There was a pause, and then she asked, "Have you ever seen a dead body before?"

"No, never," I said, just as I remembered that Sarah's mother had died a few months earlier, and that she was not an appropriate person with whom to be discussing cadavers.

The moment passed quickly, but I was embarrassed. It soon dawned on me that the lightness with which I had been approaching the visit was not a form of strength, but rather a failure to perceive the intrinsic relationship between Laura's cadaver and Sarah's mother; and further, a failure to perceive the potential relationship between Laura's cadaver and my father, who had nearly died three years before. He had been diagnosed with kidney cancer when I was a child; though his kidney was successfully removed, a diagnosis of bladder cancer had followed shortly afterward. His bladder was removed when I was twenty—the doctors were able to fashion a new bladder from his large intestine—but there were complications, and he was confined to the ICU for a stretch of several weeks. "It was touch and go there for a little while," his surgeon later told me. Nevertheless, my father survived, and, for the first time in nine years, he was

cancer-free. That was the same month Sarah's mother learned that she had co-
lon cancer.

My father's death had held enormous power for me the whole time I was
growing up. When I thought of what it felt like, the glaring fact of his imperma-
nence, I was reminded of Virginia Woolf on losing her mother at fifteen: "To
have that protection removed, to be tumbled out of the family shelter, to see the
cracks and gashes in that fabric, to be cut by them, to see beyond them..." The
prospect of that violence loomed for years. But by the time I stepped into the
cab that night, the fabric had repaired itself, and the realm beyond the fabric
was obscured. The loss of those closest to me had once again become something
that wouldn't *actually* happen. Death would intrude tangentially, killing friends'
pets, their grandfathers and even their mothers, but from me it would always
remain one step removed.

THE DOOR TO the lab was stainless steel, inlaid with a panel of opaque
glass that blazed a blinding white. When Laura opened the door to a room
full of sunlight, the space seemed—in that first instant—cheerful and fresh.
The far wall was a wall of windows, showing a near bird's eye view of the dorms
across the street, and three large, leafy plants hung from the ceiling. There were
heavily marked blackboards on the two end walls; two skeletons with blood-red
pelvises dangled in the corner. The room itself was long and thin. Eight stainless
steel tables were arranged lengthwise in rows of four, and on these tables were
eight bulky shapes, concealed by sheets of neon green plastic. The only disconcerting aspect was the smell, which was not as overpowering as I'd imagined, but
cloying and faintly vile nonetheless. And I was surprised that the bodies were
simply lying there—I had assumed they would be put away when not in use.

Laura's cadaver was in the near left-hand corner, next to her dissection
tools and the bowl in which she placed the organs during class. She prepared to
lift the sheet and paused: "Are you ready?"

"I'm nervous!" I said. I knew that the woman had died at 87, and that her
name was Nancy. But that I had no vision of what the sheet would reveal was
incredibly disconcerting. I didn't know whether to look away and see the body
all at once, or to watch as Laura pulled back the plastic. I ended up watching
with half-closed eyes, but the cadaver—which needed to stay wet—remained
partly masked by several layers of clear plastic. When Laura folded these back,
my first reaction was not horror but surprise: Nancy didn't look human at all.

"I know," said Laura. "Some look a lot more alive than others. I think she's been dead a long time." The cadaver's skin was a light beige color, and her body was misshapen, wrinkled and hard—she resembled a deflated, human-shaped balloon. Her limbs and torso lacked the curves of a live body, but her hands, still wrapped in plastic, were perfectly formed and cemented into loose fists. I touched them through the bag, at the bottom of which pooled clear yellow liquid. I had read that medical students usually cite seeing their cadaver's hands as the most emotional part of the process—the moment when they are able to connect their cadaver to the living person he or she once was—but the hands didn't bother me. "They don't bother me either," Laura said. "I think because I was expecting that they would."

What did bother me was the cadaver's face, which was still covered by a plastic bag and stiffened into an expression of disapproval. Her eyes were closed; her stringy, reddish hair was plastered to her skull. She had been lying on her face when she was stored, and as a result her nose was flattened and angled to one side. Most disturbing was her wiry black mustache, the kind of mustache that repels me even when I see it on old women who are still alive. Later I asked Laura if she felt any fondness toward her cadaver. She admitted that while she was abstractly thankful to Nancy for donating her body, she did not feel bonded to her in any way. "I'm not attracted to her as a human being. Maybe I would have felt a connection to another cadaver. There's one who still has nail polish on her hands. Or if it had been a child, god forbid. But I don't know. The mustache..." She trailed off.

Laura had started dissecting the thorax several weeks before, and there was a large incision down the middle of the cadaver's chest, and through one of her breasts. Parting the skin, Laura revealed a layer of muscle that was fibrous and looked like canned tuna fish. ("A lot of students have become vegetarians since this began," she said.) Opening the chest made the fetid smell much stronger; it became difficult to breathe through my nose. Laura removed the ribs, and then picked up a dense brownish lump the size of an apple. It was the heart. I peered into the hole the missing heart had made; I could see a few circular valves, but that was all. The formaldehyde had colored everything—skin, muscles, heart, and bones—the same light dull brown, and it was difficult to distinguish the body's various parts. There was no trace of the plump and variegated organs I had imagined describing before. Laura returned the heart and repositioned the ribs, and I helped her fold back the flaps of skin, which felt tough and rubbery. I studied the face one last time before replacing the plastic.

I looked at a second cadaver before we left. It was not against the rules, but it made Laura uncomfortable, and she made me pull back the sheet myself. Later she explained her uneasiness: "Whenever I feel like my actions are not strictly for the sake of science, I start feeling disrespectful. When I first started, I was more curious about their private parts than other parts, and it made me feel awful." This cadaver had been a large man, and looked slightly more lifelike and kindly than the first. His eyes were partly open, but though I bent down to try and see his eyeballs, I couldn't make them out. He had short black bristles on his face, as though he hadn't shaved in a few days, and I thought how hair—which is dead to begin with and looks no different on them than on us—was the most difficult part to see. Before covering him up, I could not help looking at his penis, the base of which another student had already started to dissect. The pubic bone of the first cadaver had repulsed and shamed me slightly. It had been covered in long, sparse hair, and seemed, indecently, to rise higher than the rest of her. But looking at this man's penis gave me a weird feeling of comfort. It lay between his legs, and fat and muscle erupted from a few diagonal cuts around its base. For the first time since entering the lab, I felt pleased by the mass of fat and muscle that must lie behind my own skin. For the first time, the concept of possessing an extraordinary but fallible body made perfect sense.

"Let's go," Laura said. "I hate it here." I could have stayed longer, but hurriedly covered the second cadaver and dumped my gloves and apron in the hazardous waste container by the door. I walked to the subway through cold, bright air; I felt dazed, and wholly distinct from those I passed. The scent of formaldehyde came and went in waves, and though I'd scrubbed my hands, my fingers still smelt sweet. Once on the train, I started to imagine my fellow passengers in bags—slimy and sickening, stretched out on stainless steel tables. I was not particularly upset, but now that I had seen the cadavers, I never wanted to think of them again. They struck me as ghoulish and distasteful. The thought of Nancy in particular—of how repellant I had found her mustache—made me feel guilty. I remembered what Laura had said about her professor's emphasis on respecting the bodies: "I feel like it's impossible to respect them. We're cutting them up, looking at them in places they didn't want to be seen when they were alive. How can they be respected when they're so vulnerable?" But Laura was dissecting Nancy for the sake of medicine. What was my excuse?

I was exhausted when I got home and immediately curled up in bed. I napped for five hours, and when I woke up, it was dark. Before falling asleep, I had hugged my own body to me—it suddenly seemed delicious. Earlier I'd asked Laura if she had become any less attracted to her boyfriend since anatomy class began. "No, not at all," she said. "If anything, I'm more attracted to him. I feel lucky to be touching a body that's healthy and warm." I knew what she meant. I thought of the bodies I had touched, imagined their insides—soft, pulsing, bloody, and alive. And I remember, as I drifted off, reconciling myself to the day's events: death was simply not something I had to worry about for a while.

"EVERY JOURNALIST," JANET Malcolm wrote in 1989, "who is not too stupid or too full of himself to notice what is going on knows that what he does is morally indefensible. He is a kind of confidence man, preying on people's vanity, ignorance, or loneliness, gaining their trust and betraying them without remorse." These are the opening lines to *The Journalist and the Murderer*, Malcolm's extended meditation on the journalist-subject relationship, a relationship, she contends, that is "invariably and inescapably" unequal. Malcolm takes as her exhibit the lawsuit of convicted murderer Jeffrey MacDonald against the writer Joe McGinniss, arguing that their predicament (McGinniss allegedly feigned belief in MacDonald's innocence in order to retain his trust), can be seen as "a grotesquely magnified version of the normal journalistic encounter." In particular, Malcolm is troubled by what she calls "the dire theme of Promethean theft, of transgression in the service of creativity, of stealing as the foundation of making." Although she acknowledges that a subject may occasionally accept what has been written about him, "this doesn't make the writer any less a thief."

The *Journalist and the Murderer* gave rise to much controversy when it was originally published, not least because of Malcolm's failure to acknowledge her own role in an ongoing libel lawsuit that involved several of the kinds of journalistic improprieties of which she had accused McGinniss. "Malcolm appears to have created a snake swallowing its own tail," Albert Scardino wrote in the *New York Times*. "She attacks the ethics of all journalists, including herself, and then fails to disclose just how far she has gone in the past in acting the role of the journalistic confidence man." Gratifying as it may be to witness the deflation of a writer as smug as Janet Malcolm, however, any condemnation of *The Journalist and the Murderer* that rests upon its author's own duplicity is an evasion of the central issue. Errol Morris levels a more compelling criticism when he argues, in his book *A Wilderness of Error*, that Malcolm's transformation of the association between MacDonald and McGinniss into "a generic problem of journalism" is "like creating a general theory of relationships based on Iago's relationship with Othello." Then, too, there is the matter of the work's self-righteousness and maddening rejection of nuance: Why include the phrase "without remorse" at the end of that second sentence, for instance, unless you are more interested in riling up your reader than you are in making a good faith argument? And yet, legitimate though these objections are, they do not diminish the potency of the ethical dilemma Malcolm describes. Indeed, *The Journalist and the Murderer* remains our best articulation of the tension that arises whenever we sit down to write about real people—a tension, I would suggest, that is even more problematic for the personal essayist or memoirist than it is for the journalist.

Implicit in Malcolm's contention that the relationship between a journalist and his subject is "lopsided" is that their *contract* (spoken or unspoken) is lopsided. But at least there is usually a contract. In the case of MacDonald and McGinniss, it was agreed that MacDonald would neither share his story with another writer nor sue for libel; in return, he would be given 26.5 percent of McGinniss's advance and 33 percent of his royalties. Heretical as these terms may seem—"I think Joe should be ashamed of himself," David Halberstam said of the arrangement—they would likely appeal to the subject of a memoir who has agreed to nothing at all. (This is assuming, of course, that you don't call befriending, associating with, or giving birth to a nonfiction writer an indication of consent.) The lack of rights afforded such a subject is no doubt why some memoirists attempt—or *say* they attempt—to put in place a contract of their own, one that goes far beyond the terms to which most journalists commit themselves. "I showed my manuscript to the people I was writing about and let them say whether it was appropriate or not," writes Jill Ker Conway in "Points of Departure." "I think it's an invasion of privacy not to." Ian Frazier says something similar: "I told almost everybody who is in my book what I wrote about them; I asked their permission." Annie Dillard did the same, "promis[ing] to take out anything that anyone objects to—anything at all. I don't believe in a writer's kicking around people who don't have access to a printing press. They can't defend themselves." I imagine such solicitude is the exception; the majority of writers I know wait until their final galleys to reveal what they have written, precisely so as to avoid making the kinds of changes that their subjects might demand—changes, it is worth noting, that would likely lessen the value of the work even as they absolve the writer ethically. But *would* they absolve the writer ethically? We already know how Malcolm would respond: a subject's endorsement does not change the fact of a writer's thievery.

At the same time, many nonfiction writers, including those who extend extraordinary protections to the living, do not feel the same accountability to the dead. "I couldn't have written *The Road from Coorain* while my mother was living," says Conway. "She would have struck me dead." Says Dillard: "I tried to leave out anything that might trouble my family. ... Everybody I'm writing about is alive and well"—the implication being that those who are *not* alive and well need not be granted the same consideration. But why should writing about a corpse relieve the writer of moral responsibility? Who is less capable of "defending himself" than a dead man? Moreover, doesn't this illogicality suggest that the impulse on the part of the nonfiction writer to assuage his living subjects, far from being the principled gesture he would have us (and himself) believe, is rather an attempt to shield himself from blame? To his credit, Frazier seems to acknowledge something similar when he says that guilt—the "headwind that you sail into" when writing memoir—"is a form of narcissism." Describing the experience of writing about his great-grandfather, he imagines the "outrage" the old man might have felt had someone pointed at Frazier in childhood and said, "This little kid... is going to tell a lot of people what your life meant, he's going to be the sole repository of your good name." And yet Frazier's solution, messy and refreshingly cynical, is not a solution at all: "give all your money to charity," he says, "or whatever makes you feel less guilty, and then you can work, because the reader doesn't care how guilty you feel."

Work: Has it not been curiously absent from this discussion, a discussion that hinges, after all, on the question of whether subject or creation is more deserving of the writer's loyalty? This void is partly the fault of Malcolm, who preempts all inquiry on the matter in her first paragraph. "Journalists justify their treachery in various ways according to their temperaments," she writes. "The more pompous talk about freedom of speech and 'the public's right to know'; the least talented talk about Art; the seemliest murmur about earning a living." Perhaps Malcolm is suggesting an impregnable divide between art and journalism, or perhaps she is merely making the point that artistry is an invalid justification for journalistic source betrayal; regardless, her implication is that "transgression in the service of creativity" is—for the journalist—at all times unethical. Less clear, however, is her attitude toward the responsibilities of the memoirist or personal essayist. Although Malcolm draws a sharp distinction between the writer of fiction and nonfiction, arguing that the former is "entitled to more privileges" than his fact-bound counterpart, she tends to use the terms "journalist" and "nonfiction writer" interchangeably, and never acknowledges that the genre of nonfiction comprises many more subsets than journalism alone. Is this an oversight on Malcolm's part, or does she *mean* to imply that the literary nonfiction writer is as treacherous—and as culpable—as his journalistic colleague? Might Annie Dillard cite the prospect of a "world without light" as a legitimate excuse for writing about family, or is she no more justified than Joe McGinniss in "talking about Art"? The answers to these questions, problematically elusive, are also immaterial to the nonfiction writer who is seeking Malcolm's approbation: the quandary at the heart of *The Journalist and the Murderer* goes unresolved, and Malcolm's continuing career as a journalist suggests that she, like all nonfiction writers who recognize their perfidies and even so refuse to relinquish their pens, has also chosen work. "There is an infinite variety of ways in which journalists struggle with the moral impasse that is the subject of this book," she concludes. "The wisest know that the best they can do ... is still not good enough."

THE DAY AFTER my visit to the lab, I received a call from the vet: my cat Thomas had tested "equivocal" for Feline Immunodeficiency Virus, the feline equivalent to HIV. "What does 'equivocal' mean?" I asked.

"It means he's somewhere between positive and negative."

"But what does that mean?"

"We don't know yet," she said, and recommended I bring him in for a more definitive blood test. She told me that some FIV-positive cats live long, happy lives, and that others die quickly. My mother told me worrying wouldn't help. "Think of Grammy Jean," she said. "She was alone for five years while my father was at war. I remember asking her once if she was worried all the time. 'You just can't live your life like that,' she said."

The next week I woke early to take Thomas to the vet. I was already dressed when I noticed the dead mouse. It was on its back, its little teeth bared; its grey fur was matted, as though chewed on, and one of its hind legs was bloody. I yelped, and that night dreamed that the walls and windowsills of my childhood home were swarming with rats.

My parents arrived from Boston the following morning; British and Australian immigrants, they had expressed an uncharacteristic interest in joining me for Thanksgiving. My father carried up the bags and promptly stepped on a second dead mouse that was lying on the carpet. "Ah—a nest!" he exclaimed. We put the turkey in the fridge, went for a walk along the river, and then sat in my living room waiting for the kettle to boil. When there was a lull in the conversation, my mother looked at my father and then at me. "We have some bad news, I'm afraid."

I looked at my father. "You're sick."

"Yes," he said.

Several weeks before, his routine CAT scan had revealed black spots on his lungs. There were three possibilities: it could be lung cancer, which was untreatable. It could be kidney cancer, which was untreatable. Or it could be bladder cancer, which was more often than not contained with chemotherapy. Because my father's oncologist had recently retired, it took nearly a month to schedule and receive the results of a biopsy. My parents had learned only the day before that the black spots were bladder cancer.

"Oh darling, it's been awful," my mother said. "You can imagine—while you were worrying about Thomas, I was worrying about Dad. But there was no point in telling you until we knew something ourselves."

"But bladder cancer is good?" I asked.

They hesitated. In the past few weeks, my father had also been complaining of back pain, and his new doctor thought the disease may have already spread

Jonathan Dalton, *And Then It Was Done*, 2011
32" x 24"
jonathandalton.ie

to his bones. A bone scan scheduled for the following week would decide the matter definitively.

"What does it mean if it's in your bones?" I asked, remembering that Sarah's mother had died very soon after the cancer had shown up in her vertebrae.

"We just don't know," my mother said.

"It's bad," my father said.

I could feel tears rising in the back of my throat, but they rose no further. I was not surprised. It seemed inevitable, as though I had been distrustful of my father's health all along—as though part of me had never stopped believing he would die while I was still slightly too young to be fatherless.

That night we rented *March of the Penguins*—eggs cracking in the cold and fluffy chicks being carried off by vultures. We were still watching the opening credits when there was a scrabbling sound in the kitchen: Oscar, my other cat, had caught a third mouse. He held it tightly in his mouth and ran in excited circles around a kitchen chair. The mouse was only a baby; still trapped between Oscar's jaws, it waved its little legs and a minute later died. My father scooped it up and dropped it down the garbage chute like the rest, and we continued with the film. But the incident had made me anxious, and I was unable to concentrate. When Oscar later sat on my lap, I was repulsed—I could not dispel the image of the mouse struggling inside his jaws.

My parents left as soon as the movie ended. I was brushing my teeth and Oscar hovering by the stove when he suddenly lunged at something underneath it. He emerged with a fourth mouse that was very dark grey and even smaller than the third. "Okay, Oscar, drop it," I said, assuming he would kill it as quickly as he had the one before. But instead he carried it into the bathroom, and when Thomas and I followed him, he turned on us, crouched low, and hissed. I was frightened—I had never heard him make such a sound before. "Please, Oscar, just kill it," I pleaded. "Please just kill it, please." I watched as again and again he let the mouse run alongside the bathtub, only to attack it when it reached the wall. In its brief moments of freedom, the mouse sat motionless on hind legs, front paws raised. It was already wounded, but I lacked the courage to kill it myself. "Please just kill it," I repeated, crying now. "Please, Oscar, just kill it."

The mouse refused to die. It made a break for the living room, skirting the contours of the wall, and there Oscar caught it again and batted it across the wooden floor; he caught it again, and this time succeeded at lifting it into the air with his two front paws. When he finally dropped it, the mouse ran into the closet and inside one of my boots. I became hysterical. "Oscar, please just kill it," I wailed. The words had become comfortable, a kind of prayer. "Please, Oscar, just kill it. Goddamnit, Oscar, kill it!" I sat on the floor and sobbed. There were so many times that my father had slipped past death—how could he possibly do it again? I tried to perceive the world without him; it seemed insufferably dark. And yet the longer I sat sobbing, watching Oscar claw at my boot, the more conscious I became of the thematic promise of my situation. One half of me was utterly consumed by grief. But the other half was plotting, arranging the events of the past week into a coherent narrative of death: I was writing the story of the cadavers and my father and the mice even as it happened. I understood that this severing of myself from myself was the very violence Dillard had described, but I was still appalled by my elation, by the fact that even on this first day I could not protect my father from the ruthlessness of a writing mind.

Oscar eventually retrieved the mouse and carried it back to the bathroom. It had grown weak; now when he dropped it on the floor, it simply lay there. It was still alive when, 45 minutes after the initial pounce, I could stand the game no longer and swept it into a dustpan. Once inside, the mouse curled up with its eyes closed. Its wounds were hidden, and it looked peaceful, as though it were sleeping. I was still crying when I took it out into the hall.

I called my father soon afterward to say that Oscar had caught mouse number four. "Tomorrow we'll block up the mouse hole," he said. I told him I felt sorry for it. "Oh, Katharine," he said. "Your heart's too large. You saw the movie—nature's cruel."

D URING HIS SOLE conversation with Janet Malcolm, Joe McGinniss quoted her a passage from a Thomas Mann essay:

> The look that one directs at things, both outward and inward, as an artist, is not the same as that with which one would regard the same as a man, but at once colder and more passionate. As a man, you might be well-disposed, patient, loving, positive, and have a wholly uncritical inclination to look upon everything as all right, but as an artist your daemon constrains you to "observe," to take note, lightning fast and with hurtful malice, of every detail that in the literary sense would be characteristic, distinctive, significant, opening insights, typifying the race, the social or the psychological mode, recording all as mercilessly as though you had no human relationship to the observed object whatsoever.

As well as lamenting the fact that an unlearned jury would likely not be swayed by this defense, McGinniss spoke of "compartmentalizing" the feelings of friendship he held for Jeffrey MacDonald. While ever mindful of his status as "the author," "the first letter I got from the guy, written eighteen hours after

his conviction, brought tears to my eyes. I felt genuine sorrow." McGinniss's predicament is admittedly extreme—I don't think anyone would challenge the notion that he crossed an ethical line—but his description of an internal divide between his author self and his human self is uncannily familiar. "I am of an indefensible order of the human," says Wiley Silenowicz, the alter ego of fiction writer and memoirist Harold Brodkey, reflecting upon the fraudulence of his position. "It is cheap and special to be like me: you never have to live, or know how people live: you never have to feel except as notes for scenes." In addition to highlighting the layer of invulnerability with which a writer approaches his own life—the same invulnerability I first noticed in my attitude toward the lab visit—Brodkey is uneasy about the moral implications of the artist's role. But while "indefensible" is also Malcolm's word, the suggestion here—one with which Mann would almost certainly agree—is that the very duplicity that is indefensible for the human is, for the artist, a requirement.

Almost exactly one year after the events I have described, my father died of bladder cancer in his lungs and spine. I was not with him at the time, but I boarded a train for Boston that same hour, and I remember so vividly the experience of sitting in the quiet car, trying to wrap my mind around his death, while at the same time *watching* myself in the quiet car try to wrap my mind around his death. By then I was accustomed to this doubleness, this hovering daemon—I had embarked months ago on a book about my father's life, and the daemon's frequent appearance, not wholly unpleasant, struck me as both necessary and forgivable. I was equally unconcerned by the kinds of ethical questions that had once seemed pressing and now seemed naïve, so that when I opened the door to my parents' living room—the body lay in a hospital bed where the dining table had been, a white sheet drawn to its shoulders—it did not occur to me that my father, my subject, was now more vulnerable than he had ever been; or that my book, thick with his transgressions, was not now more acceptable, but less.

Nearly seven years have passed since then, and in that time—during which the writing life and its requirements have ceased to be a novelty—the urgency of these moral concerns has only continued to diminish. My book is complete; I am nervous when I imagine the reaction of its living characters, but I don't plan on showing it to them until it is too late. (Thomas, by the way, is fine—his second blood test came back negative.) And yet, as I write this, it occurs to me that the way in which the ethical ambiguities of this profession receded from view has a similar feel to the way in which death receded from view; and I wonder whether—in the same manner that the child who saw with terror what lay beyond the fabric was in some respects wiser than the woman I would become by 21—the aspiring writer who was for several weeks consumed by the brazenness of her betrayal might not have a message that is equally worth keeping in mind.

Your father is no different from that cadaver, she would say. Look at him. Look at him: from the threshold he is himself, but when you move closer, you will see that his face morphs into something other, something fantastic, something so simultaneously like and *unlike* the person he was the day before. He is not embalmed, of course: if you dissect him—and you *will* dissect him—he will bleed. But he is pale, and, though his skin is slack, he, too, will give the impression of being immensely hard all over, as if that skin were made of wax. And then, when you move closer still and see the top of his head, you will notice that his hair is matted and oily, thinner than you remember it, and suddenly you won't want to touch him; you will hate being in that room with him, and you will flee without looking back.

Alen MacWeeney, *Tinker's Wedding Photograph, Ireland*, 1967

symposium
what is marriage for?

Henri de Toulouse-Lautrec, *The Bed*, 1893

A MATTER OF LIFE
AND DEATH

by Timothy Aubry

So for your face I have exchanged all faces,
For your few properties bargained the brisk
Baggage, the mask-and-magic-man's regalia.
Now you become my boredom and my failure,
Another way of suffering, a risk,
A heavier-than-air hypostasis.

-PHILIP LARKIN

Often at night I dream that I've found some dangerous object lying on the floor and swallowed it. I sit up, coughing violently, trying to force it back out. I turn to my wife and tell her that I've ingested something potentially fatal, and what should I do? If she wakes up grouchy, she snaps, "Be quiet! I'm trying to sleep!" Startled, I recover myself, realize it's just the same nightmare I always have, and feel acutely embarrassed, hoping my wife won't remember the interruption the next morning. Other times, she rubs my arm and says gently, "It's okay. You're fine. You didn't swallow anything. Go back to sleep, babe." The next morning she asks me, "How do you even know I'm there? I mean, aren't you dreaming? Why do you have to get me involved?"

Being left alone in my room in the dark used to be the scariest part of my life. I've been having night terrors as long as I can remember. At a pretty young age, I figured out that monsters hiding under the bed or even regular human intruders did not pose the greatest threat to my existence, and having seen a few too

many episodes of Michael Landon's *Highway to Heaven*, about an angel who tends to the needs of dying children, I directed my fears at a more likely possibility: disease, and more specifically, Cancer.

One time, when I was around eight, I had a violent flu, and the whole time my older sister kept giving me significant looks, like she wanted to tell me something. Though I was pretty out of it, I couldn't help but notice, and I became convinced that this was it. Dr. Elisofon had already delivered the news to my family: I had Cancer, I was dying, my sister knew but she didn't want to tell me, and I was just going to have to accept it.

Eventually, I discovered why she'd been giving me all those concerned stares. A couple nights before, my father, apparently, had gotten in very late. Still awake, my mother had said, "I don't expect you to come home for me anymore. But when your son is running a 103 degree fever, you might think about leaving the bar before 2 a.m." To which he had responded, "If you knew where I actually was tonight, then you'd be *really* mad." And thus it turned out that the big secret responsible for my sister's displays of anxiety was not Cancer but Divorce. My mom had decided to wait until I was feeling better to tell me. I wasn't dying, but my parents were splitting up. Life and death, marriage and divorce—ever since then, they've been all mixed up in my head, each one, at times, standing in for one of the others.

The problem with marriage, we all know, is the endlessness of it. Plenty of things we do will have long-term repercussions, but in what other situation do you promise to do something for the rest of your life? Not when you choose a college. Not when you take a job. Not when you buy a house. During childhood, you pick up many habits that are probably going to be lifelong, like walking, talking, reading, and sleeping, but once you've got those down, you start to feel like you're at greater liberty to decide what things you want to do and what things you want to stop doing. Especially when you're a young adult the apparently infinite multiplicity of possible choices—possible jobs, possible friends, possible cities, possible girlfriends or boyfriends—can sometimes fool you into thinking you have an infinite amount of time to try out everything. But once you're married, you've significantly cut down the options, and it suddenly makes your life feel shorter—like now there's a direct line between you and your own death. You've just gotten on a train and you won't get off until the very end of the track. In your final moments, if you stick to your promise, you'll still be doing the same thing you're doing now, dealing with the same person, possibly having the same arguments. And that commonality between now and then makes that far-off time, when you're old and sick and about to die, a little more imaginable. Which is scary.

Apparently even my father didn't quite escape this predicament. Although they were no longer married, my mother was still there with him in the hospital on the day he died of lung cancer at age sixty. And she even managed to subject him to one of their old familiar rituals, though he wasn't exactly in a condition to notice. Apparently after the nurse declared him dead and shepherded me, my sister and my two aunts out into another room, while we were all hugging and crying, my mother stayed in the room with my father's body in order to give him a final piece of her mind. "How *could* you?" she asked him. "How could you take such bad care of yourself and abandon your two kids like this?" My parents had been divorced for over fifteen years, and my father was dead, but my mother wanted to get in one last good fight.

I was stunned when my mother told me afterwards what she had just done. You had to have some pretty strong feelings, after all, to stand there yelling at a corpse. Did my mother still love my father? Perhaps, but I also think his death had taken something important from her—something distinct from love that marriage offers to us all. Watching her two kids collapse into sobs, she'd looked at their faces and thought about how they'd have to spend the rest of their lives fatherless, with one less person really looking out for them. Though they were both technically adults, one pregnant with her first child, they'd seemed to her especially vulnerable and helpless, and she wanted someone to blame. The causes of their distress were too big to comprehend and pretty much beyond anyone's control: disease, aging and death. So my dad, who could at least have tried to quit smoking, represented a much more tangible and more satisfying target for her grievances.

Marriage gives you someone to blame— for just about everything. Before you get married, when you feel depressed, you think to yourself, "Is this it?" And by "it" you mean life. Is this all life has to offer? Just one day followed by another? The same dreary routine? Etc. But after you get married, you think to yourself, "Is *this* it?" And by "it" you mean marriage. If your life feels monotonous, devoid of possibilities, static, two-dimensional, whatever, you don't blame your life; you blame your marriage. As a thing that's supposed to fill up your days until you die, your marriage becomes like an emblem of your life, like a kind of plastic insulation that's pressed all the way up against the very borders of your existence. It's much easier to blame the stuff lining the walls than the room itself. And there is, you sometimes remind yourself, just a little space between the lining and the outer boundaries, and thus it allows you to trick yourself into thinking if you could just get into that space between where your marriage ends and your life continues, or if you could somehow tear down the plastic, escape the confines of your marriage, life would suddenly be vibrant and rich and unexpected and mysterious again. So maybe the greatest gift marriage gives us is the chance to fantasize, to imagine that there's more to life than there actually is, and it accomplishes this by assuming responsibility for all the misery and dullness that we would otherwise equate with life itself.

But it's not actually marriage that does this: it's your spouse. One saintly individual steps forward and volunteers to be the fall guy, to absorb the entirety of your existential bitterness for decades to come, so that you can think life isn't quite as bad as you once feared, since everything that's wrong with it is actually your spouse's fault. Even if you don't ever act on your feelings, from this point forward you can believe that you don't have to die in order to escape from the dreary reality in which you sometimes feel trapped; you can just get divorced. Your marriage partner, in other words, allows

you to hold onto your hope. It's a profound gesture of total, thankless altruism, if you think about it, but you don't think about it, because, by virtue of the particular service they're providing, you're too busy feeling resentful to feel the appropriate gratitude.

Much to her chagrin, and at the cost of her own hopes of sleeping soundly through the night, my wife's presence intrudes all the way into my private nightmares. Even when I should be getting away from everything that's troubling or annoying me, into some otherworldly place where I can forget who I am and what I believe my life has become, my wife is still somehow there. And not just an imagined version, but the actual physical person, right at the threshold of my bad dream, ready to pull me back into the room, either kindly or cruelly, so I can think, as I regain my sense of reality and watch her as she tries to get back to sleep: Thanks to you I'm no longer afraid. I thought I had eaten something deadly, but I was wrong. What a relief to realize that you're still here, I'm not dead, and we're going to be together like this for as long as I can imagine.

ON NOT KNOWING WHAT YOU'RE DOING

by Mark Hopwood

There is a question about what marriage is, and then there is a question about what it might be. I am interested in the latter. In our society, marriage is still widely used as a tool of social exclusion and oppression; it has been over-idealized, over-commercialized, and half of the time it ends in divorce. Nevertheless, there is something about marriage that presents a deep challenge to the way we think about the most important choices in our lives.

First, marriage is an act that we undertake despite the impossibility of really knowing what we are committing ourselves to in undertaking it (I'll say more about what I mean by this below). Second, it is also an act whose meaning is determined less by our own individual understanding and more by the wisdom of a community—living and dead—that surrounds us. Beyond the obvious change in perspective involved in committing yourself to another person, marriage presents a fundamental challenge to our conception of ourselves as individual rational agents, independent of others and in sole control of our own destiny. In marriage we become—or at least, we *ought* to become—more deeply conscious of our reliance on sources of meaning much larger than ourselves.

Marriage is not the only act that involves an inevitable element of not-knowing-what-you're-doing. Recently the philosopher L.A. Paul created a buzz that spread from academic blogs to the NPR website when she posted an online draft of a paper entitled "What Mary Can't Expect When She's Expecting." In the paper, Paul argues that a widely held assumption—that it is rational for a childless person to decide whether to have a child by reflecting on what it would be like to have one—is mistaken. Paul's reasoning, simply put, is that a childless person cannot decide whether to have a child on the basis of what it would be like to have one because she does not *know* what it would be like to have one. Having children, at least for the first time, is what Paul calls a *transformative experience*. "Before someone becomes a parent," she writes, "she has never experienced the unique state of seeing and touching her newborn child. She has never experienced the full compendium of the extremely intense series of beliefs, emotions, physical exhaustion and emotional intensity that attends the carrying, birth, presentation, and care of her very own child, and hence she does not know what it is like to have these experiences."

What Paul says about having children seems to me to ring equally true of marriage. Until you have spent a lifetime in the company of another person, you can't possibly know what it's like to do so. When we get married, there is an important sense in which we really don't know what we're doing. This doesn't make marriage a complete leap into the dark, of course—you can be pretty sure that another person is well-suited to you, that you have similar goals, that you love each other, and so on. Even so, no matter how much you know about another person on the day of your marriage, you still don't really *know* what you're doing in marrying them. This doesn't make you wrong or irrational to do it anyway; it's just part of what it is to be human. Living as a finite being means projecting oneself toward the unknown.

The title of Paul's paper is inspired by a classic article by the philosopher Frank Jackson, entitled "What Mary Didn't Know." Jackson asks us to imagine a brilliant scientist, Mary, who spends her whole life inside a black and white room. Although Mary, with the help of books and videos (screened on her black and white TV), comes to be an expert on the science of color perception, she has never actually seen the color red for herself. When she first steps outside her room and sees a red object, Jackson argues, she will learn something new: *what it is like* to see red. Until she actually has the experience of seeing red for herself, Jackson argues, there is no way that Mary could come to know what it is like to see it.

Paul helps us understand how real life experiences, like having children or getting married, are similar to Mary's experience of seeing red for the first time—but there is also an important difference. Whereas Mary is alone in her colorless room, we inhabit a social world, and that world plays a crucial role in preparing us for transformative experiences. Take the example of another such experience: falling in love. It is practically a cliché that, if you have never been in love, then you cannot possibly know what it is like. At the same time, however, we do expect people to recognize the experience of love when it comes along. "When it happens," we say confidently, "you'll know." One might wonder how these two pieces of popular wisdom could possibly be consistent with each other. If we really did not know what falling in love was like until it happened to us, how could we ever know that it *had* happened to us?

The answer, I think, lies in our capacity for metaphor—i.e. our ability to think of one thing in terms of another. In their book *Metaphors We Live By*, the linguist George Lakoff and the philosopher Mark Johnson list six of the many different metaphors associated with love: *Love is a Journey*; *Love is a Physical Force*; *Love is a Patient*; *Love is Madness*; *Love is Magic*; *Love is War*. These metaphors are not merely poetic or decorative; they give systematic structure to our thought and language. The metaphor *Love is a Physical Force* underlies a whole range of expressions:

I could feel the *electricity* between us. There were *sparks*. I was *magnetically drawn* to her. They are *uncontrollably attracted* to each other. They *gravitated* to each other immediately. His whole life *revolves* around her. The *atmosphere* around them is always *charged*. There is incredible *energy* in their relationship. They've lost *momentum*.

Part of the reason that we're able to recognize love when it comes along is that such metaphors allow us to imagine something we haven't experienced in terms of something more familiar. Even the expression "falling in love" has a metaphorical root. Until I fall in love myself, I don't know exactly what it will be like, but the range of metaphors associated with love do at least give me a sense of what kind of experience to expect. These metaphors, we might say (to deploy another metaphor) prepare the cognitive ground for the experience of love to take root. If, when I do fall in love, I find myself saying something like: "*Now* I know what it means for my whole life to revolve around another person," there is an element of genuine discovery in that statement, but *also* an element of recognition. I may not have known what love was like, but I knew the kind of thing that I was looking for.

It is our access to imaginative resources like these that makes our situation different from Mary's. Our social world provides us with a rich and complex set of metaphors that help us to imagine what it will be like to undergo transformative experiences. And it's not just that the metaphors with which we are provided help to prepare us for these experiences; they actually play a central role in structuring the experiences themselves. If I am exposed early and often to the metaphor *Love is a Physical Force*, I am likely to experience my relationships differently than I would if that metaphor were completely foreign to me. It is not just that someone who has been surrounded by metaphors of electricity is more likely to *describe* her experience in terms of sparks flying; she is more likely to *feel* sparks flying. That is why we so often find parents attempting to instill certain metaphors in their children: "Love isn't all about chemistry, you know; it's hard work."

All of this brings us back around to marriage. In his book *Moral Imagination*, Mark Johnson offers an analysis of a series of discussions with married couples conducted in the 1980s by the anthropologist Naomi Quinn, focusing in on her conversations with one particular interviewee, "Alex." At the beginning of his marriage, Johnson observes, Alex tended to think of marriage in terms of a specific metaphor, i.e. *marriage is a resource.*

> I thought it was all going to be wonderful. You know it was—the problem of sex was going to be solved. You know I was an adolescent or barely out of adolescence, you know—this was a wonderful idea ... there really are some things that I knew about and that I wanted. A companion and friend. Probably the most ... that seemed important then—to have someone there all the time that you could rely on. And talk to all the time about things. Somebody to help and somebody to help you, you know, that seemed like a real good idea. That seemed like something we got

out of the marriage. Somebody always there.

The metaphor *marriage is a resource* helps Alex to form a conception of what he is doing in getting married. It gives him a way to understand the unknown (i.e. being married) in terms of the more familiar (i.e. exchanging resources with another person). Over time, however, the metaphor begins to show its limitations. The longer his marriage continues, the less sense it makes to Alex to think in terms of what he, as an individual, is getting out of it. He moves toward a new understanding of marriage, one that Johnson suggests is grounded in the metaphor *marriage is an organic unity.*

> I got the first promotion [in the U.S. Navy] with the idea that the second one might be coming. I think that's how it was and that was quite successful because Shirley got pregnant right away. And she, you know, when I got back from Guantanamo [at that time, just a U.S. naval base] she told me and we told the news to everybody and it was a really big deal. And I think that the apartment and the baby and all of that stuff really began to come down on us, you know, and we started believing that we were truly a couple. And we were truly a family and really married.

What does it mean for Alex to say that he felt "really married"? How is he so confident that he knows what that feels like? The answer, I think, is that he finds himself able to make use of a metaphor—i.e. marriage is an organic unity—that is drawn from the community and the tradition of which he is a part. We do not know what Alex and Shirley's marriage ceremony looked like, but it is not unreasonable to think that it might have included some reference to the metaphor of organic unity—to the idea that, in marriage, "two people become one." I think it is also quite possible that, at the time of the wedding, Alex did not really *understand* that metaphor, at least not in the way that he understands it now. This is not to say that he didn't understand what the words meant, but rather that he wasn't yet equipped to see what it *really meant* for a marriage to be an organic unity. It was something that he needed to experience for himself first. Now that he has experienced it, however, the metaphor is there to be picked up and used, like a tool whose purpose only becomes clear when the problem it was designed to solve arises.

If this is right, then we might say that a wedding is a ceremony in which two people, using words they don't fully understand, make a commitment whose consequences they don't fully appreciate. Depending on one's perspective, that is either a damning indictment of the institution of marriage, or evidence that it deserves its place alongside birth, death and falling in love as one of the great transformative experiences of life.

What is clear on either account is that marriage is connected to a particularly deep form of dependence on a wider community, which expresses itself in the metaphors that constitute the marriage. To take just one particularly striking example of the latter: at the end of a traditional Jewish wedding ceremony, a wine glass is covered by a piece of white cloth and crushed under foot. This is an act rich with metaphor, one whose potential meanings are almost endless. Breaking a glass is an irre-

versible act; it is one that has connections with celebration, but also with violence and danger. From a historical perspective, it echoes the destruction of the temple, the idea of being definitively separated from one's home. We can imagine someone saying, decades later, that they were only just beginning to understand what they were doing in crushing that glass. One might see this lack of knowledge in advance as a reason to be suspicious of marriage, but one might also see it as an example of the value of trust in one's community to provide sources of meaning that go beyond one's own individual understanding.

The trust that has been placed in religious communities to act as gatekeepers has been—and continues to be—abused by some. To deny the right to marry to entire sections of society is not merely to deny those people the right to visit each other in hospitals and avoid punitive inheritance taxes (important as these issues are). It is to deny them access to a set of imaginative and metaphorical resources that have been built up over centuries and that are contained within marriage rituals and liturgies. These metaphors stand as a reminder of something that all of us have in common—that at the most important moments of our lives, we never quite know what we are doing. It is a strange paradox of the debate over marriage equality that the guardians of marriage, those who might be expected to understand the endlessly mysterious nature of the institution better than anyone, have somehow become so confident that they—unlike the rest of us—*really* know what marriage is.

JOINERS AND QUITTERS

by Sam Brody

There are two "right answers" to the question of marriage on the American left today. Let's call the people who give these answers the Joiners and the Quitters. (The conservative right would be the Keep-Outers.) In many ways, the split between the Joiners and the Quitters is the same divide faced by civil-rights movements throughout U.S. history, whether on behalf of women, workers, African-Americans or queer folk: Joiners demand that an excluded group be granted access to some set of common rights and privileges, while Quitters argue that the very existence of those rights and privileges is the problem and that the solution lies in their total abolition. Such abolition may take the form of a frontal assault, but is more likely to appear as a secession from normality: the creation of a counter-culture, the quitting of the system. The Joiners vs. Quitters distinction is also the distinction between moderates and radicals, or reformists and revolutionaries, and it is what gives the left its tension. When the issue in question is a "cultural" one, it sometimes maps onto the distinction between philistines and bohemians, or squares and hipsters.

With respect to marriage, it seems that the current climate on the left allows one to be a Joiner, a Quitter, or even both together, as expressed in this immortal tweet by Feminist Hulk on March 26, 2013: "HULK SUPPORT QUEER AND FEMINIST CHALLENGES TO MARRIAGE AS INSTITUTION. HULK ALSO CHAMPION SAME-SEX MARRIAGE. HULK VAST, CONTAIN MULTITUDES." One frequently encounters this attempt to have one's satisfying civil rights victory and eat it too. The logic seems to be: Sure, marriage may be an obsolete relic of a time when women were passed from one male householder to another like chattel, but dammit, if the law is going to confer tangible material benefits on married couples, then same-sex couples deserve equal access to those benefits.

It's hard to say which is more prevalent: this muddled compromise, or the two starker positions it mashes together. It's certainly not too difficult to find Quitters who insist that the gay marriage movement is a huge detour. They have little sympathy for what they see as the hobbyhorse of well-to-do bourgeois couples, out to save money on their taxes and be accepted as normal Americans, since American heteronormativity is exactly what needs to be attacked. Gays in the military? Don't fight their wars! Gay marriage? Don't prop up the breeders' Holy Family! From this perspective, the throngs outside the Supreme Court are little more than dupes of otherwise normative gays who will do anything to avoid being associated with the real scary queers—the proud queens, transfolks, pansexuals, omnisexuals and assorted other radicals who *do* pose a threat to the sexual security of straight America.

By the same token, one can easily find Joiners—Andrew Sullivan has been the most persistent and the most prominent—eager to trumpet the conservatism of the gay marriage movement, claiming that traditionalism is its greatest strength. The fact that most self-identified conservatives oppose gay marriage is seen as a temporary artifact of post-Reaganite rightward political drift. In time, as even rural Americans get used to the idea of the gay couple down the street holding the neighborhood potluck and coaching Little League, resistance will ebb away and gay married couples will simply be woven into the national fabric, as unremarkable as their straight neighbors. Maybe there will even be some salutary change to American normality, worked from the inside, as gay married couples provide straights with a model of egalitarian partnership.

This last possibility indicates that even the Joiners are not totally reconciled to the marriage status quo. They recognize that gender inequality has an ineradicably negative impact on the state of marriage, and that the problem can't be solved by means of a conservative restoration of an imaginary Golden Age in which both men and women understood their proper roles. Their hope is that an infusion of new blood into the stale institution will revive it. The Quitters have an answer, of course: there's no difference between this argument as it relates to marriage and to other spheres of life. Capitalism doesn't change when there are more women CEOs, and government doesn't change when there are more female officeholders. In other words, the office influences the occupant more than the other way around, and it's sheer fantasy to imagine that feminine compassion or gay egalitarianism can transform the patriarchal institutions to which they so fiercely fight for admittance.

The Joiner/Quitter debate poses stark alternatives, no matter how many would prefer to stand on two branches, trumpeting every achievement in the struggle for gay marriage while simultaneously forecasting the future abolition of heteronormativity writ large. Progressives love to be on the right side of history, and to forecast the inevitable sweeping away of cultural-conservative opposition on the receding tides. But the possibility always remains, nagging, that what has been achieved is *not* in fact a "step forward" but only sideways, or even backwards, if it pushes back the day when the real victories are won.

And as it turns out, this argument has been going on for over a hundred years.

•

Let's travel back, then, to the turn of the last century, when bohemians lived in Bohemia, or in its general vicinity. A young Erich Mühsam endured repeated beatings at the hands of his father and his schoolmasters; they were trying to kill the anarchist poet in him and let the respectable bourgeois pharmacist be born. In 1900, 22-year-old Erich relocated to Berlin and made the acquaintance of the *Neue Gemeinschaft* [New Community], a kind of mystical-intellectual discussion group founded by the brothers Julius and Heinrich Hart. He found the Hart brothers pompous and their secular communal mysticism mostly useless, though he did take one valuable thing from the encounter: the friendship of Gustav Landauer, a notorious anarchist activist eight years his senior. Both men quit the New Community in haste, but the friendship they made there would last for decades.

Landauer encouraged Mühsam's aesthetic and political pursuits, and the two would become frequent collaborators in the years ahead—their greatest and most ill-fated collaboration being the proclamation of the Bavarian Council Republic on April 6th, 1919 (it lasted six days). Both men believed in the radical transformation of society into a self-governing network of democratic councils: workers' councils, soldiers' councils, peasants' councils. In this sense they were comrades, far closer to each other politically than to any others outside their small circles. Yet even within this close-knit friendship there was room for radical disagreement, especially on the issue of marriage.

Mühsam was in many ways a representative bohemian of his time; in 1904 he moved to the famous artists' colony in Ascona, Switzerland, where he spent four years living communally with like-minded vegetarian socialist artist types (his own art was theater—drama and cabaret). Like other anarchists, he stood for free love, women's rights and an open attitude towards homosexuality. Unlike many communists and socialists of the era, Mühsam insisted that these issues were not separate from or secondary to the struggle for economic and political revolution. "The personal is political" may be a slogan associated with the feminism of the 1960s and 70s, but activists like Mühsam and Emma Goldman already preached it at the turn of the century; it was obvious to them that one could not be a revolutionary in public and a reactionary in the home. Cultural philistinism, they thought, went hand in hand with the central bureaucratic state, the predatory capitalist economy and the hierarchy of the church.

Landauer, on the other hand, thought that the battle lines could not be drawn so clearly. Other anarchists in his milieu occasionally called him "the conservative revolutionary," since he was given to nostalgia about the Middle Ages and could often be heard defending marriage and the family from libertine attack. Landauer considered the conservative label a misunderstanding. His position could not be reduced to a simplistic revolutionary/reformist dichotomy; he was neither a Joiner nor a Quitter, but something else entirely.

In 1910, a Russian aristocrat, Maria Tarnowska, went to trial in Venice for allegedly inciting one of her lovers to murder another one. The case was a sensation, drawing international attention both to the progress of the trial and to the sordid details of Tarnowska's personal life. Landauer commented in his paper, *Der Sozialist*, that the case showed the perils of free love and its disconnect from anarchosocialist struggle. He then offered Mühsam a platform in a subsequent issue of *Der Sozialist* to disagree. In an article called "Women's Rights," Mühsam declared:

> As long as we live in the present state, in a society with unhealthy institutions and values, we cannot predict the ways in which decadence and strength will express themselves in private life under socialist conditions. ... It is a completely arbitrary demand that people who are in close relationships should remain "faithful" to one another. The state makes these demands largely in light of inheritance laws—they have nothing at all to do with socialism.

Mühsam did not rule out the possibility that marriage and the family would continue to exist under socialism, but he argued that to proclaim these a social foundation under current conditions was to fall into a conservative trap. The important thing was to maintain the intense focus on achieving women's rights and sexual liberation in the here and now.

Landauer responded in his turn with a wide-ranging article, "On Marriage." He protested against any interpretation of his words as diminishing the energy required to struggle for the rights of women. In our current society, it may well be the case that intimate life is regulated by bureaucratic systems of coercion, just as public life is. This does not mean, however, that marriage—and here he distinguishes marriage from "monogamy," which he by no means exclusively recommends—has no basis in human nature. In a just society, marriage would *really become* what conservatives say it *already* is: the basic unit or cell of society, which instantiates in microcosm all the values and relations that we want to see manifested in society as a whole. For Landauer, marriage was not only ineradicable but an essential channeling of the deepest human energies: "All our intimacy, all our holy things, all our fantasy and mysticism, all our religion dwells in this covenant of two sexes, with the progeny growing from their unification, and so also all our lust and animal delight."

Since his general anarchism was predicated on the immediate realization of socialist projects, rather than waiting for the Revolution-with-a-capital-R to break out as the inevitable result of the march of history, Landauer saw the defense of marriage as a socialist project. If one *really* imagines the relationship between spouses as an egalitarian, loving phenomenon within which each member constantly strives to improve his or her consideration for the flourishing of the other, in word and in deed, then that relationship is a test case for social relations more generally: if you can't create a miniature utopian society with *one* other person, you can't expect to do it with *millions* of other people.

To be sure, such solidarity is difficult—but this is exactly why it is essential. The constant negotiation necessary for a successful egalitarian marriage is a school for democratic decision-making. One cannot build one's personal life around relationships that founder as soon as they encounter difficulties and at the same time hope to create a lasting social structure that encourages solidarity rather than selfishness and brutality. A community of people who know how to be married, Landauer thought, is a community of people who know how to negotiate across difference.

At the same time, permanence is not to be valued above all else. Landauer's own life reflected his commitments, in that both of his marriages involved functioning as a unit within a particular milieu: he married Grete Leuschner, a needleworker, while he was involved in labor-based anarchist politics, and later Hedwig Lachmann, a poet, when he withdrew from politics to focus on philosophy and criticism. The marriage to Lachmann lasted for 18 years, until her life was cut short by illness; Landauer composed a tribute to her called "How Hedwig Lachmann Died" and distributed it to their closest friends. One year later, Landauer himself would be murdered by proto-fascist troops of the *Freikorps* as penalty for his involvement in the council republic; his friend Martin Buber would write that the loss of his wife had given Landauer a death wish.

•

Landauer's position gained few followers. It was less intuitive than that of Mühsam and his fellow Quitters, which drew on the fact that marriage was enumerated by conservatives among the guardians of law, order and right conduct (assuming that the reactionary list of things to support provided the best guide of things to oppose). And it wouldn't be attractive to Joiners either, since it assumed prior engagement in a fight for radical change across social and economic institutions. Nonetheless, a contemporary version of Landauer's position could be a powerful interlocutor for the various critiques and defenses of marriage we encounter today.

Take the conservative position. Ryan T. Anderson, a Heritage Foundation fellow and co-author of *What is Marriage? Man and Woman: A Defense*, recently spoke to an assembly of the Alliance Defending Freedom (a conservative legal group pursuing cases it deems threats to religious freedom), and claimed that "the argument for marriage hasn't been heard and rejected; it simply hasn't been heard." As framed by Anderson and other natural-law advocates like Princeton's Robert P. George, marriage provides the optimal environment for child-rearing by endowing each child with a mother and a father, each of whom acts as an irreplaceable element of a family unit that requires both. Long before our culture was enmeshed in the same-sex marriage controversy, Anderson argues, "far too many people bought into a liberal ideology about sexuality that makes a mess of marriage: Cohabitation, no-fault divorce, extramarital sex, non-marital childbearing, massive consumption of pornography and the hook-up culture all contributed to the breakdown of our marriage culture." Not only are mothers and fathers not interchangeable, Anderson argues, but rational arguments underlie the values of permanence, exclusivity and monogamy that in turn underpin marriage. (He has little to say about the fact that *really* "traditional" marriage doesn't historically involve much exclusivity or monogamy, but that's another matter.)

Anderson may be anthropologically, historically and philosophically wrong about natural law, and therefore wrong about marriage, but he is right that there are few on the left who take conservative arguments seriously, rather than simply dismissing them as bigotry.

The left is often so caught up in its internal battles that it neglects the contest with conservatism. Occasionally one gets the sense that it is considered embarrassing even to contemplate debating conservative ideas, as though they might corrupt or infect. It is worth asking, however, even if the appeal must be made on strategic grounds rather than by reference to the lofty ideals of public discourse, where the power of the conservative position comes from. The "pro-life" movement has fought on for decades after *Roe v. Wade*; the "defense of marriage" movement is gearing up to do the same thing.

Joiners, who seek only to gain admittance for gays to the institution of marriage as we know it, may concede the praise of permanence, exclusivity and monogamy, and contest only the claim that the mother and father have eternal, specific roles written in natural law. Quitters, by contrast, argue that such concessions go too far; yet in the process they seem to fit the caricature that conservatives present of the left, seemingly committed to the destruction of all stability and tradition. For all their radicalism, however, the Quitters pay too little attention to whether the dissolution of the marriage bond isn't completely in step with the march of capitalism, under which "all that is solid melts into air." In an era when many young people have more "connections" than friends, is it really liberation to imagine our relationships as a constantly forming and re-forming nebulous mass, related to completely amorphous and contingent feelings and desires? Don't many of the lefty criticisms of marriage start to seem like capitalist defenses of consumer choice?

The conservative vision of marriage, in which a Father does Father-Things, a Mother does Mother-Things, and no untoward hanky-panky ever takes place, is indeed a microcosm of the patriarchal vision for society as a whole (the authority of a father over his household is a classic model in political theory, alongside that of the ship's captain, for the authority of the state). It deserves to be met by a vision of love and commitment that is open and flexible, but not subordinated to the consumerist logic of individual whims. A left committed to such a vision might discover resources to combat the social disintegration of post-industrial life, without the false panaceas of nationalism, trade solidarity, or state-sponsored religious initiatives. Or as Landauer once put it, summing up both a commitment to utopianism rooted in the present, and a belief in the intimate ties between the personal and the political: "The message is: It is *in you!* It is not on the outside. It *is you.*" The utopian imagination must be directed inward, from which point it can radiate out to the neighbor, the spouse, the neighborhood, the city, the country and the world.

ALTERNATIVE
ARRANGEMENTS

by Clarisse Thorn

For a long time, I had zero personal interest in marriage. I discouraged partners from mentioning it. I sarcastically belittled it when it came up. The only weddings I would attend were adorably weird and semi-subversive. (Picture a wedding between a progressive Presbyterian pastor and a Unitarian astrophysicist, where the cake was shaped like a stack of books containing four titles: *I, Robot*; *The Color Purple*; *Traveling Mercies*; and *The Princess Bride*.)

So it was a bit of a shock to realize I'd begun truly wanting to get married. Somewhere in my mid-to-late twenties, as I began to consciously imagine having kids and picturing a more settled life, I found myself longing for a husband.

•

When my first book was translated into German, a review in *Spiegel* started like this:

> The American author Clarisse Thorn cultivates her contradictions. She describes herself as a "fanatical feminist" fighting against sexism. She inclines towards complicated lovers and generally has more than one of them. And she is a sadomasochist who takes her perversion seriously.

Although it is entertaining to imagine what the reviewer would make of my new-found desire for marriage and kids, I tend to think that the "contradictions" between feminism, alternative sexuality and marriage have always been overblown. In any group of people, some will take on more traditional values and some won't. Just as in any group of married people there will inevitably be perverts, many groups practicing alternative sex will include members that want to get married. Yet the argument is often made that marriage is inherently conservative, and that an alt-sexual commitment to openness and creativity in personal relationships conflict with it. Indeed, alternative sexuality in itself is often cited by conservatives as destructive to the institution of marriage.

Shortly after Massachusetts legalized gay marriage in 2003, an article appeared on the conservative website *WorldNetWeekly*. The author proposed that gay marriage would inevitably pave the way for ... drumroll ... S&M marriage!

> This ruling, forbidding any "second-class citizens" will surely allow sadomasochist marriages as well as sodomist ones. Let us predict that the Very Rev. I.M. DeSade, a sadist, wishes to marry his masochist lover, Paynes Pleasure. The ceremony is conducted by another S&M clergyman. He wears a cassock, surplice—and, in place of stole or tippet, he has a large chain around his neck. He carries a whip. This first sadomasochist wedding includes the sadist groom using that whip to give the masochist bride two dozen lashes well laid on—as the male bride exudes cries of delight and the congregation cheers .... Welcome to New Morality in Massachusetts.

I particularly love the assumption that S&Mers aren't already getting married. News flash: heterosexual S&Mers are getting married left and right—right under everyone else's noses! (Usually, however, there are no floggings at the wedding.) A lot of us have kids—and always have.

Polyamory, too—the practice of having multiple lovers who know about each other—is seen as incompatible with marriage. Google "polyamorous marriage" and you find poly people advocating for legal marriage rights, poly people claiming that it will never happen, and conservatives bemoaning the downfall of our once-great nation. A 2013 *Washington Post* article describes poly-activism within the Unitarian church, and notes that many Unitarians resent poly activists: the activists are criticized for appearing too extreme, for demanding too much too soon, and for risking "tamer" political advances like gay marriage in their quest for visibility.

But polyamory, done right, has much to teach marriage. A lot of polyamorous conversations cover ground like: How can we talk about our other relationships? If there is a "primary" couple involved, then what limitations do they place on "secondary" relationships? Some poly couples even use careful written contracts to document their relationship agreements, such as the circumstances in which a primary partner gets to "veto" or cut off a secondary relationship.

I know many monogamous people who take cues from poly conversations on topics like defining a relationship, dealing with jealousy and so on. Too many monogamous marriages have suffered from a lack of vocabulary and structure for engaging forceful emotions like jealousy. Personally, even when I have monogamous relationships, I value my poly experience because it helps me to examine my assumptions and clearly lay out my preferences.

There are tons of different poly relationship setups—each with their own jargon—and each an invitation to think about making intimacy more intentional. For example, a "vee" is a three-person relationship shaped like a "V," where the person at the apex has relationships with two other people, but the two of them have little or no relationship to each other. "Polyfidelity" is a multi-person relationship wherein the participants do not have relationships with outsiders (like monogamy, but with multiple people). And I've mentioned "primary" and "secondary" relationships, which are exactly what they sound like: a primary relationship is considered to be more important or central, with more responsibilities, than a secondary relationship.

For some polyamorous groups, all parties in the relationship are equal. Their members may outright reject legal marriage for that reason. A few form co-housing families (like co-ops), sometimes with children being brought up in the group. Plenty of poly people are already legally married to one partner—whether that partner is a "primary" partner or not—and they may even live with other partners. One of my friends in the Bay Area co-signed a mortgage with his partner's other lover. Actually, based on my circulations among the poly subculture, I would conjecture that the majority of poly people live in pairs—and for some, it's only partly because they want to pass for "normal."

Like gay marriage, the concept of polyamorous marriage invites participants to ask: What is the point of marriage, anyway? What will be the point of *our* marriage? How do we expect it to ensure fidelity? How are we acting as life partners to one another, and how is this different from our other relationships? If we want to have kids, how should this marriage allow us to provide them with love and care?

•

But there's another sex-related community with a revealing perspective on marriage: the asexual (or "ace") community—people who identify as feeling no sexual and/or romantic desire. Some aces feel little to no sexual desire; others feel little to no romantic desire; others feel little to none of both.

As a movement, asexuality has been around for more than a decade. Ace sensibilities are globally rare, so the community's organization is greatly enhanced by social media. The most visible ace group is called the Asexual Visibility and Education Network, and it's headed by my friend David Jay. When I started writing this article, I asked David to have lunch with me and talk about marriage. Some asexuals do get married, and I wanted to know more about why and how.

"A lot of close ace relationships mimic sexual relationships," David said. "But we're doing this thing that's not really built for us, so we have to find our own path. A lot of aces don't see how to fit themselves into our cultural image of long-term commitment. Sometimes, people with a strong non-romantic connection end up getting married—I have ace friends who say, "We're not a couple, we're a set." They figure that they want to live together, spend a bunch of time in this relationship, and have a party

about it, and marriage is one way to do that. The relevant question is: Do you have intimacy in your life? And how are you building that? What do you want intimacy to look like in the long term?"

On a napkin, David diagrammed the "asexual relationship triangle," with the initials S, C and P at the angles. He explained that the community sometimes talks about intimacy with partners (romantic or non-romantic), intimacy with communities, and intimacy with self. For communities, an ace might say that "this activist group I'm part of is a primary relationship," or "this band is a primary relationship." And taking care of yourself, prioritizing intimacy with self over intimacy with other people—that's still seen as a valid form of intimacy.

I asked about children. "Raising kids is a community-level thing," David pointed out. "There's a lot of ace anxiety about how there aren't a lot of good templates for community co-parenting." This anxiety is something I've seen in the polyamory community, too—and even among monogamous people in the "normal" Western world. Are we really all going to do this nuclear family thing given that resources get scarcer every day?

We've come to the point where young people can discuss, publicly and ad nauseam, our sexual options. The "traditional family" has responded by clinging grimly to its status as the best way to raise children. So we're now in a position where hard-won individual freedoms allow people of all genders to try creative approaches to intimacy, yet if we don't support institutional alternatives to the traditional family, then we haven't taken our creative approaches to intimacy to their logical conclusions.

•

A big part of getting older is developing a serious set of intentions about relationships and partners. I used to have so many relationships that "just happened," and I simply don't have that anymore. I'm much more careful about how relationships start, now that I am looking for a partner with whom to raise kids. But it's so hard to be rational about these things—it's hard, and maybe it's foolish, because after all I do want someone to love as well, not just a person to live with.

Of course, alternative sexual arrangements are especially complex when the goal is to build a relationship to last. It's inherently harder work than monogamy, with more moving parts. The poly community often smooths over stories of unstable poly situations, but there are plenty of stories of people leaving primaries for secondaries—even when the primaries had lots of careful discussions and boundary-setting. There are also stories of people neglecting primary relationship responsibilities, distracting themselves with fun times with secondaries. A polyvangelist could argue that these problems wouldn't have happened if there weren't already issues in the primary relationship, and that might be true. Yet it's just as easy to argue that it's not worth risking a relationship that might be more stable—or might be just plain easier—if it were monogamous.

In my ideal world, I'd have a polyamorous S&M marriage with the expectation of kids—but polyamory and S&M are both things that I would compromise (and have compromised) for relationships with the right people. One model I've been playing with lately is suggesting monogamy for the early part of a relationship in order to build stability—but placing an expectation on the table that we'll discuss polyamory in six or eight months or something. The problem there, though, is that a partner—especially one who's unfamiliar with poly—may be willing to think about "poly later," but end up being unwilling to actually do poly later. So taking this approach means taking that risk.

Even though I'm a sex writer, I have moved away from defining sex as the most important part of a relationship. Maybe this is part of getting more flexible about my sexuality over time—or just part of my bone-deep desire for kids. Or maybe this is just part of getting older: sex starts to recede in importance and we hold tighter to other values and desires. I think to myself, " I'm a sex educator! I'm a modern woman! My sexual rights are undefeatable and indefatigable! I deserve to have it all!" Yet the more I look at the questions surrounding modern marriage, and sex, and femininity, the less I feel like I know. I'm still figuring it out: If I do get married, then, what can I hope for? And what am I willing to compromise?

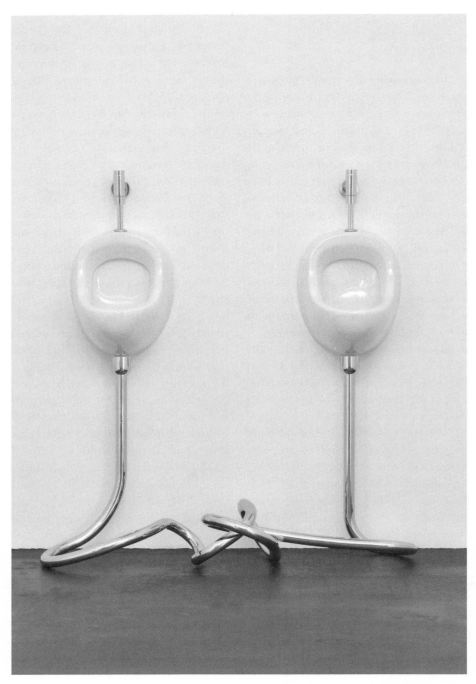

Elmgreen & Dragset, *Gay Marriage*, 2010

NATURAL LAWS

by Jeremy Bell

Writing in this year's January-February edition of the *New Humanist*, Jason Wakefield lists and rebuts 31 "homophobic" arguments commonly made against the legal recognition of same-sex marriage. Some he brands "*insidiously* homophobic," since they have a deceptive veneer of reasonableness. One such "insidious" argument is that homosexual couples "cannot have children and so should not be allowed to marry." Wakefield retorts that elderly or infertile heterosexual couples likewise cannot have children and asks rhetorically whether they too should not be allowed to marry. He warns his readers not to be duped by the air of fair-minded sobriety with which "religious campaigners" put forward this and other speciously reasonable arguments. Such arguments are mere rationalizations, and their proponents wolves in sheep's clothing. He goes so far as to claim that it is "entirely justified" to call *all* "proactive opponents" of the legal recognition of same-sex marriage "bigots" and "homophobes."

Wakefield is unusually outspoken, but many supporters of "marriage equality" share his sentiments. (Justice Anthony Kennedy expressed something similar, albeit in more moderate language, in his majority opinion in *U.S. vs. Windsor*.) The argument he so easily rebuts, that homosexual couples "cannot have children and so should not be allowed to marry," is a truncated and distorted version of an argument that, rightly formulated, seems to

me sound. However, in view of the widespread belief that only homophobic bigotry could motivate opposition to the legal recognition of same-sex marriage, I shall not straightaway attempt a full and exact statement of this argument. I shall instead begin by saying something about myself, the circumstances under which I came to take an interest in same-sex marriage, and how my thinking about it developed. I hope in this way to put readers concerned with motives in a better position to judge mine.

I first gave serious thought to the subject of same-sex marriage four years ago. At the time I had long considered myself exclusively homosexual and had only recently broken up with my partner of nearly five years, largely as a result of the strain (familiar to so many in today's world) of trying to sustain a long-distance relationship. Though my ex-partner and I had hoped to be together all our lives, we had only rarely discussed the possibility of marrying, should the option ever be open to us. I think the idea held some appeal for him; it held little, if any, for me. Marriage equality was not then the burning political issue it has since become and I had no strong feelings about it one way or another. Like Wakefield, I suspected that opposition to it was motivated chiefly by repugnance to homosexuality as such. However, unlike Wakefield, I was inclined to distinguish between sheer "homophobia"—dislike or hatred of homosexuals—on the one hand, and moral condemnation of homosexual acts, on the other. Some think this distinction unimportant, or even unreal. It is true that people who condemn homosexual acts often harbor feelings of visceral antagonism toward those who engage in them, and it goes without saying that this is no accident. All the same, my own experience had taught me the importance of the distinction. Like all homosexuals, I knew the sting of hearing offhand caustic remarks, sometimes touched with real malice, about "fags" and "poofs." I had on one occasion been at the receiving end of vitriolic verbal abuse punctuated with graphic allusions to homosexual practices, which, the day after, I could not recall without feeling sick. These were examples of homophobia. By contrast, an old and good friend who was also a devout and staunchly orthodox Catholic had continued to treat me with unfeigned respect and kindness after I had told him of my being in a homosexual relationship, without ever condoning the relationship or wishing me well in it. Again, one of the best teachers I have ever had (someone who is not in any usual sense "religious") has made it clear in his writings, though not, to my knowledge, in his classes, that he regards homosexual acts as immoral, yet it would never have occurred to me to call him "homophobic."

This is not to say that I considered moral condemnation of homosexual acts innocuous. On the contrary, I considered it potentially devastating in its consequences, perhaps more so than raw homophobia. An acquaintance of my Catholic friend, himself also Catholic, had once spoken in my hearing about homosexuals needing to "have their heads bashed in." He was joking, or half-joking, but his remark was still an unpleasant reminder of the brutality that homosexual men and women have suffered, and sometimes still suffer, at the hands of those raised to believe that homosexual acts are immoral. I was also familiar with accounts of vulnerable homosexual teenagers, especially boys, being driven to suicide by shame at their own desires and dread of admitting them to their family and friends. Thoughts of such things haunted me when I read or heard earnest, unimpassioned condemnations of homosexual acts by apparently well-intentioned moralists. Nonetheless, I found it impossible

to believe that all who profess to hate the sin without hating the sinner are simply malicious, stupid, thoughtless or self-deceived. I was thus in a quandary. This was one reason that I began to think seriously about same-sex marriage in the wake of my relationship's collapse. I wanted better to understand the thinking of apparently good-hearted and intelligent people who condemn not just same-sex marriage but homosexual practice as such.

Naturally I wanted to believe that moral condemnation of homosexual acts is deeply misguided, whatever its motives. Strange as it may sound, however, I was not confident of this. I do not mean that I had nagging feelings of guilt about my own desires and choices, or that I had been unwillingly impressed by arguments for the immorality of homosexual acts. Rather, the very idea of calling a loving couple's consensual sexual acts immoral had always been alien to my sensibilities. Precisely for this reason, I could no more positively reject the idea than accept it. I could only, as it were, stare blankly at it. Before I could be confident of its being misguided, I needed to make the idea real to myself.

•

If two men or two women celebrate their love for each other sexually, what, if anything, importantly distinguishes their act from that of a man and a woman who do likewise? This question was my starting point. A possible answer occurred to me immediately: that coitus can lead to pregnancy, while no homosexual act can. This is, indeed, so obvious that it may seem trivial. But it did not, on this occasion, seem trivial to me. On the contrary, for the first time in my life it struck me as profoundly important. I was of course already familiar with the argument that, since the sexual organs have a natural, procreative "function," homosexual acts are "unnatural" and hence wrong. I had also encountered the related, vaguer argument that, even apart from their procreative function, the male and female sexual organs are naturally "fitted" or "geared" to each other and that homosexual acts are therefore, again, "unnatural," hence wrong. Neither of these arguments had ever greatly impressed me. But although it is fashionable in many circles to ridicule them, I think it is dishonest to suggest that they are *patently* ridiculous. A homosexual friend once remarked to me, in an unguarded moment, that the male body was "not designed" for anal intercourse. Outside of gender studies seminars, few would disagree. Similarly, unless it is a mistake to believe that *any* bodily organs have natural functions—a wildly implausible idea—it would be obtuse to deny that a natural function of the sexual organs is procreation. (This is why they are called "genitals.") To be sure, nothing directly follows from either of these facts about the morality of homosexual acts. I shall later argue that the procreative function of the sexual organs does have a bearing on the morality of homosexual acts. However, what first struck me four years ago was not that these acts fail to fulfill a natural function of the sexual organs. It was rather that their lack of procreative potential deprives homosexual acts of a natural *meaning* that coitus has, or at least can have.

A man and a woman engage in coitus, the woman falls pregnant and, nine months later, she gives birth. Together the couple have brought a new human being into the world, of their own flesh and blood. Having a child is so commonplace an event that we rarely reflect on how momentous it is. The couple may not intend or even welcome it, but this does not diminish the unique wonder of procreation. It seemed obvious to me that the generation of new human life is not, so to speak, a mere side effect of coitus. That an act of loving bodily union should lead to the conception of a child composed of material from both parents' bodies—a child with whom, in turn, the parents normally wish to share their love—is surely more than a brute biological fact. It is fitting, seemly, that things should be this way. The procreative potential of coitus bespeaks an apparent *order* that is at once biological and spiritual. Of course, not all pregnancies result from coitus between people who love each other. Nor does coitus in most cases actually lead to pregnancy. Nonetheless, it is hard to take seriously the suggestion that, when it does, this is no more than an instance of cause and effect, like rain after condensation. Pregnancy is an effect that reveals part of the intrinsic meaning of its cause.

I have spoken of the apparent "order" manifested in the causal connection between loving bodily union and conception, and of the "meaning" of coitus. These expressions may occasion some misgivings. To speak of "order" may seem to imply intelligent design. I shall say more about this later, but for now I will say only that we may acknowledge an instance of apparent natural order without regarding it as evidence of design. The word "meaning," on the other hand, may in this context strike some readers as merely emotive. At the very least, it may seem unhelpfully vague. I admit that its precise force is difficult to grasp. When I sought to express what impressed me so strongly about the connection between coitus and procreation, it was the first word that occurred to me, and I still think it apt. And while claims about the "meaning" of human acts may be somewhat obscure, they are not flatly unintelligible.

Yet to say that pregnancy and childbirth are mere incidental consequences of coitus, intended or not, welcomed or not, hence to deny that they reveal something about the act's intrinsic meaning, is in effect to treat coitus as a means to the end of reproduction—one with which we could dispense, with the aid of technology. Aldous Huxley envisaged this possibility in *Brave New World*. His utopia has abolished conception *in utero* and entrusted the generation of new life to Hatcheries and Conditioning Centers, where fetuses mature in "decanting bottles." Sex no longer serves a reproductive function and the very word "mother" arouses embarrassment and revulsion. If we are appalled at these arrangements, as Huxley intended, we should ask ourselves why. Disregarding their authoritarian enforcement and their sheer antiseptic grimness, they have a clear rationale. As well as serving to control population size, they do away with the severe costs of natural procreation: the inconvenience of pregnancy, the pain of labor and the attendant risks to the woman's health. True, they also destroy the family, but we can easily conceive of less radical arrangements, whereby couples give their sperm and ova to lab technicians, who manufacture children that are then returned to their parents to be raised. Such arrangements may be technically feasible in the wealthier parts of the world within the next few decades. If the intrinsic meaning of coitus is only the celebration of conjugal love, there seems to be no reason to object to its separation from procreation, if effective contraceptives and alternative means of reproduction exist. Indeed, given the costs of natural procreation, perhaps it would even be

irresponsible *not* to sever the two in this way. Is it mere sentimentalism or lack of imagination that makes us contemplate a formal severance of coitus and procreation, if not with horror, at any rate with unease?

I found myself unable to deny that the procreative potential of coitus imbues it with a unique and profound meaning, one that no homosexual sex act can have. Nonetheless, it was not clear to me that this showed anything about the morality of homosexual sex acts performed by loving and faithful partners. Just because such acts lack this meaning, it does not follow that they are not good in their own way. Surely they are just as much expressions of love and mutual commitment as those of heterosexual partners. For this reason, the lack of procreative potential in homosexual sex acts did not seem to me obviously relevant to the subject of same-sex marriage. If there is nothing immoral in such acts, there can hardly be anything immoral in two men or two women solemnly contracting to remain faithful and devoted to each other till death—and same-sex marriage would presumably consist in no more than this.

I should at this point remark that I gave virtually no thought at this time to *marriage*, in contradistinction to sexual relations and procreation. Even four years later, the precise meaning of marriage is not wholly clear to me. However, it seems clear to me now—and I think I dimly recognized this even four years ago—that the question of the morality of homosexual practice is directly relevant to the question of whether governments should legally recognize same-sex marriage. If homosexual practice is immoral, then solemnly contracting to enter into a lifelong homosexual union is assuredly immoral. Some might argue that, just as governments reasonably tolerate other immoral behavior (such as lying), so too they can reasonably recognize same-sex marriage, even if it is immoral. But the analogy is false. Certainly governments can reasonably *tolerate* both homosexual practice and mutual pledges by homosexual partners to remain faithful and devoted to each other till death, just as they can reasonably tolerate private citizens describing such partners as "married." But legal *recognition* is a different matter. It is by no means obvious that governments should either recognize or refuse to recognize any kind of marriage, whether "traditional" or otherwise. (They neither recognize nor refuse to recognize lifelong friendships, for instance.) Legal recognition has an unavoidable symbolic, as well as a merely practical, dimension. If a government legally recognizes same-sex marriage, it thereby implicitly affirms the moral legitimacy of homosexual practice.

•

My reflections four years ago led me no further than I have so far indicated. While they did not convince me that there is any clear, plausible moral objection either to homosexual practice or to same-sex marriage, they did leave me with a lingering sense of disquiet. I was still unashamedly attracted to other men and I had not abandoned hope of some day resuming my former relationship, but I was unsettled. In retrospect, I would say I was unprepared to think through all the implications of affirming that the natural connection between coitus and procreation demands our respect and perhaps our reverence. To speak in this way is to imply that, regardless of our wishes or even our needs, nature's arrangements with regard to procre-

ation have for us a certain moral authority. But this seems unintelligible unless nature's arrangements more generally have for us some sort of moral authority.

Though rare today, belief in the existence of such an order has a long and venerable history. Both Plato and Aristotle looked to nature as in some sense a standard for moral judgment. The Stoics sought to live "according to nature." Medieval theologians identified the moral law with the "natural law," as contemporary Catholic theologians still do. Even today, when a "disenchanted" view of the natural world goes largely unquestioned, appeals to nature as a standard for moral judgment have undeniable rhetorical power. We can readily appreciate, for example, why the ghost of old Hamlet describes his own murder, at his brother's hand, not only as "most foul," but also as "most unnatural." And if we do affirm the existence of a natural moral order, the suggestion that the natural procreative *function* of the sexual organs also has intrinsic moral significance begins to look more plausible.

Perhaps nature has established in coitus a connection, demanding a certain respect, between sexual pleasure, the celebration of love, and the begetting of offspring. One might concede this much but argue that the natural order in coitus is irrelevant to homosexual practice. Homosexuals would perhaps be glad to combine sexual pleasure and the celebration of love with the begetting of offspring, but they cannot do so. While it might be wrong for heterosexual couples formally to sever coitus from procreation, it could not be wrong for homosexual couples to engage in sex acts that are by nature *unapt* for procreation. However, if the natural procreative function of the sexual organs demands our respect, no less than the natural connection of the three elements in coitus, it follows that a homosexual couple's sex acts cannot be anything other than an abuse of their sexual organs. That homosexual desire in many cases has a genetic or hormonal etiology and is therefore itself, in one clear sense, "natural," makes no difference. As Aristotle observed, nature sometimes "blunders," often with tragic results. Psychopathic personality traits may in some cases be due to low cortisol levels or lesions on the orbitofrontal cortex, and these are certainly "natural." Nonetheless, if they are among the causal conditions for a person's harboring a desire to inflict pain or worse on his fellow creatures, they are just as certainly natural defects. A "natural" desire to abuse one's procreative capacity is equally a natural defect. The reality of "natural defects" does not tell against, but rather underscores, the existence of a natural order. In seeking sexual pleasure and loving union in a way intrinsically unapt for procreation, homosexuals do violence to this order—violence essentially the same in kind as that perpetrated by Huxley's fictional eugenicists.

I am aware that this train of thought will strike many as outrageous. To begin with, the idea that there is a "natural moral order" may seem absurd. Whether we like it or not, surely the natural world *is* fundamentally no more than a vast quantum of energy in constant flux, with no intrinsic "meaning." In any case, the suggestion that natural arrangements in general reflect an all-encompassing moral order seems quite implausible on the face of it. Do the collisions of asteroid belts or the collapses of far-distant stars have moral significance? Even if we consider only living beings, their parts, and their immediate natural environs, the suggestion seems far-fetched. Earthquakes and cyclones destroy thousands of lives and are no less "natural" than the climatic conditions that first make those lives possible. Terminal cancers are as much natural growths as vital

organs. When female spiders eat their mates after copulation, or when cuckoos destroy other birds' young and deceive the parent birds into rearing them, nature is assuredly running its common course. Can we really descry a moral order in such arrangements? Ridiculing the Stoics for seeking to live "according to nature," Nietzsche characterized nature as "boundlessly extravagant, boundlessly indifferent, without purpose or consideration, without pity or justice, at once fruitful and barren and uncertain"—and was he not right?

Quite apart from the dubiousness of appealing to nature as a moral standard in the first place, the argument just sketched about the procreative function of the sexual organs might seem to prove too much. If sexual pleasure and loving intimacy are not to be separated from procreation, then not only are homosexual sex acts wrong, but so are all heterosexual sex acts other than coitus, to say nothing of solitary masturbation. Even coitus, it would seem, is wrong if the couple practices contraception, or if one of the partners is infertile or sterile. Would any reasonable human being accept these consequences?

But a fully disenchanted view of nature involves difficulties of its own. If all that exists is energy in flux, morality can have no foundation in the nature of things. Nietzsche saw this clearly. In flatly declaring that "there are no moral facts," he was merely acknowledging a necessary corollary of the view that nature is "boundlessly indifferent, without purpose or consideration." To be sure, he also speaks of human beings "creating" meaning. "Evaluation is creation," his Zarathustra grandly declares. When people today speak of "creating" or "making" meaning, they pay knowing or unknowing tribute to the seductive power of Nietzschean rhetoric. But the notion that human beings "create" meaning is, I believe, simply false to our daily experience. Suppose we hear of a soldier throwing himself on a grenade to save his comrades and are awestruck at his courage. If we call his act noble, are we "creating" meaning? Are we not rather *recognizing* it? Again, when we call the actions of serial killers and child molesters evil, are we not simply acknowledging a fact? It may seem more plausible to say that, when we see a snow-capped mountain peak bathed in late-afternoon sunlight and exclaim "How beautiful!" we are "creating" meaning—yet this is assuredly not what we take ourselves to be doing. We think that what we see *is* beautiful. We take ourselves to be *responding* to natural beauty, and we would likely feel that someone who could look on the same scene with complete indifference would be missing something. Quite generally, when we speak of goodness, wickedness and beauty, we take ourselves to be responding, and responding appropriately, to features of the world we inhabit. We discover meaning; we do not create or "project" it. (This is not to deny that our capacity to discern meaning is fallible and needs cultivation, as Plato and Aristotle both stressed.) Therefore if morality is not a mere illusion, it must have some foundation in nature.

Here it may be objected that morality surely has its foundation in *reason*, not in nature. Man's autonomous reason, it may be said, elevates him above the merely natural and is the source not only of morality but of all that goes under the name of "culture." I suspect that this Kantian or Hegelian view is at bottom barely distinguishable from the Nietzschean view that human beings "create" value, inasmuch as it treats reason, in Kant's words, as "self-legislating" and hence as *making* meaning, rather than discovering it. In any case, to say that morality has its foundation in reason is only to repeat that it has its foundation in

nature, since reason too belongs to man's nature. I would add that, morality aside, the very existence of mind and reason are difficult to explain if one accepts a disenchanted view of nature. That the blind motion of elementary particles could give rise to the capacity, in certain organisms, to know and understand the world out of which they have emerged, seems incomprehensible. The problem is often obscured today by loose talk of organisms acquiring ever greater "complexity" in the course of evolutionary history, as if this sufficed to explain the emergence of consciousness. Yet the distinction between the conscious and the non-conscious is not, on the face of it, a matter of degree, but of kind. Neurophysiological complexity may be a precondition for thought, but it is far from clear how it could *explain* it.

When I first thought seriously about same-sex marriage, I had already for some time been preoccupied with the question of how mind and morality can belong to the natural world. Indeed, this was itself an additional reason for my giving thought to sexuality and its "natural" meaning. A year later, I was firmly convinced that a disenchanted view of nature is untenable, given the existence of mind and morality. Arguments to the contrary seemed to me, by this time, little more than sophistic evasions. But I had also begun to think that it cannot make sense to speak of a natural moral order unless one is prepared to acknowledge this order as the work of (supernatural) *design*. I said earlier that one may acknowledge an instance of *apparent* natural order as such without regarding it as evidence of design. I had by this point gradually (and reluctantly) come to doubt whether natural order could possibly be more than *merely* apparent if it were not the work of a designer. I had also begun to think that, if mind cannot emerge from non-mind, and if nothing comes from nothing, then one has no choice but to believe in the existence of a non-human—or rather superhuman—mind that is somehow the origin of human minds. In short, I was leaning toward theism. And the following year, after much brooding and not a little agonizing, I converted to Catholicism.

I have given only the most cursory indication of the reasons that, humanly speaking, led me to take this step. I have passed over many possible objections to the arguments summarily rehearsed in the preceding paragraphs, and I have said nothing about why I was drawn to Catholicism, rather than to any other form of theism. I may have given the impression that my conversion was a merely intellectual affair, when of course it was not. As with many converts, friendship with believers played an important role. I owed much to the old friend mentioned earlier, and still more to another, dearly beloved friend of more recent years, whose support at the time of my conversion meant more to me than I can say. Among the inevitable stresses and strains of conversion, none was more painful for me than that of explaining my decision to my former partner. I had come to believe that, to the extent that our relationship had been one of more than deep affection and mutual care, it had been gravely wrong on both our parts. Telling him so was the hardest thing I have ever had to do or, I hope, ever will have to do. I count it as one of God's mercies that, badly hurt as my ex-partner was, he has remained a close friend.

•

The idea of a natural moral order undeniably presents difficulties. From a theistic perspective, however, these difficulties are not obviously intractable. The starry heavens above me, no less than the moral law within me, may fill my mind with awe, whose rightful object is Him who made both. The austere grandeur of inanimate nature serves to glorify the Creator, as does the moral order manifested in the human frame. The apparent brutality and waste in the animal kingdom admittedly remains perturbing, as does the misery that seems endemic to human life. The reality of natural defects or "blunders" itself seems difficult to reconcile with the existence of a benevolent creator. If one believes in the fall of man, one may regard defects and corruptions in human nature as incidental to our fallen state, and the near-ubiquity of suffering as serving a punitive and corrective purpose. The problem of evil (in the broadest sense) arises for any cosmology that acknowledges its existence at all. Christian theism indeed brings this problem into stark relief, since it boldly affirms that, notwithstanding the reality of evil, God is all-good and all-powerful. Whatever its difficulties, however, I had come to believe, as I say, that the only logical alternative to theism is a bald "naturalism" that denies the reality of good and evil altogether.

I earlier remarked that the argument from the procreative function and meaning of coitus might seem to prove too much. Since I have mentioned my conversion to Catholicism, readers will not be surprised that I accept that argument's implications regarding contraception, non-coital sex and masturbation. Catholic moral teaching in general purports to be rationally defensible and the fundament of Catholic sexual ethics is the principle, laid down in the famous (or infamous) 1968 papal encyclical *Humanae Vitae*, that the unitive and procreative meanings of sexual intercourse are not to be separated. (I might say in passing that, at the time that I first thought hard about homosexuality and procreation, I knew nothing of this encyclical beyond its name and its ban on contraception.) The Church teaches that sexual intercourse is only licit within marriage—a teaching that I presently accept on faith, since, as mentioned earlier, I am not as clear about the meaning of marriage as I would need to be in order to accept any such teaching on merely rational grounds. The Church does not, of course, prohibit couples to marry who are incapable of childbearing; nor, subject to certain conditions, does it prohibit marital coitus during infertile periods. It is a fair question why not. In recent debates about same-sex marriage, the most prominent Catholic defenders of "traditional" marriage have been the so-called "new natural lawyers," John Finnis, Robert P. George, Patrick Lee and others, who argue for an essential connection between marriage and procreation. Their most thoughtful critics, such as Andrew Koppelman and John Corvino, have claimed—I think rightly—that they fail adequately to explain why, given their principles, infertility is not an obstacle to marriage. As we have seen, Jason Wakefield (the same-sex marriage proponent with whom I began) puts the same question to the supposed "bigots" and "homophobes" who argue that procreation is in some sense essential to marriage.

What distinguishes the "new" natural lawyers from more traditional natural law theorists is their refusal to appeal to the natural "function" or teleology of the human reproductive system. This refusal is motivated partly by the wish to avoid reasoning fallaciously from an "is" to an "ought" (the biological function of the genitals *is* procreation, therefore one *ought not* engage in sex acts intrinsically unapt for procreation) and partly, I suspect, by unwillingness to enter deeply into metaphysical questions. I

believe it is this refusal to appeal to the procreative function of the genitals that ultimately accounts for the inadequacy of their efforts to justify the marriage of infertile couples.

Catholic apologists should not disguise from themselves or from others the real difficulties in defending this aspect of Catholic moral teaching. In a 1964 exchange about contraception with the liberalizing Dominican Herbert McCabe, the philosopher and convert Elizabeth Anscombe openly acknowledged that it is far from obvious how to justify the marriage of elderly women on the principles of traditional Catholic sexual morality. However, precisely if one grants that nature's arrangements have a certain moral authority, one may reasonably infer two things from the biological facts. Firstly, though coitus is naturally connected to procreation in a general way and derives its meaning in part from this connection, nonetheless the human reproductive system is not so designed that coitus should usually, or even often, lead to conception. Therefore, secondly, one does not act against nature if one engages in non-contraceptive coitus, knowing that conception is unlikely to occur, or even certain not to occur. The infertile periods in women of childbearing age, the rarity of conception even after coitus during fertile periods, the onset of menopause and, despite all these, the lack of seasonal variation in human sexual desire, together leave little room for doubt that the natural moral order does not demand of spouses that they restrict sexual intercourse to periods when they can be reasonably confident of its leading to conception. And if sexual intercourse that will probably or certainly not lead to conception is licit in principle, it is at least plausible to think that, by extension, the marriage of men and women naturally incapable of having children is also licit. This is compatible with recognizing that the biological function of coitus and of sexual pleasure is procreation, that the connection of the three must be respected and that, hence, *willfully* to sever this connection is to violate the natural moral order.

This thumbnail sketch of Catholic sexual ethics and what I take to be its rationale obviously leaves many questions and possible objections unanswered. The major stumbling block for many is of course the very idea that natural arrangements might have for us a certain moral authority. (Provided they do, the inference from "is" to "ought" need not be fallacious.) I have sought to explain how I came to take this idea seriously and why I still see no reasonable alternative, short of outright nihilism, to some form of natural law theory. Not all contemporary thinkers who take a similar view are Catholic natural lawyers. Leon Kass and Philippa Foot, for instance, both acknowledge the need for ethics to be grounded in some way in nature. I have suggested that the idea of a natural moral order is ultimately untenable without theism, because meaningful "order" presupposes design, and hence a designer. However, an atheistic natural law ethics is not patently incoherent, and a natural law defense of "traditional" marriage need not and should not appeal to theistic, let alone specifically Christian, premises.

•

It might seem that all I have said only goes to show that Jason Wakefield is right after all. My argument against the legal recognition of same-sex marriage is simply an argument for the immorality of homosexual practice and,

in fact, I have said comparatively little about marriage. Does this not confirm Wakefield's charge that opposition to same-sex marriage is inherently homophobic?

I have suggested that one should distinguish between homophobia and moral condemnation of homosexual practice, something Wakefield would likely deny. Wakefield is, however, right at least to this extent: the argument that homosexual partnerships do not deserve to be called "marriages" because homosexual sex acts are intrinsically unapt for procreation cannot be formulated in such a way as to allow for the marriage of elderly or infertile heterosexual couples unless it appeals to the procreative function of the genitals; and, in making this appeal, one unavoidably commits oneself to the immorality of homosexual sex acts. In truth, one commits oneself to a great deal more than this. A consistent sexual ethic based on recognition of the procreative function and meaning of sex is far more severe than most people today, homosexual or heterosexual, are prepared to tolerate. It is useless for principled opponents of same-sex marriage to pretend otherwise. The merely "conservative" argument that we should not tamper with a time-honored institution is both intellectually unsatisfactory and rhetorically weak, and arguments drawing on sociological studies of same-sex parenting are, I think, inconclusive at best. If one wishes to make a principled case against same-sex marriage that will hold water, one must in effect mount an all-out assault on the sexual mores that have been dominant in the West for the better part of the last half-century.

This being so, the campaign in the U.S. against same-sex marriage seems to me likely to fail, at least in the short term. In writing this piece, my primary intention has not in fact been to aid this campaign, worthy though I think it is. I have chiefly wished to address people in certain respects like myself—that is, people with strong homosexual yearnings who nonetheless realize that opposition to same-sex marriage and moral condemnation of homosexual practice need not be motivated by blind prejudice or sheer hate. I have implied that to refrain from seeking gratification or loving intimacy with a same-sex partner is reasonable. That doing so is difficult and fraught with pain I do not deny, especially if one's desires are exclusively homosexual. Reason has only limited power over the passions. Nonetheless, I would urge people with homosexual desires who are not wholly unmoved by what I have said consciously to resist the fashionable and cruel myth that the passions, and sexual desire in particular, simply *cannot* be controlled or moderated by reason. Every responsible adult knows that they can. Whether the argument I have made from the procreative function and meaning of sex *is* indeed reasonable is of course another matter. I have acknowledged that, as a natural law argument, it rests on a view of "nature" that raises numerous questions, some of which I cannot answer. I might add that, at the time I first resolved not to seek or hope for future homosexual gratification, the details of this argument were far from clear to me, though I had no doubt of its basic soundness. To act on only partially clarified insight is not the same as to make a leap of faith. To be sure, if someone is contemplating a step that may involve sacrificing one of this life's greatest joys, he or she will reasonably want as much clarity as possible. I hope this piece may be of some aid to such a person.

Steven Miller, *Blood Oath*, from *Wild Boys*, 2006

NOT FOR ANYTHING

by Alex Worsnip

Human beings are "teleologizing" creatures. That is to say: we like to understand the phenomena that we encounter in the world as coming to us with built-in functions or purposes; as being "for" something. As extensive psychological research has shown, this is a bias that comes to us naturally. For instance, young children freely describe mountains as "for climbing" or babies as "for loving," and even prefer explanations of the existence of such entities in terms of these functions. Somewhat more subtly, the bias remains in adults, intensified when they do not deliberate carefully, and, fascinatingly, when suffering from conditions like Alzheimer's that cause them to forget much of what they once knew. It has even been found residually in professional scientists.

At the same time, human beings are also "essentializing" creatures. That is to say: we have a tendency to view things as having the features they have inherently and unchangeably, even when these features are demonstrably contingent aspects of the particular social world that we happen to inhabit. Again, children provide very striking examples—in one study, they judged that boys would prefer playing with trucks to playing with dolls even if they were raised on an island otherwise only populated by women. But social attitudes to gender, race and sexuality make it clear that this bias is, once again, not confined to children.

The tendency to teleologize and to essentialize can come together to form a dangerous cocktail. Regarding a social institution like marriage, we have a tendency to teleologize—to think, as the title of this symposium seems to implicitly take for granted, that there is something that marriage is "for." On its own, that might not be such a dangerous thing. After all, marriage is a social institution that was created intentionally, for particular reasons—unlike mountains—and has a certain kind of existing social function. That existing social function, however, is not something of obvious normative significance, or indeed something that we should not feel free to reform and change as we please. But then our essentializing tendency kicks in, and we start to view marriage's existing social function as constituting something like its essence, thinking of contingent social arrangements as something unchangeable.

This tendency pollutes the gay marriage debate. So, we find people arguing against gay marriage on the grounds that a same-sex union simply *cannot* be a "real marriage," since it is part of the essence of marriage that it excludes gay people. The sometimes almost rueful tone of such proclamations reminds me a bit of the kind of power-tripping institutional or bureaucratic official that everyone has encountered at some point in their life: "Sorry, I'd love to help you, but I'm afraid them's the rules." It's nothing against gays, we're told: it's just that marriage inherently excludes them. And we can't do anything about that.

It's a strange argument: even granting the dubious premise about the essence of marriage, it's unclear what's so bad about violating an essence. If the social institution of marriage fails to match its supposed timeless essence, what exactly is supposed to happen that is so bad? Is fire going to rain down on us as a consequence? Well, maybe so, if the argument is grounded upon the idea of marriage's essence as ordained by God—indeed, this is the context in which talk of an essence of marriage makes most sense—but the arguments in question tend to at least to pretend to secularity (though they have a funny coincidence of coming out of the mouths of strongly religious people).

What is certainly true, less ambitiously, is that the word "marriage" and its associated concept have a particular meaning, one that clearly did not include gay marriages, say, fifty years ago. But concepts and words are constantly changing and evolving—that of marriage being no exception throughout history—and those of the late twentieth century have no special metaphysical or moral significance.

Arguments to the contrary reflect an obsession with categories and a misplaced belief that normative conclusions can fall out of the meanings of words. Here's another example: when Christopher Cox wrote a great piece in *Slate* about why vegans (and vegetarians) should be happy to eat bivalves such as oysters, the comments were flooded with angry responses to the effect that vegans should not do this because the word "vegan" just *means* that you don't eat any animals. But the question of moral relevance is obviously not, "is this behavior covered by the meaning of the English word 'vegan'?" but rather, "do the general *reasons* for being vegan carry over to refraining from eating bivalves?" Similarly, even if we grant that "marriage" means (or, more accurately by this point, once meant) something that could only take place between a man and a woman, the question at stake for public policy is not, "are gay unions included under the 'original' meaning of the word 'marriage'?" but rather, "do the general *reasons* for the state to sanction the institution of marriage carry over to gay unions?"

And here I think the answer is a resounding "yes." Gay marriages can be just as loving and, yes, permanent, as straight ones; and there is no evidence to support the prejudiced assumption that they are worse environments in which to raise children. But even if there were evidence to the contrary, that still wouldn't be enough to secure the argument for the anti-gay marriage lobby. Consider the following analogy: suppose that, in some particular society, there is a general statistical trend that suggests that marriages within a particular racial group were less permanent, and provided less stable environments in which to raise children, for whatever reason. Would the state then be justified in banning marriages between members of these racial groups? Surely not. The point this reveals is that sometimes particular statistical trends about social groups do not justify the imposition of injustices on individual members of those particular groups. Most simply, not every member of the group will conform to the statistic, and it is an injustice to punish them for it.

It will be objected that lack of access to marriage is not an injustice, since there are other ways to afford gay people the same protections under the law that straight people get. So-called moderates concede civil partnerships without endorsing gay marriage. So, for example, Justin Welby, the Archbishop of Canterbury and head of the Anglican church, has tried to put the anti-gay marriage point in a characteristically evasive and wooly faux-liberal manner, insisting in his speech to the U.K. Parliament that the gay marriage bill "assumes that the rightful desire for equality ... must mean uniformity, failing to understand that two things may be equal but different." Shamefully, the otherwise wonderful Liberal Democrat grandee Shirley Williams has echoed his sentiments almost exactly.

The problem with the "different but equal" reasoning, however, is that it ignores the ways in which difference is felt and experienced as inequality. Let's try another thought experiment. Famously, during segregation in the Southern states of the U.S., black people had to sit at the back of buses. This was considered an outrage. Now let us imagine how the Welby-Williams reasoning would apply in such a scenario. "Well," our Welby-Williams counterpart would say, "we totally understand why you're angry. After all, being at the back of the bus gives you differential access to the front doors of the bus. It means you have to walk for longer after getting on and before getting off, and your seats aren't as comfortable. These are clearly the harms you're objecting to—and we agree with you! So we've come up with a solution. Instead of putting the white people at the front of the bus and the black people at the back, we'll put the white people on the left of the bus and the black people on the right! The seats will be of the same quality, and they'll be in equal proximity to the front doors. There we go; problem solved—different but equal."

Obviously, this spectacularly misses the point. The very act of separating two races is in itself discriminatory, divisive and "otherising": it doesn't matter if the seats are the same. And likewise with designating gay and straight unions with "different but equal" legal standing. Given this, the burden is on the opponent of gay marriage to explain the positive reasons for separating gay and straight marriage. Of course there is a difference between being gay and being straight— but there is also a difference between being tall and being short, or being blonde or brunette. The question is whether the difference is sufficient to necessitate a differential legal arrangement. And a mere registering of some difference is not enough to answer it.

The fundamental point which gets returned to when this challenge is broached is that gay sex does not and cannot involve procreation. As Welby puts it, the proposal to allow gay marriage is actually a proposal to "abolish" marriage, because "the concept of marriage as a normative place for procreation is lost." I'm not sure what a "normative place" is (though it sounds like a lovely place to procreate), but it is obvious from a moment's reflection that the current concept of marriage does *not* designate it exclusively for procreation, since marriages between heterosexuals who cannot have children, or who deliberately choose not to have children, are legal.

Even if you ignore all of that, though, why on earth *should* marriage be so closely tied to procreation? The world is not in urgent need of more procreation—far from it. And it can't have anything to do with the need to provide stable environments for children to be raised, since one can raise children without procreating, through adoption or IVF, and in any case the legal questions of gay adoption and IVF rights are entirely separate from those of gay marriage legislation. So we are simply returned to the essentialism with which we began—marriage just *is* about procreation (or, the kind of sex that can result in procreation); that's its essence!

More complicated but equally (if not more) unpersuasive are the attempts by Sherif Girgis, Ryan T. Anderson and Robert P. George in a recent book to explain why these other non-procreating heterosexual relationships *can* be marriages, because they still involve heterosexual sex, which has the so-called *telos* of producing children. Even if, um, you do everything in your power to prevent it from ending in that result, you're still aimed at having babies, apparently. Coyly, Girgis et al. talk of the "distinctive bond" that, as they call it, "coitus" involves, which is really just a way of elevating their own sexual preferences to the status of quasi-transcendental truths about the form of the good.

As I have already argued, we should show this so-called essence of marriage—which one might suspect is really just an ahistorical way of talking about the conception of marriage we happen to have had in the recent past—no respect at all until someone shows us what its tangible value is. In the meantime, we should define our social conception of marriage in response to the considerations that matter to us, not try to deduce what matters from some supposed metaphysical essence.

This is not, it bears stressing, to say that all *values* are relative to how we think of them. On the contrary, it is precisely by giving up the idea that we should be led by marriage's "essence" in formulating legal rules that we make room for evaluating different possible arrangements against moral standards. Here there is an analogy with positivist accounts of the law. In jurisprudence, positivism is the view that what the law says is simply a matter of actual statute and precedent—the question of whether something is legal comes down to this, and not to moral questions.

Sometimes anti-positivists accuse positivism of being an amoralist position, but nothing could be further from the truth. On the contrary, it is positivism that makes room for normative criticism of the law, rather than pretending that fundamentally the law always reflects morality. Similarly, the view that marriage just is whatever we choose to make it in no way implies that there are not better and worse ways for it to be.

The essentialist view, by contrast, seems in the final analysis to rest upon a desire to preserve a particular conception of marriage for ultimately religious reasons. The reason that many anti-gay marriage campaigners won't be up front about this is that they recognize that many Americans think of religion as an inadequate basis for public policy. This attempt to enforce religious preferences on others is an instance of the ever-more ubiquitous practice of claiming the right not to have others around you do things that you don't like. Of course, once you allow these rights into your system of rights, they make rights meaningless, since for every right you can name, there's a corresponding and apparently counterbalancing right of this kind. For the right to free speech, there's the right not to have other people say things you don't like. For the right to free choice over your body, there's the right not to have other people do things with their bodies that you disapprove of. And yes, for the right to religious worship, there's the right not to have other people worship gods you don't believe in. Rights, then, lose all their meaning: everything is a tie. Given such a permissive notion of a right, rights-discourse becomes just a way of dressing up any disagreement or basic conflict of preference whatsoever.

This is likewise the implicit reasoning behind the idea that when someone else gets married to someone of a gender you don't want them to marry, it's an infringement of your religious freedom. This is rubbish: your religious freedom extends to your own practices, not your ability to enforce that religious conception on others. (I'm reminded here of a popular Facebook group, back in the day when people were members of Facebook groups just for the sake of it, called "Don't like gay marriage? Then don't get one.")

More subtly, and perhaps more interestingly, I think it can also be seen in the small but non-negligible minority of gay people that oppose gay marriage. Here the idea is often (if not always) that if gay marriage is legalized, it will become the norm for gay relationships, "forcing" them to adapt themselves to conventional standards associated with heterosexual relationships. But this seemingly radical point is really just the same old "right not to have others do things you don't like." If it transpires that the majority of gay people in relationships get married, that will be because they have chosen to do so. For those who don't like that, and prefer a gay relationship which doesn't subscribe to such traditional norms, they are free not to subscribe to them and not to get a gay marriage, but if others choose differently, that's tough: again, there's no right not to have others do things you don't like. Indeed, at the point when this reasoning is offered as a reason not to *legalize* gay marriage, it is the *opponent* of gay marriage that is the one trying to enforce their conception of what a gay relationship should be like on others. The inherent traditionalism of marriage might be a reason not to *have* a gay marriage; it is not a reason not to allow others to *choose* whether to have one. We elide that distinction at our peril.

Sir William Quiller Orchardson, *Marriage of Convenience*, 1883

MARRYING UP

by Cammi Climaco

Obligation is the sole reason to play a game that you know you will lose. While spending my first Christmas at my new boyfriend's mom's house, the smarty pants college educator got out her favorite game, Scrabble. His entire family is good at it. I explained to the family that I never really played before. "What do you usually do for Christmas, Cammi?" the brother asked me, shocked.

"Oh!" I answered, "Usually, after opening gifts, me, my sisters and all the kids sit around the room and make fun of whoever is fattest." It's a family favorite and also very competitive.

It was clear by the Scrabble scores that I wasn't like them. So clear that a longtime friend during drinks one night commented, "You married up. Huh?" At the time, I laughed; he knew all about me and my family; my dad worked in a factory, I was the first person to go to college, when we fight there's a lot of screaming and breaking shit. Sometimes the police show up. I learned how to play bocce and bet on horses. Later, after thinking about my friend's comment for a while, I became insulted and horrified—that's what people thought of me? Gold-digger? But, "gold-digger" only fits when there's gold to dig.

Meeting my husband, Warren, was the best thing that ever happened to my father. When I went to college my dad decided I should be a nurse because I could definitely get a job and those are the only jobs women get. In his defense, he was born in the early Thirties and there happen to be a million hospitals in Cleveland. He never took into account the fact that when I walked into a hospital I would automatically fill with dread and start uncontrollably crying because people "get sick." People in my family describe me as "sensitive." I decided to get a degree in art because who wants money and being sensitive is an attribute. My dad, naturally, was terrified I would pregnantly drag home some degenerate artist that would lead to years of me moving in and out of the house, borrowing money from him—and possibly to a Lifetime movie. When I brought Warren home, I could see his inner monologue whistling the song "I'm In The Money." Warren had "potential earner" written all over him. To this day the first thing my dad says to me on the phone is "How's Warren doing?" Which, in translation means, "Who cares about you, is Warren making money?"

The last thing I fantasized about, as a girl, was my wedding day. I never thought about what my wedding dress would be like. I never thought about bridesmaids, party favors, chicken or filet mignon. In retrospect, it probably would have helped if I had, because it took five years for my husband and me just to agree on a location. At 27, I never wanted to get married. I thought: married people are kidding themselves; monogamy is totally unreasonable; and everyone gets divorced. And even after being married for sixteen years, I still think that. In fact, I'm pretty sure that denial of being married is how we've managed to stay married. We don't wear wedding rings.

When I met Warren, I knew I wanted to be with him forever. He was the smartest person I had ever met, he wouldn't have sex on the first date (which, honestly, I thought was weird) and, mostly, I liked his style. He has great taste in eyeglasses and a moral and ethical compass that could cut a bitch. It was refreshing. Especially after dating a string of men that would steal pills out of anyone's mom's bathroom cabinet ("This one's a blood thinner for cancer patients, it'll get you drunk faster!").

My parents, really old-fashioned, made it known that Warren and I were "living in sin" and wouldn't let us sleep in the same bedroom any time we came to visit them. We got engaged after 9/11 and married five years later. I had to get that marriage thing rolling if my parents weren't going to die disappointed. It was the happiest day of their lives. All those years imagining us in the same bed together, fornicating. Gross! Now since we've been married the last thing we want to do when we visit them is sleep in the same tiny beds. When he says, "Can't you move over a little bit?" it means: "You dragged me to your family's house, now isn't there anywhere else you can go sleep?"

Warren and I fight. A lot. I know the difference between right and wrong, but it does get dark and soupy in places. During one of our first big arguments—I believe it was about who was in charge (me) of taking the laundry to the laundromat, sitting there for two hours, folding it, bringing it home and putting it all away—I threw a bottle of Tide at him. Near him, to be clear. He calmly stated that if I ever threw anything at him again, we were over. It led me to reevaluate my problem-solving techniques.

I've found that during our time together, my arguing style goes through cycles. After the Tide incident, I would employ "silence" as a fighting strategy. That stopped working after two or three arguments with his simple, "If you've got a problem, say something, I can't read your mind."

And my quiet passive-aggressive response, "I just wish you would shut the drawer."

When that became a bore, I began to critically reason out my concerns and issues. "If you could please shut the drawer, I would really appreciate it. The knob is leaving a bruise on my hip." It seemed to work, but after time it became ineffective. That led to screaming and yelling, "SHUT THE FUCKING DRAWER!" That got some attention for a while, but ... he eventually became numb to it, as one does. When you reach a fever pitch, there's only one way to go, without reverting to throwing things of course, and that is back to silence. It becomes effective again. The system works and takes years. I believe, in the sixteen years we've been together, we are currently in the middle of the fourth cycle. Warren has his own style that works for him as well, the Bruce Lee style of "fighting without fighting." I can appreciate it. But it's not a fight about the drawer at all. It's about money.

Even though we are both artists, our careers are completely different. As a graphic designer, he does what he loves, is good at it and gets rewarded for it financially. For me, having gotten an MFA in sculpting, I'm essentially qualified for lottery winner, mediocre karaoke singer, and pierogi maker. He makes and has always made more money than I do. Because of this, we have shared a bank account since we first met. But even though Warren has been exceedingly generous with it, I don't feel like it's not "our" money but his money, especially when I'm spending it on cute socks from T.J. Maxx. Whether true or not, I feel like we're always doing what he wants to do, from dinner to vacation, to what we're going to watch on the TV. I call it the "Warrenocracy"—a line stolen from the movie *Bring It On*. He loves it! (Just kidding.) Big deal, right? Money is what every couple fights about the most. That, and finding lube under the bed. If it's not your lube, then whose is it?

That only happened once, a few years ago.

Neither of us has cheated on the other. However, the lube incident did lead us down a dark path. I texted Warren, "I found your tube of lube under the bed when I was cleaning."

He called me immediately. I didn't pick up, left before he got home from work and stayed out at the bars until 4 a.m. He was so upset I didn't call back that he took a drill and screwed the door closed. (Also screwing himself in, but no matter, it's the gesture.) When I got home, he was awake and the door was already unscrewed (the drill holes remained). We just stood there looking at each other. He said it wasn't his lube and I said okay. We hugged then went to sleep.

Even though I believed him, (we determined it was left over from some houseguests who will remain nameless) I painted our bedroom bubblegum pink while he was at work one day. He hates coming home to an apartment that's a totally different color. But the bedroom was so bright and jarring, I had to start sleeping on the couch. Do you see what I mean now about denial? Monogamy? Bad decisions? Backfiring color revenge?

It's hard to believe that anyone would want this, gays, straights, penguins. But alas, we do (well, not the penguins), even against what we know is medieval, nonsensical. The pressure of not getting married is too overwhelming. It's also too weird. I asked one of my students, a twenty-year-old aspiring artist from California, if she wanted to get married, and she said, "Absolutely." When I pressed her on why, she said, "I just want to be normal." I told her she was out of her mind, but sure. I'm no dream crusher.

Even though we refuse to wear matching outfits, I still really like Warren and I continue to live my life as a married person. It's got its benefits, aside from tax breaks. I call him five times a day to see what's for dinner and he understood when I listlessly laid on the couch for two weeks when my mom died. We celebrate each other's success and sympathize with each other when we fail.

Instead of sex fantasies like a normal person, I fantasize about the day when I come home with a check for $1,000,000 and say something like, "How do you like me now? We are going to do whatever I want for the rest of our lives and if you don't like it I'll divorce you and buy someone that does." We'll laugh really hard and I'll say, "I'm serious." Then, we'll get a three-bedroom apartment, I'll have my dad move in, he'll finally get that unlimited time with Warren and we can host Warren's family for Scrabble night. It's unlikely, yes. Quixotic, perhaps (26 Scrabble points) ... but aren't all marriages?

Ute Klein, *Resonanzgeflechte #1*, 2009

THE LOVE WE USE

by Charles Comey

I remember walking on the white slabs of cement in the breezeway between our kindergarten and elementary school when I was five, and some older kid telling me that my friend Tom's parents had split up. After that—basically after learning of its existence—I remember dreading divorce for my own family. My mom says I used to come up behind her and take her hand and put it in my dad's.

But one afternoon when I was seven, my parents, who were wearing uncustomarily nice attire for an about-the-house weekend, explained that mom was moving out. We would be spending half our time at her new place near the fire station. A few months later my dad had a heart attack, and thereafter fell deep into his inherited Myotonic Muscular Dystrophy. I'm sure that there's a lot more to say about the circumstances, but this is the basic framework for the way 1988 turned out. Truth be told the next years— the six years after the divorce and before dad died—had plenty of joy in them, as much intimacy and indulgence as my sister and I could eat up. But as you'd expect it also had a lot of misery. And dad's household was not healthy.

Children of divorce apparently react very differently from one another as far as how they feel about marriage as an institution. Tom, for example, is now very classically a husband. For others, like my friend Greg, who has watched literally every one of his siblings (he's the youngest of six) get divorced, followed finally by his parents, marriage is out of the question. I think that I've come out more like Tom. In fact, for my part I suspect that seeing this divorce and death up close may be one reason why I seem to have a hard time even addressing, in a direct way, a question like whether or not marriage is a good thing, whether it leads to a fulfilling life, etc. When I try to ask something like that, the room sort of meta-pivots around so that the question remains a half-hearted third person plural one. For myself it's more like: *I must reconstruct a marriage or ... I'll die. Failing that, the TV will come on, I'll keep a living room that is a mix of love and entropy, and expire.* I guess that sounds disempowering. For what it's worth, now that I'm married and have a happy home, honestly, it doesn't feel disempowering at all. This is what I want. It feels more like I am fortunate enough to have complete clarity on the topic as it pertains to me.

I can certainly sketch out what it must be like to consider what married life offers in comparison to life without it. You get security, comforts, companionship, a day-to-day partnership for an orderly home, possibly the fulfillments of a total, lifelong intimacy over homemade meals, etc., etc. Then, over in the "cons" column, you need permission to go out with friends; you may become bored and absent. And, of course, it may fail explosively. This type of deliberation being basically unavailable to me, it will be better for both of us if in this essay I don't pretend to be engaged in it. It will be better if I take off from the question "What is marriage for?" by addressing another question related to that pragmatic one, and in a sense prior to it. I'm not convinced that many married people, or people planning to be married, actually ask themselves whether marriage is a good idea any more than I do. I have my excuse, as I've just explained. But when I look around at my married friends and family, I don't get the feeling that they have been entertaining much more real deliberation on this than I have. Or perhaps, to be more exact, a considered point of view is much more ready on the tongues of those that don't intend to marry. The rest of us debate whether we want to own our home, or have children; but it's not quite the same with nuptials. I am interested in why that is.

Is it just that some of us, the slower, stupider ones, fail to appreciate that marriage is no longer a given? I'm sure that that's part of it. But I suspect that it also has to do with what modern marriage is, with its great weirdness: the notion that we somehow make a commitment to continue loving.

•

The basic point I have to make in this essay will sound sort of obvious: it is that modern marriages are romantic. But when I say that marriages are romantic, I don't exactly mean that, as we sometimes hear, our marriages are founded on love, or, say, require regular sex, though those things may also be true. I'm saying that today marriages themselves are romantic. To explain what I mean by that you'll have to indulge me for a bit of a detour.

The spring and summer when I was fourteen was indefatigably social, spent, to my memory, in certain carpeted basements. At the time I liked or "like liked"—this was the terminology we used back then—a girl named Mary. Mary and I hung around to-gether a lot; she laughed loudly at the stupid crap I said, and one time in a movie theater ticket line she put her arm around me on a conspicuously thin pretext. In spite of these things I was hesitant. Now in what follows, you will forgive me a little if you know that Mary was improbably and basically perfectly pretty. I was an ugly semi-loser. I really don't think I'm exaggerating either of these assessments. We were in that little gap just before high school in a small sheltered town, when everyone is in late puberty and someone like Mary can, for a moment, be grossly miscategorized, attractive out of all proportion to the people she spends time with.

Anyway the particular occasion I want to talk about to make my small but important philosophical point, on the way, I promise, to one about marriage, is one night at the end of that summer. Mary called me unexpectedly and said I should sneak out of my mother's apartment and meet her. So another guy friend and I biked a few miles across town to where Mary and one of her friends had, it emerged, made a campfire in a clearing and laid out sleeping bags. I've probably augmented the scene somewhat in retrospect, but this is how I remember it. There were definitely sleeping bags. She, it seemed to me, started to smirk when I sat down next to her.

Nevertheless I did nothing for a long time, other than as usual trying to make myself seem worth it. I suppose I was in a state of shocked relief that this night, surely, I would finally find out that she "like liked" me; whatever else my mind was capable of had turned to gas and whistled out of my ears on the ride over. After about an hour I did come out of my happy daze a little: I found a way to put out vague feelers for how Mary felt about me, via a go-between. I awaited intel. It became 11:00, 12:00, 1:00, and, oddly, my intel didn't seem to come to anything, or only in a veiled way. Other than that I tried some heavy hinting. I half-whispered pusillanimous hooey to her like: "I like this girl, but I don't know if she likes me...," one toe always just over the line in deniability. It became 2:00, 2:30.

Curiously something else was going on that was just the opposite of these things. I think I had this fantasy that in such ideal circumstances as the crackling pine needles, the campfire, crickets and so forth, Milky Way visible between the tops of the trees, the trees moving over us reclined on the faded red plaid pattern of the sleeping bags in increasing physical proximity (the result of secret shimmying), we might slide into something else; as if once ordinary non-romantic life came so close to romantic relations as to be all but indistinguishable from them then we would cross over imperceptibly, unable later to recollect with any distinctness the time when "something more" had begun. Don't ask me what this ever could have looked like in terms of actual embodied heads and hands, with, really, our non-liquored teen selves surveilling no less then than ever.

To make a lamentably short story short, the dew fell. The sun came up. Not long after this night Mary and I dropped into the big waters of high school and my beautiful friend was whisked (or leapt) away from me by (or to) a much older and more attractive athletic hero. And then I learned for sure that Mary had indeed "like liked" me that summer. She had wondered whether I felt the same way. We had wanted the same thing.

So here is my first point, on the way to that bigger point I promised: in this scene there is no reciprocity. That might seem obvious, but bear with me a moment. What there are are all the raw materials, in some sense all the parts, of a reciprocal relation. Her feelings had, it turns out, matched and mirrored mine. Very likely, next to the campfire, we were feeling these things at the same instant, pining eye to pining eye—feelings we had about the other's complementing feelings and plans: wondering whether I was likewise wondering whether she was ... and so on.

But to reciprocate is to respond in kind. A response, literally a "speaking back," answers what has addressed it. The thing that is most confusing, and most vital, about reciprocity, and, by extension—this is what I'm getting around to—erotic energy, is that reciprocity is not just the same as mere mutuality. Something is mutual when two people are engaged in the same attitude, action, etc., in relation to each other. When an artist tells another artist that she makes great paintings, the latter may reply that the respect "is mutual." But she shouldn't say "the respect is reciprocal." This is because reciprocating involves not just symmetry in attitudes, but also some causal or conditional connection between them. (She shouldn't say the respect is reciprocal unless she means to confess that this judgment has just now been corrupted by flattery.)

Reciprocity is out of place in what ought to be an objective judgment like the appraisal of an artwork. But here's the point: it is the natural form of erotic life. And that couldn't get going under the hemlocks with me a trepidatious little vole.

If I could go back in time and meet my younger self that night (let me at this point acknowledge that we may be on this digression in part to resolve some stuff), perhaps when I'm just getting off my bike,

and put my hand on this vole's shoulder, and tell him that I've come with some words of wisdom so that he won't fumble The Glory of My Youth, I would say something like: "Look, it matters whether or not Mary has had, is having, feelings for you; it matters how she's disposed. Of course it does. But you need to get out of your head this notion that that's, like, the matter, the material. Some scene in which your disposition and her disposition take up positions, and you come forth and beam at each other officially over the pine needles, and someone offers ambassadorially: 'Well how felicitous. Now we can get on with acting on said feelings, eh?'— that's not how these things go. What you need now is exposure. Mary, I think, is actually a big girl and unconsciously understands this. You need to say something like: 'Mary, I've been too shy to tell you: I think you're so beautiful.'"

I do acknowledge that a mini-lecture is probably not the best way to advise the anxious fourteen-year-old. Probably just insisting on the last part would do. But do you begin to see what I mean? Romance has its romantic way of being, where the rule is that arousal awakens arousal.

I'm not just talking about a kind of contagiousness—that lust leads to lust in the same way that yawning spreads from person to person, without anyone meaning for this to happen. Actually that contagiousness is something that Mary and I presumably did fall into, as we basically knew—all but knew—how the other was disposed. What I'm talking about has to do fundamentally with will and enaction and, peculiarly, a sort of work. If we think of a caress or a kiss for example—aargh ... sorry this is so embarrassing—the particular sensation on our cheek or lips might matter quite a bit,

but it matters much more in self-consciously embodying what this person thinks they are up to. It is this enacted idea, this intention, that is excited body-to-body; and this is itself the idea of this very reciprocal erotic escalation. With romance we climb up out of mere dispositions and into that self-swallowing, seductive consciousness of arousal at arousal itself, which is emphatically what the kissers are implying and infecting each other with. Eventually she may be turned on by the fact that the fact that she wants him to be turned on turns him on. The latter sounds like a geeky philosopher's paradox, but it is integral to the way a kiss works.

One funny quality that romance always has—we can list it right next to its helplessness—is a kind of hyper-effectiveness, where effort, effort on its own, a manifestation of one's own will, independently of how well it is executed, can be effective. There is the wine; the wine tastes good and is, apparently, an aphrodisiac for some; but dissolved in each glass is its idea.

Speaking of "work" in this way I make it sound like all of this is orchestrated by conscious mental maneuvering. I don't mean that. When something like a kiss is happening, the thinking that ticker tapes inside a person in English, for example, is plainly obtrusive. Given that you, reader, are reading this, it is quite likely that you like me have let the intellect get so hulking it can no longer hide behind the bushes at these times: you know how third-wheel it is: " ... Huh, well this is actually happening right now in this unremarkable room...," etc.

My son is one year old, and is very affectionate. Now he gives his big pumpkin-face grin and squints and stretches out his little arms and fingers for, it is clear, contact of the affectionate kind. Not too long ago (though it's remarkably easy to forget what he was like just a few months ago) he didn't do this in quite the same way. Now he does.

I have the feeling that it's really really tricky to put into words, in the adult rational and psychological terms we can understand, what we think is happening in a baby as this very psychological picture is itself tottering into existence. So forgive me, but as it (inarticulately) seems to me: if I say of my son that he smiles and stretches out his arms because he wants to give me a hug, well, we've got one thing. Then of course we need to add that he also wants me to hug him, and is as it were using his own proffered hug in order, in turn, to get me to hug him back. But one thing I'm pretty sure of: you can't take those two things together—to be hugging and hugged—and collect them to get an adequate account of what is up with him. He doesn't want two things, or two things together at the same time. Affection's way of being is actively awakening affection: the desire is like a tingling thing that he wants to develop in the world, *and in this way*, between himself and me.

As I say, he only recently started doing this. But for a long time, since he was maybe six weeks old, he's been doing a smile-and-smile-back thing, which is, I think, basically the same deal. Which is to say: it's not like what I'm describing requires ministrations which we are capable of only when we master the high concept of "other minds," or some such nonsense. For *homo sapiens*, erotic reciprocity of this kind is just a basic structure of emotional life that the heart works with effortlessly. Kids seem just as good at it as adults.

Abstract formulations have their use. With love and sex, such formulations always feel like one is proudly handing over a body, not realizing that it is missing organs, fluids, a face; not realizing, even, that it's dead. For what it's worth, in general terms what I think I mean by romance is that: *We manifest (and enjoy) something shared, where the shared thing is itself, in part, the causal connection between our own participation in it and the participation of the other.* I like this formula because when I stare at it long enough I occasionally catch sight of (though it's very hard to hold on to) that self-swallowing quality I mentioned, where the idea includes itself in its content, which is really the most important thing. Where I'm going with this is that I think marriages in the twenty-first century are romantic relationships in this sense, not so much because of their content as because of their structure. Because of this marriage is not normal when it comes to decision and that sort of thing.

•

Marrying for love is a relatively recent phenomenon. Timing-wise, the rise of the love match differs depending on where in Europe we're talking about but is generally said to get going in a serious way at the end of the eighteenth century. This of course had to do with all sorts of things, not least the Enlightenment and changes in certain political possibilities and values. Just as fundamentally, it had to do with home economy. We can't overestimate the extent to which for most of human history to almost everyone marriage was a way of securing the basic necessities of life—like no-nonsense: food, fuel, shelter—in a way that it just isn't anymore. A big part of the

Ute Klein, *Resonanzgeflechte #3*, 2009

nonoptional economic exchange that took place in a medieval marriage, for example, was what came from others—particularly one's parents (e.g. for the woman her dowry; for the man the inheritance of his father's farm or trade, which took place only when he married). One's parents didn't "just want you to be happy" in the way they do today. They wanted to secure the solvency of the family as a whole through time and travail, as well as the legitimacy of heirs. The community had a wedding gift too: the groom's initiation into political and economic enfranchisement. Marriage was about the brute seriousness of these transactions. Passionate erotic love was not the point, and was, at various times, even viewed as destabilizing to what marriage was supposed to be about.

To other pre-moderns, the separation of love and marriage was even more fundamental than this. The fact that men and women began not only to consider love a legitimate reason to marry but made love the centerpiece of the institution itself is one of the truly remarkable reversals in the history of our culture, and as such it is something most people have heard of. Less well known but just as interesting is the rich literary tradition that positions love and marriage as not only aloof but actually antithetical to each other. This tradition reached its most extreme expression in the "Courtly Love" of medieval Europe, but it goes back at least to Ovid. Ovid's *Ars Amatoria*, a versical how-to for getting laid in the Empire, made much of coyness and closed doors. According to Ovid passionate love can only thrive as a sort of war and conquest; consummation cannot be a sure thing, and in general compulsion of any kind is out of place. So he took it for granted that his advice had no application to

husbands and wives who were "obligated to share a bed."

Andreas Capellanus's *The Art of Courtly Love*, an influential twelfth-century tract written in the tradition of Ovid's poem, lays down the strict separation of love and marriage quite definitively. *The Art of Courtly Love*, for example, depicts a conversation in which a noblewoman, "A.," tells her admirer, "Count G.," that she cannot be receptive to his advances because she is already absorbed in the love she has for her husband. Count G. objects that she must be confused. Love, he says, is incompatible with what a marriage most fundamentally is. The two appeal to the Countess of Champagne (Marie of France, daughter of Queen Eleanor whose famous "Court of Love" Andreas may have been depicting), who gives the verdict:

> We declare and we hold as firmly established that love cannot exert its powers over two people who are married to each other. For lovers give each other everything freely, under no compulsion of necessity, but married persons are in duty bound to give in to each other's desires and deny themselves to each other in nothing.

(Elsewhere in *The Art of Courtly Love* it is explained that although there may be affection between husband and wife, love is an entirely different and incommensurable sort of feeling). In a similar vein, Heloise, the famous twelfth-century nun, adduced her aversion to marrying her lover Peter Abelard as evidence of how strong and true her passion was for him, writing to him—"You cannot but be entirely persuaded of this by the extreme unwillingness I showed to marry you."

For sure such ideas are not necessarily representative of twelfth-century conventional wisdom on the relationship between marriage and love—particularly outside the idle nobility. Insofar as we today quite explicitly and emphatically found our marriages on love—indeed, for us the social stigma is as much against a loveless home as a broken one—what the Countess of Champagne says actually poses a much more direct challenge to us than to her contemporaries. Many things have changed since the twelfth century, both for love and for marriage, but so far as I can see none of them does anything to dull the pertinence of the basic conundrum: How are the spontaneity of love and the commitments and responsibilities of something like spousehood supposed to fit together? You have to admit, even if it turns out to be unenlightened, the courtly tradition has things conceptually clear and intuitive.

When I got married I vowed to my wife, on a pulpit in front of all my friends and family, that I would continue to cherish and love her for the rest of her life. It was a kind of promise. We don't have to think of love as sexual in the mode of *The Art of Courtly Love* to see how problematic that promise is. We just have to think that we cannot control whether or not we love someone. Or we just have to think that compelled, contrived love, love delivered as promised isn't the kind of thing we would want from a lover even if it were possible. The love we want is spontaneous, underlying, underived and free. This is how it can affirm who we are. How can I commit to continue to love my wife?

I am, as I've said, about to go on to argue that marriages are romantic, that they are analogous to a kiss. How am I going to square this with what appears to be marriage's very different logic of establishment, of office and obligation?

•

Normally I take care of my son in the morning. The other night, however, there was a lot of teething—more than ever, in fact. He's an okay sleeper in general but that night he cried and cried; so we let him sleep in. This, in combination with the fact that I woke up early, meant that I had a rare half hour to look lower down on the to-do list past the usual a.m. tasks.

So that morning I went out and picked up the twigs and brittle branches that had fallen in the yard. We have a couple of old lichenous ash trees that are not long for this world. They are incontinent, I guess would be the word, in that they lose large and seemingly important parts of themselves in a big wind. I broke up the gray limbs into stove-size kindling and carted them in a wheelbarrow to a pile near the living room door. From there they can be fetched for fires in the stove starting in November.

What this means to me, what keeps me leaning over and at my morning work, is, in part, quite straightforward: this is enjoyable for its own sake (snapping sticks is something I've liked to do since I was maybe two), and, of course, the work is a means to meeting one of our oldest needs: fire, warmth in winter. In fact it is these two things together. I got to take in the wet spring air and use my hands and see something literally pile up that is unambiguously useful. The archaic almost anti-ambiguousness of work of this kind—"wholesome" would be the right word if you could subtract the goody-goody connotation—is one reason I like living in the country. The old saying is that wood warms you twice.

But I do not live out here by myself. If I did, if I were a bachelor, then, even if every motion were the same, every muscle moving the same, with all the satisfactions of the productive work I just mentioned above available to me, nonetheless the work would be done in a spirit utterly unlike that in which I actually did it. You won't understand what I am doing if you don't see the action as emotionally enveloped in a relationship; which for now, since my son can't talk rationally yet, means mainly my marriage to my wife. This is action en *famille*.

Now what is action en *famille*? One way of responding to the Countess of Champagne's challenge (a way which is not to just conclude: so much the worse for modern marriage) is to imagine marriage as a kind of metamorphosis of love. The infatuation of courtship and the calmer commitment of the achieved relationship are each given their own logic, but at different times. The endeavors of an adolescent telling a girl "I think you're so beautiful" may give way, someday, to spousehood; and one way of understanding that transition is that while the boy's erotic act aims to cross the gulf between two people, into something shared, a spousal act is done out of something standing. Not that the passions peter out exactly. Rather (according to this view, which is not quite my own), new forms of affection take over: feelings for the other such as devotion and pride, a sense that this person is in some way one's own. Above all we develop a deep, disinterested concern for this person's well-being. From this point of view, a pathos of

belonging—incredibly intense and potent in its own way—would be the perfected emotional substance of spousehood.

I actually think this is almost right. I've just never been impressed with it as anything like the full picture. It is too zoomed-in to capture the whole movement of marriage. I might, in heroic morning moods, fancy that something like this is what is animating me, and that that's all there is to it. But as soon as I hear footsteps on the stairs and a human being comes into the kitchen in all her 3D reality and proves to have eyes, ears, and a mouth, the inadequacy of such disinterestedness in describing the situation is palpable. This is not because I don't care for my wife's well-being very deeply—I do. And I suppose even if I had to keep my helpful acts of wood-gathering for her sake secret, watching over her guardian-like, I would.

But although my devotion drives me to do this—my sense that I am a husband and husbands do this—my devotion is also something I want her to feel. It is, in fact, something to be returned in kind, erotically, devotion for devotion. And the real sense of satisfaction of this work is to do it not for her sake, but for her eyes. Not literally; not that she beholds my virile act and swoons. She is upstairs. She is unlikely later to be impressed by the resulting aesthetically questionable pile of sticks. But being married, devotion belongs between us, and spousal acts bear the stamp of the living, active, commitment-at-commitment, trust-at-trust; a project that invites, implies, calls out and unfolds each of its parts.

Imagine for a moment that I really didn't care how she received and responded to my help. Imagine that she got the sense that I was indifferent to her reception of it. Whatever else this might make her feel, that I was either an angel or a self-involved douche—either way, I posit, it would make her feel like something less than a lover.

I went inside and made breakfast for the family: eggs, bacon, blueberries, leftover beet salad. If breakfast didn't have a cook, server and served, and a real need for nourishment, it would be nothing. But like the glass of wine, it is the idea of a relationship that is eaten.

•

My mom moved into her new apartment in January of 1988. A couple of weeks later she came to pick us up for our first stay. I remember that once we were all packed up my dad surprised us by pulling some glass mugs out of the freezer he had frosted up for root beer floats.

Actually, though, I recall it was exciting to move (half-move) into the new place, exploring the interesting creaking old rambling antique apartment, checking out my new room (tiny, while my sister's was like a vast drinking hall). Really in my experience that trip was less strange the first time than it was on all subsequent trips, when the two houses had begun to drift further and further apart in character. It was later that, whichever place we were, it felt like the other was some dimly recollected other life.

That June my dad had his heart attack. On that morning my sister was at a sleepover or something, and it was just me and him in the house. I don't remember it very well. I didn't realize the significance of what was

happening, or had happened, until several days later.

I remember that at first he thought he had eaten something bad. We had just come back from camping and had had skeezy sandwiches on the way home. Or so he thought, though mysteriously I had had the tuna too, and I was fine. Then he realized that there was something very wrong. What was in fact happening is called tachycardia—an arrhythmic speeding-up of the heart. My image is of my dad lying on his bed with his arm draped over his face, with the radio on. He was greenish-white, mouth dry and open. He should have called 911 immediately. Instead he told me to pick up the phone and call my mom.

My mom, when I spoke to her about this recently, just thinks he called her in this crisis out of habit. I'm sure that that's part of it. My parents were technically still married at that time—they didn't divorce for another year. It was not a bitter break up. Right up until dad died in fact they remained in some respects each other's main support in life. This was a relief to me and my sister of course. But I'm not convinced my mom is familiar with all of the complexity of his house at that time. I was there (albeit eight years old, but there). That phone call, for example, felt not so straightforward to me: whether he had me call her because she lived only a mile away, or as much as a mile away; whether he wanted me to witness, mark, measure the fact that his wife was only on the other end of the telephone and not in the room—and for her to hear her son mark this. Anyway she came. We all got into her little red VW Rabbit and drove to the hospital.

And ultimately he came extremely close to death. Later he told my sister and me the

Ute Klein, *Resonanzgeflechte #7*, 2009

story that lying in his hospital bed he had had to reconstruct the order of the tiles on the ceiling or he would die. He did reconstruct them. He didn't die. But when he finally came home three weeks later he was not the same. He was sunken all over. He had to retire from his work as an electrical engineer. Myotonia has all sorts of symptoms but the main one is that your musculature cannot properly grow or repair. So there was no going back.

As I say, it was a relief to my sister and me that my parents still loved each other. But one way of seeing the problem is that their loves no longer had to do with each other in the right way. My dad didn't have the strength to conceal from us for long that he hadn't wanted the divorce. One morning, I don't remember exactly when, on his bed, with, again, his now baggy arm draped over his eyes, he told me he was still in love with her. Meanwhile he plunged precipitously into needing help. When he got this help from her, he did not have his own love's homecoming, an answered appeal and arousal. Instead he just had her real compassion. He just had her heartfelt care and commitment, forthcomingly.

This is one way in which two people can be unwed. His love was meant for hers, and hers was merely meant for his well-being; and all his red blood leaked out of that asymmetry.

I am at my work snapping sticks, pulling some old soft moldering ones out from the clutching dead grass, for my marriage. My marriage is alive when my work explicitly and actively arouses my wife's response in kind, which is not just appreciation or approval or thanks (though those things may mark it and store it) but ultimately the transmission of erotic energy over to her reciprocal role, a response which in turn actively arouses me to rise to mine. This is, in part, how love is sustained. And it is in this that the action is captured.

We can't control love. But what I'm suggesting is that in a marriage we do want love that is at its erotic work.

•

Back in the day marriage was truly an institution. Let's say an institution is an institution and not just an ideal when there is something at stake for some significant party in the integrity of the institution itself—the observation of its form and rules—over and above the vicissitudes of any particular case in question.* This institutionality could, in turn, have to do with religion, with being integrally involved in the rest of society, or with a particular party's (e.g. men's) interest in its dominance as a norm. That general-

---

* If I follow a muffin recipe very very carefully and measure my flour ever so precisely per the instructions and get annoyed and shoo away anyone who approaches the mixing bowl with deviations, then I am conforming to the recipe. But here what I really care about is that the muffins turn out well. This is not conformity as it functions in an institution. In an institution we care about the institution itself. This latter type of conformity is what I think is in decline. Marriage for sure still functions as an institution in this way to some degree, but it's nothing like it was when an individual living in sin couldn't even get a job. We might look askance at our neighbor the notorious philanderer, but what is driving the disapproval is largely analogous to my care over the muffins—we cite its effect on his wife, his children, himself. We fault people for fucking up their marriages, but not so much because we're concerned for the fate of *matrimony*.

ized group concern used to be part of what gave marriage its seriousness and solemnity in our lives. All of this is fading fast from marriage as it is today.

A few months before our wedding my wife and I had a meeting with the very liberal UCC minister who was to marry us. We told him that we would be uncomfortable if he threw around the word "God" in the ceremony (J-word, it went without saying, off the table). This meeting was in the fall of 2008, basically right at the nadir of our plunge into the Great Recession. At the time I was living on my grad student stipend. My wife was teaching for not much money. And this had not much at all to do with why we were marrying one way or the other.

At this meeting I remember him asking us why we wanted to get married. The question wasn't: Why do you want to spend the rest of your lives together? It was: Why do you want to get married? Thus it was also unavoidably the question: What does marriage mean anymore anyway?—which, incidentally, given that this minister was actually about our age, he might have really been wondering.*

What I'm claiming in this essay, you'll remember, is that I don't have access to an answer to the first question, the personal one. To the latter I'm trying to make a contribution. I'm saying that the phrase "because I'm married" in the twenty-first century has its own form of solemnity, its own way of being more than, as we put it, "just a piece of paper."

---

* Indeed, being my height, complete with short red hair and beard, he looked and even sounded so much like me that we asked him to wear a robe at the ceremony just so any near-sighted elders and plus-ones would know which was the groom.

In the past, marriage established two firm offices: HUSBAND and WIFE. These dictated duties over and above our own mere inclinations. The roles in progressive Western modern marriages, I submit, have a different way of taking the imperative mood. "Duty" strikes me as the wrong way to think of it. Instead, as Ben Affleck breathlessly and, it appeared, accidentally said in his Oscars speech this year, marriage is work. In particular it is erotic work. HUSBAND, whatever it was in the past, is now a romantic identity—it is characterized and known by, and only acceptable as, arousal awakening arousal.

If I could hazard an easy to misunderstand formulation as to what marriage is for, it would be: marriage is for itself. But hold on. I don't mean that it is just intrinsically or immediately valuable, valuable independently of what results from it, like the way a slice of cherry pie is valued, or the way some people think that art ought to be. My whole point is that marriage is a means. But this is the thing: marriage is a means to itself. This, I'm saying, is the right way to understand how we experience and enjoy it.

It is also the right way to understand its rules. Returning one more time to my morning work, the way in which this is romantic is not that I have some sort of look in my eye that says: "I love you" or something. I need no special look. This is because we are married. A modern marriage contextualizes (and promises) that my efforts will be of this erotic kind. If my wife were to someday turn to me and say "you're no husband," it wouldn't be because I was a deadbeat or something—it wouldn't be because any particular act was or wasn't performed. It would be because what I was doing wasn't coming from love looking for her love.

•

Reciprocation literally means something like "back and forthing." But now that we have a kid, for my wife and I there is not much in the way of a temporal gap. There is no moment when we are not both acting out our reciprocal responsibilities. After breakfast was over I went out again to finish up the yard. I reached to grab a living low-hanging branch to get it out of the way, and at the last moment my eye darted before my body could change course to catch a glimpse of an outlandish caterpillar covered in red fuzz just where my hand was closing. The glimpse I recorded was of a three-inch Elmo from Sesame Street. He must have fallen from the branch as soon as I sprang back, that or exploded. I never found him and the only evidence of his existence was my fingers and palm punctured all over in red bristles.

I got many of them out. My wife had to dig out the rest, all the ones entirely buried beneath the skin, and all those stuck at odd angles between my fingers. Now my wife is always eager to do these things—she has a basically curious and let-me-get-in-there-with-the-trusty-tweezers personality for which plucking out tiny things under a magnifying glass is a nice prospect. The proper tools just sort of materialize in her hands at these times. For her too this has a very straightforward kind of satisfaction. Yet it is also the completion of a two-person movement.

One of our wedding vows, which we stole from friends, was "All that I have I give to you." One way of understanding that is: now there will be no more mine and thine. The rings we exchange here are the last things that we can ever give each other. Henceforth there is one common pool, "us."

Perhaps then my wife would feel the sting of those bristles in the sensitive white webbing between my fingers, as she would be plucking them out of our own hand.

But that's not actually what the vow says. And although such merging can be very powerful and real (in fact she happens to have told me that she could feel the pain), in the end it is not at all erotic, eliding, as it does, the gap between two people, the comportment to the other as other.

What I've been trying to show, rather, is that marriage is more like an exchange: an endless exchange, all for all. Exchanging rings enacts, more particularly, a creative erotic exchange—not just the transaction of things that we already want (as in a medieval marriage) but at the same time the transmission of desire—and is just, in ceremony, the movement we will make over and over again.*

---

* Perhaps in modern life, marriage, loosened from some of the institutionalizing forces that shaped it for most of civilized history, is in some respects more like it used to be in the very ancient past. Marcel Mauss in *The Gift* remarks how in archaic cultures marriage was often conceived as a continual exchange of gifts. But here, says Mauss, we've got to make sure that we don't import our own assumptions about gift giving and exchange back into our interpretation of what that means. In particular, Mauss's great predecessor Malinowski had assumed that there was a sort of spectrum, with a cold utilitarian trade of goods-for-goods at one end, and a pure, selfless gift at the other. Malinowski thought that, insofar as one was encountering a true gift, one must be encountering some sense of altruism in the giving. Spousal gifts would be on this latter end of the spectrum.

Mauss's big, amazing point in *The Gift* is that what the anthropological research actually shows is that Malinowski was approaching the phenomenon of the gift in the wrong way entirely. The basis of gift giving was reciprocity, and reciprocity, Mauss found, isn't reducible either to economic exchange or pure

Ute Klein, *Resonanzgeflechte #8*, 2009

I do apologize, reader. Oscar Wilde says that us married folk should not wash our clean linen in public. But I need illustration and, being new married, can hardly be expected to share something ugly.

Now perhaps you are saying to yourself here at the end: ah, but there is a disanalogy. Whereas with a kiss, a one-person kiss truly is meaningless, a dry oddity, the acts and advantages of marriage like having someone who will dig the bristles out of your hand— these are valuable regardless of anything that has to do with love or marriage.

Now reader, it is beyond my capacity in this essay to argue about whether or not actually nourishing one's body, brushing one's teeth, money, a sunny trip to the ocean, getting up out of bed, *just feel worthwhile* to the kind of thing that we are—that the felt value of these things just floats toward us. But I really don't think that this is the case for many of us. Most of us, even. Not, for example, for me, or for my dad. We have to be giving something of ourselves to make meaning in even everyday things. And we need what we give returned.

And I think that those who get married are people like this—people like me and him. And if that's true, reader, you can see why it isn't possible for a person, today, to decide that marriage is good in his own case. If someone can, then I declare that he is not married.

---

charity. In fact, Mauss interprets anthropological research as showing that reciprocity—giving, receiving, reciprocating—is a basic form of life, stretching into and interrelating religious, familial, economic and political ideals, experiences, emotions and values. It's important to get this right because, Mauss thought, "Reciprocity is the human rock on which societies are built."

reviews

Susan Murtaugh, *Really Flat Coke*, 2012

THE WORLD OF COCA-COLA

by Antón Barba-Kay

ONLY FINALLY DOES the question blunder into focus. I have already taken the trouble to walk down here, on my day off from a conference, five or six blocks from my hotel in downtown Atlanta. I have already waited in a short line to pay $16 for admission. I have already waited for about 45 minutes under a cold drizzle in a much longer snaking line. Long enough to return all my pending calls, long enough to text out a few other pleas for attention, long enough to take some pictures of the side of a Canadian tour bus—the driver: flattered by my interest in the amateur mural populated with several dozen painted busts of Famous Canadians. Me: barely containing mirth at recognizing only a face or two from among the illustrious maple-leaf melee—and long enough to make timid chitchat with the family standing behind me. (It's their third or fourth time here, today with out-of-town visitors.) The bovine conviviality of lingering in line for mass entertainment slowly gives way to a crescendo of more and more bawling children, to my irritation at being jostled one too many times by that woman's backpack, to the sense that standing this long on my feet is turning my optimistic curiosity into entitled crankiness. And it is then, and only then, that I find myself asking just what on earth I am doing, paying to undergo such damp indignities for the sake of taking a good look at what is bound to be one massive corporate orgy of PR self-congratulation. I have no idea how I've even heard of this place, no idea how it's insinuated its way to the very top of my unformulated list of Sights To See One Day in Atlanta. I mean, I don't even drink the stuff, certainly no more than like twice a year, when a trainee bartender misinterprets my request for "soda," or at some ill-conceived Fourth of July gathering where there's nothing else with which to choke down the one lonely bottle of rum that predictably survives at the drinks table. But by now I've come so far that there's hardly any turning back, and I'm finally through the metal detector and into the World of Coca-Cola.

WE ARE, ABOUT eighty of us, ushered into a waiting room with giant decorative bottles of CC, on which are written culturally sensitive holiday greetings in perhaps two dozen different scripts and languages—Joyeux Noël! Feliz Navidad! Happy Kwanzaa! (It is late December, after all—but then I can't read what the Arabic or Japanese salutations say.) A timer on the wall informs us how long our wait will be (such timers turn out to be rife within the well-oiled crowd management of the WCC), and a few minutes later we are welcomed into a large hall, covered top to bottom with various items of vintage CC paraphernalia. Television screens sensationally flash bits of "Did You Know?" trivia: "...that Coca-Cola bottles are 98% recyclable?", "...that Coca-Cola contains no artificial flavors or preservatives?", "...that Coca-Cola is locally produced and bottled?" There is something for everyone here. Come ye, environmentalists; come ye, health conscious; come ye, opponents of globalization and advocates of local labor: it is clear from the outset that CC aims to be all things to all people, to advertise sympathetically to every preference and principle. The strategy feels flat enough in an age when everything from stadiums down to park benches is brought to us by some miserably inapposite company or other, and when tarted-up assertions about quality and production are as a matter of course qualified away in the casuistry of fine print. Beverage of Choice for the Health-Conscious Environmental Underdog. As if the very saying made it so. But I resign myself to the thought that for a while I'm a guest in the company's particular little World, and anyway we all have our private corners of confabulation.

Most of our crowd is made up of families with young children; a sizeable minority are foreign tourists ("Did You Know ... that 70% of Coca-Cola's sales are international?"), and many are young couples who look to be out on dates. (In case you were considering it, I would strongly advise against attempting a family venue like this by yourself as a lone adult male. More than one parent sizes me up with something like consternation during the visit, as if scanning for a scarlet "P": at one point during a theater presentation, a father even sets his mind to rest by switching seats to interpose himself between me and his kid.) Our tour guide, Ari, is in her early twenties, pretty as you please, and brimming with southern cheer and charm. I look for it, but there is no shade of the strained rictus one so often catches from service-industry employees whose job description includes the pretense to a sunny disposition. She welcomes us to the WCC, dances a little jig while she tells us how great it is to be part of the CC family, fills us in on the history of some of the more prominent posters and objects in the room, including the most expensive one (cue oohs, aaahs)—a Norman Rockwell painting of a Huck-Finnish-looking boy holding the telltale bottle—and leads us through the various cheerleading motions one expects while touring a family museum. In what will prove to be a significant gesture later in the visit, she asks every person in the room to simultaneously shout out where they are from; she then picks out one or two places from the cacophony and makes neighborly comments about how far away that is, or how warm or cold it probably is there. There is no want of enthusiasm when she prompts us to yell that we are in Atlanta, because WE LOVE COCA-COLA!

We are then led into the "Happiness Factory," a small movie theater where we sit through a seven-minute animated CC ad called "Happyfication." It is hosted by Pete, a blue critter who appears to be a cross between a smurf and a gremlin, gifted with a groovy smoove Marvin Gaye voice. Pete guides the viewer through a series of half a dozen cute musical vignettes, all of which supply the pretext for feel-good punch-lines, culminating in a song that is nothing but a Best Of unrelated bromides: "be curious, there's so much to discover," "be giving and kind, help people in need," "be in the now, love the life that you lead," "be active, in shape, turn that frown upside down," "see the cup as half-full, not the other way round," "tinker with your thinker, keep a grin on your chin." A bottle of CC is always present as a background accessory in some form or other, and the recognizable CC jingle provides the theme for the final song, but there is no direct attempt to address or promote the product's excellence as such—the words Coca-Cola are not actually spoken. It is as if the ad directly invites the question of how it does its work, by stretching the distance between its form and intention as far apart as they can go. In spite of finding its title perfectly gross, I still feel my heel tapping along to the catchy tune, and, I admit, even trying to remember some of the winsome valedictions with which one of the characters bids the viewer goodbye—"stay fly, chicken pot-pie!" "Keep it real, little baby seal!"

I am used to thinking that commercial advertisements do their work by virtue of juxtaposition—if a product is associated with something obviously pleasant or good (family, friendship, humor, sex, charity or whatever) then some of that sheen will somehow rub off or reflect on the product. The affective *frisson*, the spritz of dopamine, that we experience with respect to one visual scenario carries over to the product, coloring our future preferences. And ever since a friend awed me during one clandestine middle school recess by pointing out the smutty patterns printed on every pack of Camel cigarettes, it has also become second nature for me to assume that such associations could be entirely subliminal, suggestive in ways of which we need not be consciously aware. (As I sit through "Happyfication," it certainly takes no great strain of the pop-Freudian imagination to construe several of the weirdly polymorphous cartoon characters as allusive to pudenda.) The WCC does not exactly refute this account, but it complicates and deepens it: the company is disarmingly forthright about how they flog their wares, about how they take their publicity to work. If "Happyfication" tacitly invites the question of how such ads operate on us, then the rest of the "museum"—is that the right term for the WCC?—turns out to have a compelling logic of its own.

HAVING EXITED THE Happiness Factory, we enter the museum proper, of which the first likely stop is an exhibit called the "Vault of the Secret Formula." We amble through a corridor displaying various myths about the CC recipe, meant to sharpen our appetite for discovering just what the genius of the product is; a throaty recording whispers "sssssecret!" as we pull open any number of the drawers stacked along the walls, each of which contains some popular rumor about the much bruited Secret Formula of CC's composition. (There is no explicit attempt to deny any of the rumors—it is clear throughout the WCC that the company revels in any kind of widespread attention, whether warranted or no.) After proceeding through the vault's faux security foyer—in which, spy-thriller style, our faces are "scanned" and "approved" by the "database" for ingress—and after a few volunteers play a brief virtual reality game about hunting for CC bottles on a nineteenth-century train, the walls close behind us, swirling images of the recognizable tobacco-colored liquid are projected all around as if to engulf us, and the music whips up to a frenzied dithyrambic climax. Here it is, finally: the Sssssecret Vault! The walls open up in a different place, revealing ... right, yes ... something that looks like a Disney version of a bank vault, wreathed in lambent dry ice mystique. The recipe for making CC is supposedly inside This Very Vault. We are not permitted to touch it, though two minutes are allotted for pictures. "Is that a real vault?" I ask the guard, sidling up in my most wink-wink confidential tone. "Yes it is, sir," he replies with the deadpan politeness he must keep on constant hand for dealing with wise guys.

It is after going through the Vault that one can then turn to the more historical and educational exhibits in the WCC, but the opening lesson feels clear: What exactly did we expect here? That they would divulge their best-kept corporate formula to us for the price of admission? There is no doubt that CC is a distinctive, tasty drink; but the drink's recipe is an opaque (if fixed) X around which the company has waged a vast marketing campaign for a century, a marketing campaign that—as Happyfication had already suggested—only tenuously relies on the merits of the product as such. Just what goes into a bottle of CC is of little consequence: nothing actually hangs on whether that Vault contains a secret recipe or a slip of paper with the word "suckers!" scribbled onto it. And so it is the next exhibit that begins to reveal the real secret, as it walks one through the transformation of the original CC product—a quack potation sold at soda fountains as the "ideal brain tonic" by John Pemberton of Atlanta in 1886—to the ubiquitous commercial presence it is today. The key transformation from "product" to "presence" seems to have been instigated by one Asa Candler, who, as a placard informs us, bought the company a few years after its creation and, even as he went about convincing more and more soda fountains to sell the product, "added the Coca-Cola logo to a host of practical, everyday

Susan Murtaugh, *k*, 2012

objects. These items, including serving trays, calendars and clocks, reminded people everywhere of the refreshing taste of Coca-Cola." The final step was the introduction, throughout the first decades of the twentieth century, of something the museum signs refer to as "lifestyle advertising"—the presentation of the product as emblematic of a certain personality, attitude and culture. The CC lifestyle, "the lifestyle of the refreshed," is, we are told, glamorous, happy, attractive, optimistic: the advertisements no longer focused on demonstrating the superiority of a beverage for the purposes of refreshment or health, but on showing cool people having fun, CC in hand.

The historical exhibit concludes with a look at some of the company's most prominent sponsorships—sports teams, athletes, the Olympic Games, the Oscars, musicians and even the armed forces. (There is a description of CC's efforts to make sure that troops stationed in the Pacific Theater during World War II had ready access to "the taste of home.") The "rubbing off" and "juxtaposition" in my initial characterization no longer feel quite accurate here: what's striking is just how utterly seamless such images are, as if the very sight of Michael Jordan enjoying a CC is in itself a tacit aesthetic claim to the unity of his athletic prowess with his other choices. Do we really suppose even for a moment that athletes are committed to the products they endorse in their everyday lives, that they depend on them for sporting success? It may still be that there is something vaguely numinous about what is taking place in such advertising—as if whatever MJ comes in contact with will be thereby imbued with his own dunking charisma (like when we squirrel away an object that has once belonged to, or even just been touched by, a loved one). But however it is that the transference works, it is also clear that we take in our star-struck perception of endorser-and-product all at once, as single immediate insight into what is admirable. We take in the suggestion that we are seeing the kind of person who consumes a given product. I think this is why we are at once dismayed and maliciously delighted to hear top athletes talk about their own performances with all the nuance of grizzly bears attempting to make soufflé, and why public opinion is not entirely wrong to insist that celebrities behave as wholesome role models. No matter how many times we tell ourselves that many of them are corrupt human beings who just happen to excel at one isolated skill, we are nevertheless not effortlessly capable of discriminating that skill from the rest of who they are. Our visions of the beautiful and good are each of them a unified, coherent *thou shalt*—to sift what really should properly belong in them is a secondary and not at all straightforward task. "Is lifestyle advertising what stitched Coca-Cola to national consciousness and the whole world?" giggles the sign at the exhibit's exit, "We'll never know! But it's refreshing!"

That we should perceive advertising images as seamless claims to meaning is interesting (and revealing) in its own right, but still feels more or less familiar as I keep myself moving through the museum. The placards' blithe candor is of course unnerving, in that the company can count on my willingness to continue to be manipulated even once it has outlined how the manipulation works. But then it does seem like a more convincing description of contemporary advertising than my previous thoughts about the sinister marketing geniuses subliminally—and therefore mechanically—coercing us to buy certain things. (Okay, okay, not that that would have been prominently displayed on the walls here, even if it were true. Or that the two approaches should be incompatible.)

The next stop is a small, actual packaging plant, where one can see an assembly line of bottles neatly being filled up, carbonated, capped and crated. Two or three workers supervise the (almost entirely computerized) process, oblivious to our ogling from behind the glass; and the placards tout facts about the great pains that the company takes to ensure that the flavor and aspect of the product is strictly uniform and universal. "Printed on every bottle is a unique code that indicates where and when all the ingredients and the packaging were manufactured. It also specifies the precise time and place the finished beverage was produced." The assembly line is entrancing as only assembly lines can be: the severe homogeneity of each and every bottle directly inviting the thought of how various their eventual fates might prove. Passing up a chance to photograph myself with a man in a CC polar bear costume (it's now nearing closing time, and his fur has been rendered unphotogenically tacky by the no doubt hundreds of children who have lovingly mussed it during the past seven hours), I ascend to the second level of the museum for the final stations of the unfolding argument.

ONCE UPSTAIRS, I encounter another exhibit, the "Pop Culture Gallery," which features a mix of CC-themed memorabilia and prominent episodes in the company's history. There is a description of how an attempt to change CC's recipe in 1985 led to public hysteria of such magnitude that the company was forced to backtrack, and to reintroduce the original product as "CC Classic":

> People carried protest signs, wrote songs in tribute to the original recipe and emptied grocery stores of the last remaining cases of "old" Coke. Com-

pany leaders knew the new formula for Coke had scored well in blind taste
tests and expected the initial uproar to subside once people had sampled
the product. But they had not anticipated the depth of consumer loyalty
to a brand that had been virtually unchanged for generations. Stung by
increasingly angry and vocal critics, on July 11, 1985, exactly 79 days after
the new version had been introduced, the Company announced the return of the original formula...

A few angry letters are proudly displayed, and the whole fuss is spun into a
ringing success for CC—as indeed it is—showcasing the company's sympathetic
responsiveness to consumers' needs, along with the unexpectedly deep commitment of the latter to the specific taste of CC. The urge for sameness trumped
any possible improvement in quality.

As if on cue to reinforce this point, one of the roving tour guides—Bill, a
pudgy, balding man in his mid-thirties, whose eager-beaver ("in training") manner is somehow redolent of his being domiciled in his parents' basement—
walks up for no obvious reason to start telling me about a 1971 television ad,
called "I'd Like to Teach the World to Sing," to which he then points me. The
ad features a group of attractive young people of all colors, garbs and ethnicities,
all standing, evenly spaced, side by side on an Arcadian hill, all beaming and
facing the same direction, all singing the same flower-powerful tune: "It's the
real thing, what the world wants today/I'd like to buy the world a Coke and
keep it company..." As I put these words to the page, I realize that it all sounds as
hopelessly kitschy and zombified as the rest of the museum, and that of course
it figures that the phonier our mass culture becomes, the more we are prone to
a sort of Robespierrean anxiety about what should count as authentic, and that
this only makes us bigger suckers for phony authenticity—for "the real thing,"
for the "classic" CC taste. The actors in this ad are clearly lip-synching, after all.
But from Bill's logorrheic palaver of Fun Facts I gather that CC actually went to
the trouble of putting exactly one young person from every single country in the
world on that hill, and perhaps it's that detail that causes me to pay attention in
a different way, to feel gripped by a moment of close attention.

It's a theme that recurs again and again in the marketing campaigns I watch
later in the museum: the fact that CC is the same for all people and all places,
that it is "one of the unique things we all share," that *at this very moment*—and
please try to picture this—in every single country in the world (except, licitly at
least, in Cuba and North Korea: Bill again), in practically every single Lebanese
city and Portuguese town and Papuan hamlet and Antarctic outpost, someone
is taking a sip from the same product, is tasting the unmistakably selfsame fizzy
savor, to the tune of 1.7 billion servings every day. Setting the commercial per-
versity of it aside, there is something immediately beguiling about this thought,

downright visionary even. We share any number of other things in creaturely solidarity, to be sure. We all long for and argue about the same things every day, the very things that make it possible for us to hold onto the thought that, say, art, philosophy and religion offer us windows onto what is purely universal. True as that may be, CC's case still stands out for its clarity and palpability. Not only do art, philosophy and religion require a certain amount (even if merest modicum) of cultivation in order for us to be able to enter into their discipline, but they remain in some respect intrinsically hopeful; they are not methods of transferring controlled information, but pledges of an idealism that more resembles the act of flinging bottled love letters into the ocean. I do not mean this as criticism. They must be such because, in order to speak to us directly, they first require that we each take the trouble of interpreting them through our own experience. But within the intimacy of our mouths, within the palate pleasures of carbonated sugar, such ambiguities are bypassed in favor of what looks like a much more direct form of communion—immediately shared because it is as raw and uneducated as it is distinctive.

Even the taste of drinking water admits of some variation from place to place. I've visited jungle villages in Central and South America where there was no electricity, where the children were malnourished and lousy with treatable disease, where the women were unashamed of their bare breasts, where nearly no one spoke a European language, where the living conditions could hardly be more different from my own in every single other respect—and yet there too CC was, preposterously, always ready available, there too we had this one common pleasure and practice and name. The company boasts that "Coca-Cola" is the most widely understood term in the world, second only to its twin in vague optimism, the word "okay."

If you are like me, then you are used to envisioning a communist society—Marx's protestations about the "free development of each" notwithstanding—as a sort of wretched Soviet hive, in which every trace of individuality has been grimly stamped out in favor of drudging conformity. "I'd Like to Teach the World to Sing" stops me cold because—maudlin as it sounds—it offers a flash of what it would be like for everyone in the world to really live as conscious participants of the same way of being and doing, what it would be like for us to be reprieved once and for all from the burdens, comparisons and antagonisms otherwise intrinsic to political life. What surprises me is not only the thought that CC markets itself in such a way as to appeal to a deep human hunger for uniformity, not only that it offers us an image of eschatological brotherhood, but that, in a sense, it already embodies it, already holds that place for us, by being universally same, universally shared, and universally present. CC is an obviously defective expression of that hunger, voided of ethical substance and attached to the purse-strings of a shamelessly profit-driven Atlanta juggernaut, but it is an image of a particular possibility nonetheless, and, yes, for a moment I do find myself thinking that it's all sunshine, that tour guide Bill may not be so crackers after all when he tells me, with an utterly straight face, that "Coca-Cola has always been an ambassador to the world."

I thank Bill and move on to the next exhibit, where I stand in another short line to watch a ten-minute 4-D feature called (again), "In Search of the Secret Formula." It chronicles the zany hijinks of professor Rigby Addison Whetwhistle—a scientist with mad hair and posh British accent, natch—who, with the help of assistant and pet ferret, sets out to discover just that, the Secret Formula. None of this would be worth mentioning, and it's all pretty lame, except that the conclusion they finally draw is again unexpectedly frank. The pursuit of the Secret Formula soon ceases to be about chemical ingredients alone, and Rigs ends by summing up his researches into what makes a Coke a Coke under the headings of four "U's": Unforgettable flavor (the X in the Vault, check), Uniform quality (bottling plant, check), Universal availability (sorry Cuba/North Korea, but check) and ..."You!"—here Rigs and assistant unexpectedly apostrophizing in tandem to the fourth wall—"You, my dear people, are the heart of the secret; it's you who have made Coca-Cola part of your daily lives. Coca-Cola is more than what's inside the bottle, it's an experience that's unique to each of us, yet something we all share—special moments and memories, the secret formula for Coca-Cola is all of those things. What could be more refreshing than that?"

A separate series of monitors in the foyer to the 4-D film has already prepared us for this, showing unscripted bystanders, apparently filmed just outside the WCC, relating their favorite memories involving CC—a first date, a childhood fishing trip, a famously hot Ohio day, and so forth. It's clear that these people are not speaking about just anything; however it is they've been selected for this video appearance, their eyes light up with vim and conviction as they gush about the reasons why they prefer CC, how much it means to them. I don't make much of this at the time—people get worked up about the darndest things—but after a bit more aimless wandering, I decide that I'm tired enough to sit down in the "Perfect Pauses Theater," and it's there that it dawns on me.

The Theater is playing CC ads from a range of countries and decades on a forty-minute loop, a scattered audience wandering in and out at will. The versatility of the ads is again striking: they look and feel manifestly different, depending on their target demographic. There is a funny Spanish ad in which a pair of young pals discuss whether or not CC advertises by means of subliminal messages—as they all the while intently gape at images of a CC being poured onscreen. There is a Canadian ad that cleverly pitches CC as a counter-cultural emblem of a 1968-style student uprising. A Brazilian ad depicts the product as a prop for the antics of a fun-loving, insouciant bunch. A rather staid Chinese ad stresses character building and friendship. India, Argentina, Russia, Nigeria, Japan: my mind starts to drift off into generalized intercontinental tutti-frutti. Until something shows up on screen that jerks me back sharp. Because suddenly I feel a lump forming in my throat, and with a pang I realize that I've seen these images of a goofy dog in search of refreshment before, that I first watched this ad during the 1994 World Cup, that I saw it as I sat with a group of friends hopefully watching Mexico play Norway, crowded around the living-room floor, munching chips and drinking Cokes and agonizing at the television with all our young lungs' muster, and that I've lost touch with every single person in that room, that they were all dear to me then and that time has since washed all of them out of my life, that even those players on the television are long gone, and that this ad this jingle this drink are all that's left of that moment, and I have to take a deep breath because it slays me.

M ANY OF THE ads I end up seeing invite the viewer to reflect on precisely this theme, on CC's presence and role in our own childhood, on our own formative memories of friends and family. It begins to feel less and less as if CC is simply aiming to sell itself by making cameo appearances with the beautiful and successful—its claim to memory is a claim to be one of the few things that endures unconditionally and unwaveringly same, to bind us to our own history not just as a sidekick, but as a constitutive element of that history. "Always Coca-Cola," chimed the company's slogan throughout my teenage years. I am all at once in sympathy with the chagrined folks that made sure that the new CC recipe did not replace the old one: if "I'd Like to Teach the World" and its kind show how it is that CC is universal in space, the appeal of temporal permanence feels equally, if not more, acute. Who cares what the thing tastes like, when what matters is that it allows us to keep directly in touch with our most intimate nostalgias, as easily as buying and opening a bottle? It may as well whisper "No, time, thou shalt not boast that I do change..."

As I leave the theater, still rattled by this thought, I catch sight of a series of placards that turn out to add one further twist to the museum's argument. Do you know what Santa Claus looks like? The roly-poly guy with God-the-Father beard, floppy cap and red-and-white pajamas, right? Know why you think that? "Through the centuries, Santa Claus had been depicted as everything from a stern bishop to a mischievous elf," but in 1931 CC commissioned Haddon Sundblom, illustrator, to sketch images of Santa for a new advertising campaign:

"Unlike earlier versions of a stern and sometimes scary figure, Sundblom's Santa projected a warm and friendly personality that helped shape the image of Santa that lives on in the minds of children—and adults—all over the world." The colors of Santa's ensemble are no coincidence: they were expressly conceived to look good on bottles and cans of CC.

The implications of this seem staggering—I feel as betrayed as when I found out a few years ago that the Happy Birthday song is the copyrighted property of Warner/Chappell—but they are also of such dimensions as to be clean out of sight. Are we in any meaningful sense abetting the CC company when we draw on that familiar, friendly likeness of Santa? Or is the advantage only in play when we see him on a CC can? Did CC perform a service for us by standardizing Santa, in an age when the egalitarian passion for homogeneity is ascendant? And if it did simply perform that service, why should it matter that it's CC that did so, rather than anyone else? It strikes me once more that CC's universality is only possible because it seems perfectly spineless, perfectly indifferent to content. Jolly red Santa has only become ubiquitous because he is nothing but a polished mirror in which—bowdlerized and defanged of whatever dark mischief he got up to during the middle ages—we find reflected the thin acquisitive mythology suitable to our cultural situation. And yet the fact remains that that mirror is brought to us by CC. When we invoke that Santa, that banal-benign childhood fixture—a character subject to such feverish speculation up until the disenchantment of the world circa age eight—must we not in some sense also invoke the original source of his personality along with him? Or is it that no clear-cut division between our holiday practices and his CC connection can be traced anymore?

The final exhibit allows visitors to taste a range of CC company drinks marketed to the idiosyncrasies of local palates from all different continents. CC itself remains everywhere the bestseller—and the company owns Fanta, Sprite and several other prominent soft drinks—but the CC company's portfolio stands at about 3,500 different beverages worldwide, and one gets the sense that they've gone out of their way to choose some of their most outlandish productions. Because, of course, the more unpalatable we find some niche concoction from Bangladesh or from Namibia, the greater the wonder that we all have a shared taste for the flagship product. But after two or three such unsavory discoveries, I concede I'm too tired to play the CC sommelier, and look for the way out.

Each visitor is handed an 8-ounce glass bottle of CC upon exiting the museum—a parting gift—only to then debouch into the gift-shop, where I can't but smile at myself as I stop to buy a few expensive postcards. When I'm finally outdoors again, I stand blinking for a few moments as my eyes adjust to the uncertainty of deep twilight. A numerous Indian family is arranging itself for a picture: each of them stretching out their souvenir bottle before them with deliberate, toothy grins. They are obviously modeling themselves after one of the CC ads they've seen inside, for a snapshot that will duly take its place in the 2012 Atlanta Family Vacation photo album. And so it goes.

I look up at the WCC's building, and try to make out whether its attractively streamlined aluminum style itself counts as "pop" or as "pop art" or as a pop imitation of pop art, until it again occurs to me that, as with the Norman Rockwell painting inside, the distinction is pointless tail-chasing. There is something unquestionably shabby about commercial advertising—its venal pandering, its demeaning, stultifying repetitiveness—the very thing that prevents an advertisement from, in principle, being a true work of art, a full expression of human freedom. But then my mind wanders to one of the best Frank O'Hara poems ("Having a Coke with You") and then scenes from some of my favorite films come tumbling along after it—from *Late Spring* (Noriko and Hattori memorably cycling by a CC ad) and *Nights of Cabiria* ("This car's got everything! Even Coca-Cola!") and *It's a Wonderful Life* (the CC ads in Mr. Gower's drugstore) and *Doctor Strangelove* ("You're going to have to answer to the Coca-Cola company!")—and I realize that it's all true. That the distinctions between advertising and art are no longer as impermeable as all that. That we can no longer assume today that certain commercial brands are any less universally present to our experience than the trees and the stones. That this silly sugar water is one of the things we have come to hold in common dominion—"Napoleon blew it, Hitler blew it, but Coca-Cola's gonna pull it off!" cracks Jimmy Cagney in *One, Two, Three*. That I now understand why I've paid and devoted time to watch this company's advertisements. That it's not just the World of Coca-Cola.

Derek Overfield, *Capaneus Scaling the Theban Walls*, 2013
Diptych canvas, 47" x 25"

OUTRAGE

by Cole Carter

WHENEVER I HEAR big political news I reflexively reach for my phone to check Twitter. I scroll down in the timeline to whenever the news—Thatcher is dead, an Excel error gave us austerity—first hit, and then scroll back up to watch the gradual emergence of right-thinking opinion among the left-liberal writers who make up my feed. I don't turn to Twitter to learn about the event, but to see how "we" feel about it. Through a series of tweets and retweets (some sincere endorsements, some meant to display the enemy in all his cravenness), a consensus gradually emerges, and after reaching the top and refreshing I can put my phone back in my pocket, happy to have a ready-made opinion to wield.

To get one's news in such a highly mediated fashion is clearly dangerous. The ersatz dialogue which occurs on Twitter can give the misleading impression that all opposing opinions have been given a fair hearing, and thus that the dominant opinion at the end of the day must be the inherently superior one. No need to weigh the various arguments yourself, Twitter already did the work for you. Touted for its promotion of decentralized and democratic dialogue, Twitter more often enables the rapid formulation and dissemination of orthodox opinion. At the same time, if you maintain a bit of critical distance, watching the construction of conventional wisdom on Twitter can teach you plenty. You can see which arguments trump others, which positions are taken to be unassailable, what affect works best. Taken as a whole, it's an unprecedented wealth of sociological data.

Observing Twitter in this way, one quickly notes that an addiction to outrage seems to afflict writers across the political spectrum. Opponents are castigated for being insufficiently scandalized by the atrocity of the hour, and authors of offending posts are roundly demonized and ridiculed. Silver linings are rarely sought in bad news, common ground with adversaries seldom found. The right is arguably more reliant on this Manichaean rhetoric, but the left has a strong habit too. As opinion crystallizes on Twitter, posters become increasingly uncompromising, attracted to whichever position most strongly attributes moral purity to their own side and depravity to the other. Meanwhile, anyone who would criticize an outraged writer's moralistic tone risks appearing too callous or naïve to realize the enormity of the crime at hand—whether it's Obama's visit to

171

an Amazon warehouse or a university's experimentation with MOOCs. Outrage may look like moral bravery but, on Twitter at least, it is safe as can be.

As an example, let's consider the Internet left's response to the Rana Plaza disaster in Bangladesh—or more accurately, the Internet left's response to Matt Yglesias's response to the Rana Plaza disaster. Yglesias is a frequent target of leftist outrage, which he intentionally courts and seems to relish. Within hours of the building collapse, Yglesias wrote a post on his *Slate* blog entitled "Different Places Have Different Safety Rules and That's OK," in which he argued that Bangladesh's lower workplace-safety standards are justifiable considering the country's reliance on cheap labor. Yglesias intended his post somewhat narrowly, as an argument against uniform international safety standards, but, quite rightly, it was interpreted in the broader context of the unfolding tragedy and quickly denounced for its gross insensitivity.

Yglesias's post was glib and tone-deaf, but the gleefully venomous response to it was absurd. Suddenly, the issue was not the disaster in Bangladesh—a true outrage if there ever was one—but Yglesias's apologia. "Does Matthew Yglesias Enjoy Murder?" asked the writer formerly known as Mobute Sese Seko in the title of a much-circulated piece. A crowd-funding page was set up to raise the money for Yglesias's one-way airfare to Dhaka. As the fatalities mounted in the following days, Yglesias was repeatedly taunted with tweets like "Reminder: the Rana Plaza building collapse death toll is over 800 and you still look like a sack of mayonnaise." Yglesias eventually apologized—rather ungraciously—but he continued to receive more scorn from Twitter's left than more culpable figures like, say, Sohel Rana and the fashion executives whose clothes the Rana Plaza workers died making.

The paroxysm of outrage distracted many leftist writers from the real issue, and caused them to miss an opportunity to say something about a world in which such disasters are just a cost of doing business. Those writers could have responded to what Yglesias actually wrote—it would have been easy enough to dispense with his arguments. They could have foregone the moralizing and instead argued for the global labor standards that Yglesias was dismissing. Instead, Twitter's left wing opted for shaming the outsider and elevating themselves. Forget how blithe and ill-considered Yglesias's position was—at least he set forth a political argument. By expressing only outrage, his critics risked nothing, but they also gained nothing, aside from Yglesias's reluctant retraction.

The world gives us no shortage of things to be outraged about, and in the right context outrage can be politically useful as well as morally appropriate. But outrage can also be reactive and unreasoned, and too often it leads us astray. It is understandable that the left, in its prolonged weakness, has come to rely on such defensive rhetoric. Over the past four decades, as unions were

busted, wealth redistributed upwards, and Iraq invaded—all with electoral sanction—the American left has had little to enjoy besides the sense of righteous
camaraderie which outrage can provide. But if the left has any ambitions for
the twenty-first century—if it hopes to bring about good, not just decry evil—it
must kick its outrage habit.

ONE RECENT EPISODE illustrates how reactionary outrage can mis-
guide and harm us, how it can cause us to marginalize ourselves and undermine our political goals. The resounding condemnation of *Zero Dark Thirty*
by the left-liberal establishment was not an inconsequential, Twitter-confined
tumult like the Yglesias affair. The scope and effectiveness of the campaign
against the film were truly impressive. *Zero Dark Thirty* was released to consider-
able anticipation and widespread critical acclaim, only to be rejected with unani-
mous outrage in the court of respectable political opinion. At the Oscars, after
enduring two months of attacks, the movie mustered just a single Sound Editing
award, which was almost more insulting than being shut out entirely.

Glenn Greenwald, a writer who has built his career on left-libertarian outrage, led the charge against *ZDT*, condemning it—by his own admission—before
he even saw the film. Greenwald didn't think he needed to wait for the movie
to be released. He agreed with Andrew Sullivan, who wrote that "the mere facts
about the movie, as reported by many viewers, do not require a review. They
demand a rebuttal." Those "facts" concern *ZDT*'s alleged misrepresentation of
the role of torture in the hunt for Osama bin Laden. *Zero Dark Thirty* suggests
that it did play a role, and for Greenwald and many others that meant *ipso facto*
that the film glorifies torture. Accordingly, *ZDT* was painted as propaganda.
The Green Berets for the War on Terror, and all respectable people quickly took
their distance. The film may be artfully made, said the critics, but it is morally
repugnant. The usually restrained Chris Hayes accused the filmmakers of "col-
luding with evil." In the *Guardian*, Naomi Wolf compared the director, Kathryn
Bigelow, to Leni Riefenstahl. Outrage became obligatory, attentive engagement
with the film was deemed unnecessary, and florid, moralizing takedowns mas-
queraded as reviews.

What troubled *ZDT*'s critics was the prospect that the film would convince
Americans that torture led directly to bin Laden's death, and thus that torture is
an indispensable part of the American security strategy. Critics of Bush's interrogation policies pointed out for years that the argument against torture should
not be based on the claim that it never works—such an argument concedes

Screenshot from *Zero Dark Thirty*, 2012

too much, and is almost certainly incorrect. Yet the critics of ZDT invariably reverted to the instrumental case against torture in their reviews of the film. They repeatedly insisted that torture did not contribute in any way to locating bin Laden, as if admitting that it did would scuttle their case. As Richard Beck noted in the *Los Angeles Review of Books*, this is shaky ground to stand on. It is impossibly naïve to believe that although the CIA may have been systematically torturing terror detainees for years, not one of those interrogations produced anything of relevance to the hunt for bin Laden. Leon Panetta, CIA director at the time of the bin Laden operation and no apologist for Bush's enhanced interrogation policies, told *Agence France-Presse* after seeing ZDT that "[T]here's no question that some of the intelligence gathered was a result of some of these methods."

The factual case against ZDT is therefore not as strong as its critics assert. But even if torture made only a minor contribution to the locating of bin Laden, would the critics really have preferred Bigelow to leave the CIA's torture program out of the film entirely? ZDT's focus is on the hunt for bin Laden, but it is also the first major film to grapple with the War on Terror in its full chronological and geographical expanse—to leave out the torture which all acknowledge became routine would have been to whitewash history.

Jane Mayer of the *New Yorker*, one of the best writers on Bush-era interrogation and detainment policy, made the common complaint that *Zero Dark Thirty* "sidestep[s] the political and ethical debate" that the torture program provoked, and describes the film as "a police procedural, devoid of moral context." Comparing ZDT unfavorably to *Lincoln*, she wrote that "if [Bigelow] were making a film about slavery in antebellum America, it seems, the story would focus on whether the cotton crops were successful." Mayer suggests that Bigelow could have provided the allegedly lacking moral context by depicting the internal debates on the legality and morality of torture that took place in the Pentagon and Justice Department. Never mind that this would have changed the focus of the film entirely, while also risking preachiness—is it really necessary that viewers be led by the hand through the moral case against torture? Can't they supply the moral context for themselves?

Furthermore, it is hardly the case, as critics like *Dissent*'s Brian Morton have claimed, that ZDT suggests torture is "virtually the *only* reliable means of gathering information from prisoners." The first major disclosure from a detainee is obtained by disorienting him with lies and plying him with food, after days of torture have failed. Vital information is also gained through bribery and surveillance. Regardless, it is foolish to judge the film solely on its portrayal of the efficacy of torture. Despite the monomania of the critics, the film asks a bigger question than whether or not torture is a useful interrogation technique.

Many of the film's subtleties were overlooked by critics whose views were jaundiced by outrage, but no scene has been more willfully misunderstood than the last. In the film's final moments, after bin Laden has been killed, Maya, the CIA agent at the center of the story, boards a plane to take her away from Pakistan. The pilot asks her, "Where do you want to go?" These are the last words spoken in the movie. Maya says nothing, and after a moment she begins to cry. Having obsessively pursued a single goal for nearly a decade, she is unable to say what she wants next. The scene could be criticized as heavy-handed had it not been so widely misinterpreted. Matt Taibbi refuses to see any "regret or ambivalence" in Maya's quiet weeping, telling anyone who does so that they are just reading it in. "The posters don't say 'WE SOLD OUR SOULS TO GET HIM,'" Taibbi writes, "they read, 'THE GREATEST MANHUNT IN HISTORY.'" Morton, in his review, asks a series of sarcastic rhetorical questions as to why Maya might be crying, then concludes: "Who knows? The movie gives us no clue about why she's crying, but it seems very deep." These two capable reviewers have let their outrage turn them into philistines, displaying their refusal to think seriously about the film as a badge of honor. They write as if we should take our cues on how to interpret a film from the promotional posters, as if it's unreasonable to ask the audience to grapple with the complexity of a character's emotions.

There is, of course, relief in Maya's tears, but there is no sense of triumph—the movie never gives us a moment of fist-pumping celebration, certainly not in this final scene where a lonely, neurotic woman bursts into tears after being asked such an apparently simple question. To me, Maya's reaction betrays a sense of purposelessness as the project to which she has dedicated years of her life comes to a close. That the filmmakers chose to end on such an emotionally ambivalent note suggests that they did not want the audience to leave the theater high-fiving one another, filled with unalloyed pride for those rough men standing ready to torture and maim those who would harm us. The film doesn't end with exultation—it ends with a reminder of "the desolate, empty nature of revenge," as Michael Wood put it in the *London Review of Books*. I think that the filmmakers wanted viewers, jarred by the film's purposeful anticlimax, to ask themselves the questions that the critics insisted the film was ducking, namely: Was it worth it? Were the crimes we committed, the wars, the paranoia, the militarization of civilian life, the international animosity, a fitting price to pay for the vindication we felt when that one man was shot dead in front of screaming women and children?

Popular Oscar-nominated films that ask such important questions do not come around very often. *ZDT* could have been a jumping-off point for a discussion of how the War on Terror has transformed our national life, but that opportunity was squandered for the pleasure of righteous outrage. *ZDT*'s detractors knew when watching the film that the death of bin Laden was not worth the brutality that the film depicts, but they could not imagine that the larger American audience would be sophisticated enough to think so critically. If, as the critics insist the film tells us, torture got bin Laden, then surely the American audience will be unable to resist the conclusion that torture is justified. As Beck wrote, the critics "imagine that 'real Americans' were being made tools of power through one of their most important social rites: moviegoing." Rather than engaging with those real Americans as intellectual and moral equals, the critics chose to embrace their own self-imposed alienation from the body politic, relishing the sense of moral superiority which their manufactured outrage produced.

I T IS NATURAL that, after the traumas of the Bush years, the left is easily piqued by anything that suggests approval of torture, or that expresses support for our belligerent post-9/11 foreign policy. But the reception of *Zero Dark Thirty* revealed that the left's outrage reflex is overdeveloped, causing us to miss political opportunities and mistake friends for foes. Instead of engaging ZDT and its vast audience, we drew in our ranks as if under attack and congratulated ourselves for our elevated sensibilities while implicitly condemning the unfeeling multitude who shored up the status quo by remaining silent. If the left maintains this clannish, defensive posture, it will be difficult to bring about the political changes we desire. The politics of outrage is devoid of transformative potential because it is necessarily reactive—if we start a political conversation with outrage, then we have started it on the enemy's turf. Even Reagan, a master of backlash politics during his tenure as governor of California, realized that he had to strike a gentler, more aspirational pose in order to successfully advance a national political agenda. Outrage may be useful for marshaling the true believers, but the fellow travelers who make up the bulk of any movement must be won over with sweeter stuff. The Twitter-enabled spasms of leftist outrage over the latest neoliberal plot are not aimed at winning converts by stirring the consciences of those outside the fold. Rather, their reward is the satisfaction that comes with identifying oneself as one of the initiated, someone who recognizes certain pieties and reacts appropriately when they have been violated.*

---

* Penny Lewis gives an example of the self-marginalizing effect of leftist outrage in her recent book on the anti-Vietnam War movement, *Hardhats, Hippies, and Hawks*. Lewis tells us that the moralistic rhetoric of many protesters ("Hey, hey, LBJ, how many kids did you kill today?") made

Kyung Sunghyun, Untitled, 2010

But the left's politics of outrage is not only ineffective as a rhetorical tactic—it fundamentally misrepresents issues of great importance. Look again at the response to *Zero Dark Thirty*. Brian Morton ended his *Dissent* review by stating that "of all the ways in which our political culture has changed since 9/11, the widespread acceptance of torture may be the most profound." This is a bizarre claim. First, though support for torture has gone up since 9/11, the most recent and widely cited poll still shows that a majority of Americans oppose practices such as waterboarding and the chaining of naked prisoners. Second, President Obama's executive order of January 22nd, 2009 explicitly banned such practices, which suggests that the supposed pro-torture transformation of our political culture may be a bit overstated. Here, outrage needlessly marginalizes the leftist critic, who could count large numbers of Americans—including the President!—among his allies if he wished.

Outrage can also cause us to misrepresent or mythologize the past. Morton, for instance, claims that before 9/11, our alleged toleration of torture would have been unthinkable. "*We were a people who didn't torture*—whether or not this has ever been completely true, it was a bedrock element of our idea of ourselves." As Samuel Moyn pointed out in a magnificent essay on the politics of torture in *The Nation*, this story of regression doesn't match the historical record. Moyn tells us that torture's current status as an unspeakable taboo is actually quite recent, tracing its origins to the international human rights movement, which gained steam following the end of decolonization in the early 1970s. Throughout the early twentieth century, and for centuries before, colonial Western powers (the French in Algeria, the British in Malaya, and yes, the United States in the Philippines) were torturing their subjects with hardly a twinge of guilt. Only when newly independent native rulers began to practice the interrogation techniques they had learned while fighting in colonial armies did Westerners enshrine torture as the most unspeakable of moral horrors. And even after Amnesty International got going, as Morton clearly knows, torturers operated with American support throughout the Seventies and Eighties in the Cold War's post-colonial hotspots.

---

it difficult for some working-class sympathizers to identify with the anti-war movement. It seemed to these reluctant activists that the protesters were not only denouncing the war, they were judging "the soldiers, their families, people who supported the president or believed in the country." These "real Americans" weren't incorrigible hawks—as Lewis shows, there was much stronger anti-war sentiment in the working class than is typically acknowledged—but they objected to the protesters' presumption of moral authority, their "sitting on high and telling everyone else how to live their lives." Working-class Americans became more involved in the anti-war movement as the war dragged on, but in its early years the movement was a decidedly middle-class undertaking, its social base limited in part by its histrionic outrage.

Neglecting this sordid history, and projecting one's own ideals backwards onto a supposedly more virtuous past, leads to a politics of stifling moralism. There is no pre-lapsarian state that our government could return to if only we shame it into doing so. As Mark Fisher, citing Wendy Brown, pointed out in a recent blog post for Verso, the rhetoric of outrage suggests that the state is a sort of "momentarily misguided parent" rather than "a codification of various dominant social powers." The democratic nation-state has never lived up to its legitimating ideology of egalitarian liberalism. Simply pointing out this perennial inconsistency is not helpful. The state has always operated under the influence of those with a vested interest in the injustice of contemporary social arrangements—concessions have been won only with great effort and at great expense. To think otherwise is to misunderstand the historical role of the left as well as the contemporary political scene. Our project is not a defensive, juridical one—it requires constructive, political action. If we want a world without torture, indefinite detainment and assassination, we have to build it.

Yet the left cannot afford to limit itself to such clear-cut moral issues. The left's taste for outrage encourages a minimalist politics which, as a result of a triage of an almost unlimited supply of atrocities, seeks to curb only the most willful and obvious abuses of power. As the possibility of transforming society has receded, the left has contented itself with condemning the worst aspects of the present system. Moyn tells this story of shrunken ambitions in his *Nation* essay. During the Reagan years, as the Old and New Lefts fell into disarray, writers like Judith Shklar, Richard Rorty and Elaine Scarry crafted a new, more modest program for American liberalism—not to establish an empire of liberty or build a Great Society, but simply to minimize suffering and cruelty. This brass-tacks utilitarianism might have felt refreshingly pragmatic coming after the bombast and empty theorizing that characterized the campus left of the 1970s, but it cannot anchor a political movement. It does not explain what causes suffering in our society, and it does not help us to envision a less cruel world. It gives its adherents no practical political orientation—just the command to do no harm.

This contentless ideology underwrites the reactive moralism on display in the response to *Zero Dark Thirty*. Lacking a robust sense of historical purpose, the American left only feels sure of itself when it stands in opposition to obvious atrocities like torture. The passion devoted to these moral issues makes up for a loss of conviction on other fronts. But we shouldn't let our defeats discourage us so thoroughly. As Moyn says, we cannot "allow the worst that our governments have done to continue to distract us from the task of imagining and enacting the best we can make them do after the emergency is over." We have to give our political imaginations more freedom than the politics of outrage will allow.

BUT A REVIVED utopianism will amount to nothing if the left doesn't change the way it relates to the American people. The most troubling aspect of the response to *Zero Dark Thirty* was the deep distrust of average Americans exhibited by the film's detractors. Convinced that the film would dupe the American public into supporting torture just as it was duped into supporting the invasion of Iraq ten years before, the critics sought to discredit the film before it could corrupt its credulous audience. Moviegoers were treated as wayward children unable to make their own judgments.

The critics assumed that there was a moral gulf between themselves and the average viewer of *Zero Dark Thirty*, who would no doubt be all too susceptible to the violent jingoism the film was supposedly peddling. They imagined the theaters filled with members of the "silent majority," constitutionally conservative people always willing to support our country's military adventures in the name of national honor. The Republicans have been winning elections while invoking the support of these "real" Americans since 1968, so it is understandable that some on the left have come to believe that our country must be inherently right wing after all. Embittered by the repeated betrayals of the American electorate, many on the left have ceded populism to the right and have grown comfortable with their marginal political position, their sense of purity making up for an absence of influence.

Such parochialism is harmful and unnecessary, especially when a window of opportunity seems to be opening for the left. The culture wars are subsiding, and demographic trends are in our favor. The right has run out of external enemies to accuse us of appeasing. The Communists are gone, and the "Islamofascists" will not replace them. The specter of "actually existing socialism" no longer haunts us. Economic inequality is once again seen as an injustice, one that hundreds of thousands will take to the streets to protest. In the years of austerity ahead, the left will find a receptive audience in the underemployed, overworked and indebted. If we pay attention to the problems that affect these "real" Americans, try to explain the origins of those problems and put forward a vision of a better society, we might be able to develop a new left populism. Instead of conceiving of ourselves as the conscience of a morally blind nation, we could start to see ourselves as a political movement, capable of building ideologically diverse coalitions and implementing progressive policies.

If the left wants to be a political force in the not-too-distant future it has to learn to see allies, not adversaries, in the American people. If we want to give their disaffection political expression, we have to learn to speak with confidence. Pedantic moralizing won't mobilize Americans. Listening to them might. People are ready for something new—and if the left doesn't give it to them, others will.

Boris Pelcer, *Enlightenment*, 2013

ENLIGHTENED

by Jon Baskin

THE NAÏVE VIEWER of HBO's remarkable and now-defunct tragicomedy, *Enlightened*, may be forgiven for assuming, having gone through the first four or five episodes, that the show's title is meant as a joke at the expense of its protagonist. After all, there could hardly seem a less enlightened "hero" than Amy Jellicoe (Laura Dern), whom we meet at the start of episode one crying her eyeliner out after being transferred from her division at a Los Angeles-based pharmaceutical company, partly for sleeping with her boss. Following a baroque meltdown in the hallways of the office, Amy adjourns to a Hawaiian retreat, Open Air, where she claims to receive a life-altering wisdom. But the show really begins with her return to L.A., where she endeavors, with a sunny obliviousness broken by temper tantrums and occasional fits of self-reflection, to apply that wisdom to her everyday life.

The first several episodes all follow what becomes a familiar arc, commencing with Amy expressing hope about some aspect of her new life (getting her job or her ex-husband back, making a new friend, starting work at a homeless shelter, etc.), and concluding with her disappointment—and often her rage—when things do not work out as she had planned. Both the hope and the disappointment are typically articulated in Amy's lucid, sentimental, and often surprisingly moving voiceovers, beginning with her statement of purpose, set to a montage of nature images and men and women cavorting around a bonfire on a beach in Hawaii:

> I'm speaking with my true voice now. Without bitterness or fear. And I'm here to tell you, you can walk out of hell and into the light. You can wake up to your higher self. And when you do, the world is suddenly full of possibility, of wonder, and deep connection. You can be wise. You can be patient. ... You don't have to run away from life your whole life. You can really live. You *can* change. And you can be an agent of change.

The speech is remarkable for its frantic combination of nearly every variety of new age pabulum. Yet such an observation may not protect the viewer entirely from hearing, behind Amy's words, the always-inspiring vibration of a human being desiring to change her ways. In fact the voiceover demonstrates all on its own what the show itself will go on to exhibit at length: the potential of virtually every word we speak about enlightenment to be delusional, superficial, fraudulent, empty—and at the same time to be sincere, courageous, rich with the possibility of spiritual transformation or awakening.

I have spoken to detractors of *Enlightened* who believe that director Mike White does New Age movements a disservice by presenting as their representative such an obviously compromised individual. But White has not made a show about the select few able to devote decades to training under a guru or perfecting their meditation posture at monasteries. He has made a show about the much larger subgroup of Americans who, having limited resources and time, seek nevertheless to transform their lives in accordance with the highest principles. Amy is an illustrative, if slightly exaggerated, representative of this demographic, and the show does more than justice to the way such a person will tend to be viewed by those around her. Amy's ex-husband Levi (Luke Wilson), her mother Helen (Diane Ladd), her co-workers Tyler (Mike White) and Krista (Sarah Burns), all share the naïve viewer's initial suspicions, interpreting Amy's lectures about change, fulfillment and the search for a better world as thin screens for her narcissism, emotional neediness and desire for revenge. "I just don't want to jeopardize everything because you're pissed about your life," Tyler complains when she tries to enlist him in her plan to bring down Abaddonn, the company they both work for. His worry is echoed and amplified by Amy's mother and by the *LA Times* journalist, Jeff Flender (Dermot Mulroney), who asks her what kind of "revenge play" is motivating her attempt to sell him on a corporate whistleblowing story in Season Two.

Neither the viewer nor Amy's friends and family are unwarranted in their suspicions. Amy *is* paranoid, impatient and almost criminally self-involved. At night, she entertains violent fantasies about those who treat her poorly, and dreams of others she is convinced live free of anguish, all the time failing to see how she herself contributes to the anguish of those closest to her. The genius of *Enlightened* is just that it lays bare a soul, like most souls, in which the narrowest of passions bump up against the most noble of aspirations. Indeed it shows how the process of enlightenment itself, or the yearning for it, can bring out simultaneously the best and the worst in us. On the one hand, the desire for personal betterment exacerbates in Amy the sins of self-involvement and self-delusion. At the same time, Amy's idealism, her hope for herself and for the world, seem slowly to work a change in her and those around her, prompting them to examine whether the lives they lead are really as satisfying or as full as they might be. "You saw something in me that didn't exist, or maybe it did" Levi admits in Season Two, "Maybe *you're* my higher power."

Enlightened was billed by HBO as a comedy, and at times it can be very funny—especially in the scenes set at Abaddonn, which unspool in the deadpan register of *The Office* or *Office Space*. But White has ultimately lit his world with a different kind of light. Consistent with the show's emphasis on transformation, the camera itself proves capable of converting suburban driveways, office parking lots and chain-restaurant dining rooms into sites for reflection no less provoking than the Pyramids or Walden Pond. ("People drive by here and they see a school and a field," Levi observes in Season Two, as he and Amy sit in the bleachers of a familiar baseball field near their homes, "I see heaven ... and hell.") Meanwhile, the voiceovers magnetize the episodes up out of the realm of easy sarcasm and into the vicinity of hard and pertinent questions: What is the relation between personal betterment and the betterment of society? Is self-improvement really separable from narcissism? And what anyway *is* enlightenment?

T HAT LAST QUESTION is addressed, famously, in a short essay by Kant ("An Answer to the Question: What is Enlightenment?"). As usual, and with liberal use of italics, Kant gets right to the point:

> *Enlightenment is man's emergence from his self-incurred immaturity.* Immaturity is the inability to use one's own understanding without the guidance of another. This immaturity is *self-incurred* if its cause is not lack of understanding, but lack of resolution and courage to use it without the guidance of another. The motto of enlightenment is therefore: *Sapere Aude!* Have courage to use your own understanding.

Although all men are in theory capable, Kant goes on to say, of overcoming their immaturity by means of their reason, only a few are actually trained to take advantage of their freedom. Consistent with the optimism and faith in progress that characterized his time, however, Kant believed that not just the elitely educated but the wider public, too, would eventually enlighten itself, so long as "artificial measures" were not devised to keep them in a state of unfreedom. We may not live in an enlightened age, he declaimed, but "we do live in an age of *enlightenment*." Everyone would soon have the option of becoming enlightened; all it would take was courage, a good will, and the desire to shake off one's chains.

Enlightened bears witness to the fact that we continue to live in an age of enlightenment (the show makes a punch line out of Open Air's hefty price tag, but the retreat operates on principles that will be familiar to most viewers from local yoga classes, free meditation centers, Alcoholics Anonymous, and the self-help sections of neighborhood bookstores), although whether Kant would recognize it as such is an open question. When Kant speaks of enlightenment, he takes his bearings from the European movement to reform society along the lines of reason and science—and against the dogmas of authority, tradition and faith. Although addressing himself initially to the individual (*Sapere Aude!*), Kant thus primarily conceives of enlightenment as a collective project, capable of freeing society from the domination of church and crown and spawning in their place encyclopedias, schools of philosophy and a free and mature politics of self-governance. In the twentieth century, various European detractors of Kant's idea of enlightenment (Adorno and Horkheimer, Foucault) objected that the historical Enlightenment was neither as rational nor as reliably progressive as its advocates pretended—but they did not question the premise that the *goal* was the rationality, or maturity, of society as a whole.

In America, however—as Tocqueville noted repeatedly—enlightenment did not develop in *opposition* to religion, nor was it conjoined with a practical political science or with efforts to improve social literacy and living standards. Instead it was ever linked to the spiritual project of awakening or (what Jonathan Edwards called) Great Awakening—a project that took it almost as its duty, one might say, to liberate the individual from the dreamworld that the Enlightenment had wrought. This is not to imply only that American thinkers privileged the individual over the political—although Thoreau did believe the time had come for men to attend to the *res privata* with the vigor they had formerly reserved for the *res publica*—but also that they prescribed for both the individual *and* society not knowledge or understanding so much as energy, intensity, zeal. "Sleep lingers all our lifetime about our eyes, as night hovers all day in the boughs of the fir-tree," wrote Emerson, in a passage of "Experience" that would be answered at the close of that archetypal book of the American Enlightenment, Thoreau's *Walden*:

> We are sound asleep nearly half our time ... I do not say that John or Jonathan will realize all this; but such is the character of that morrow which mere lapse of time can never make to dawn. The light which puts out our eyes is darkness to us. Only that day dawns to which we are awake. There is more day to dawn. The sun is but a morning star.

The idea seems to be that, in America, to fail to live one's life is not so much to fail to make use of one's understanding as to fail, so to speak, to get up in

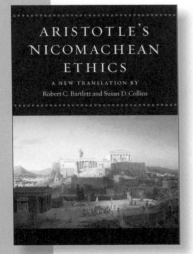

the morning—with the alternative being not ignorance or backwardness but lethargy, sleepwalking, or (what Emerson called) conformity.*

But how do we know if we have gotten up in the morning? The danger and obscurity of the American form of enlightenment have to do with the ambiguity of its criteria for fulfillment. If enlightenment does not show itself in stable scientific knowledge or social progress, then how can we distinguish it from its fraudulent (or merely benighted) imitators? *Enlightened* is studded with scenes of Amy waking up to her alarm clock, but as viewers we are prompted simultaneously to ask whether she has really *awoken*, say, to "that morrow which mere lapse of time can never make to dawn"—or, as she again puts it, to her "higher self." Perhaps one *can* change—but does *she*?

W HAT SAVES *ENLIGHTENED* from ever falling into didacticism, or full-fledged parody, is its circumspection in relation to precisely this question. Moreover, it repeatedly dramatizes the tension between Amy's commitment to her inner awakening and her desire to "wake up" her society. Frequently, Amy's quest to become an "agent of change" is shown to distract her from her own unfinished process of self-improvement, or becomes an excuse for her to discontinue it. The two projects even require contradictory virtues. To improve the world, Amy needs to be self-assured, combative, single-minded and sometimes ruthless. To change herself, she has to learn to question her motives and to accept ambiguity and doubt, a process that culminates at the beginning of the final episode, when she asks, "Am I my higher self? Or am I in the mud? Am I an agent of change? Or a creator of chaos? Am I the fool? The goat? The witch? Or am I ... enlightened?"

She is both and all, as any watcher of the show by then knows—although this is a knowledge that is for Amy hard won. The first season of *Enlightened* is largely about Amy's attempt to transform herself *completely*, banishing all that is inconvenient or complicated for the ideal version of herself she envisions in the aftermath of Open Air. "We can be free of our sad stories ... and what's left is pure life," she reflects, drifting down a river in a kayak with her ex-husband Levi

---

* I am limiting myself here to distinguishing between American and European notions of enlightenment; of course an even wider chasm separates Western from Eastern notions. To some extent, though, the American version of enlightenment can be read as a Western appropriation, or application, of the Eastern version; certainly Thoreau and Emerson both drew heavily from Eastern source material—as do the majority of today's native New Age programs.

in episode four. "Every single thing can be transformed." The scene is followed by a blow-up with Levi over his drug use, after which the two of them abandon the camping trip for a cheap motel in town where Levi can get high. By the end of the episode, Amy acknowledges that, "you can try to escape the story of your life, but you can't. It happened. My story isn't the one I would have chosen in the beginning, but I'll take it. It's my story."

The final lines are delivered back in the garden of her suburban childhood home, where she has lived with her mother since returning from Hawaii. The garden serves as a visual touchstone, often opening and closing episodes, and representing the past that Amy so desperately wants to get free of. Throughout the season she alternates between dwelling in that past and dismissing it; the words, "I'll take it, it's my story," thus resonate as progress as she looks out over the familiar flowers and the swimming pool that no one ever uses, which the camera reminds us contain a certain beauty, even as they remind Amy of all she considers stultifying and belittling about her backstory. One aspect of Amy's personal enlightenment would then be the acceptance of what is familiar and native, alongside the "new world" she always imagines existing at the opposite pole from where she stands. To "awaken" in this sense (a very Transcendentalist one) is to see what is meaningful about whatever ground happens to be beneath one's feet.

Season Two, at once snappier and less quixotic than Season One, revolves (with the notable exception of episode three, the masterfully told tale of Levi's visit to Open Air) around Amy's attempt to expose wrongdoing at Abaddonn, a crusade she places in the context of the failure of the American economy. Amy's platitudes about wealth inequality and corruption ("People are living under the illusion that the American dream is working for them, and it's not. Because it's rigged by the guys at the top") are redeemed somewhat by the risks she takes in attempting actually to do something about them. Nevertheless the issue of Amy's motivation continues to yank her public mission back into the domain of the *res privata*. At times in Season Two, Amy is motivated by revenge, personal passion (for Jeff), and megalomania. At one point she is described (not without some justification) as a "mental patient," while Jeff asks if she is an idealist, a do-gooder or just someone who "wants to have her name in the paper."*

---

* As viewers, too, we may be prompted to question our motives and passions as we watch the story in Season Two unfold. In the final episode, Amy says she feels "satisfaction" as she gets to see the Abaddonn CEO Charles Szidon (James Rebhorn) flip out over her "betrayal"—and that feeling of satisfaction may spread to the viewer. But what are we taking satisfaction from? Person-ally, I took satisfaction from watching the smug and powerful brought low. Is that how someone *enlightened* would feel?

Nevertheless, there are moments in Season Two where it seems Amy will get everything she dreams of: the destruction of Abaddonn, a fulfilling relationship with Jeff, entrance into a new, politically active world where "things happen." "Can you make your own heaven in this life?" Amy wonders. "Can you really get all you ever wanted?" Predictably, much of Amy's expectation is disappointed—Jeff drifts away as the story goes to press, while Amy's relationships with her mother and ex-husband remain complex and troubled. Less predictably, Amy herself begins to question the wisdom of her starry-eyed aspirations. "I'm waiting for my new life to start. Abaddonn is over. My past is over," she tells Jeff over the phone in the penultimate episode, but her voice is wistful, unsure. "That's a good thing," Jeff responds. It was Jeff's assuredness that had attracted Amy, his single-minded focus on exposing evil and enlightening the world. But, having gone through with her plan to expose the company she works for, Amy has begun to perceive the false comfort in such self-certainties.* To challenge authority, she begins to realize, entails having the courage (as Kant might say) to think for herself—not simply to substitute one set of truisms for another.

Enlightened has the courage and resolution to conclude there, with an Amy who is not sure about anything, least of all her own enlightenment. Even in the somewhat rushed finale (which bears the scars of White's not knowing whether HBO would grant him a third season), Amy falls prey to some of her worst old temptations, in one scene verbally assaulting her coworker Krista in the hospital on what turns out to be a false pretext, while in others demonstrating a poise and composure that would have been unthinkable in Season One. It is as if the show wants to leave us with the idea that there is ultimately no way of being certain whether the quest for enlightenment is indeed one long and futile charade, or whether it is the only thing capable of rescuing us from a long and futile charade. And perhaps there is no way of being *certain*. One may suspect that *Enlightened* seeks to recommend enlightenment to its viewers at least insofar as it paints a dark and daunting picture of a life lived in its absence.

Unfortunately for us, we are now compelled to live in the absence of *Enlightened*, which was canceled last fall by HBO after only two seasons. One wonders if it would have enjoyed a longer run had White chosen a more appealing protagonist. Amy was, in many respects, the opposite of the charismatic heroes and heroines of the new television: Tony Soprano, Don Draper, Walter White, Hannah Horvath. Such figures demand our attention despite treating others

---

* Her growth in this area is expressed by the final decision she makes, to go see her ex-husband, Levi, rather than Jeff, after getting fired from her job. The two of them sit together on the old, familiar steps outside his apartment. "I've just done something crazy," she tells him. "What else is new?" he replies.

poorly and doing little to improve the world (often the opposite). In contrast, Amy tried to do good, and to improve as a person, yet she alienated not just her acquaintances on the show but also—judging from the ratings—most potential viewers of it. Well, the enlightened are often annoying. The light which puts out our eyes is darkness to us.

1994

by Megan Walsh

PEOPLE THINK ABOUT 1994 now because Kurt Cobain died then, which causes one to squint through the year, misremembering the end of that era as encompassing all of it. It has always struck me that 1994 ought to be one of those years we commemorate, though there's nothing so momentous as Cobain's death to put a point on the thing that it was. I'm older now, which has let me look at the year as a body of work, as opposed to from within it, which was how I experienced it the first time around. At eleven, 1994 was the first year I could be present in culture with any sophistication. Still naïve to the blunt devices at its foundation, I could begin to appreciate its finer-grained offerings beyond blue raspberry breakfast flakes and syndicated sitcoms. I was in sixth grade, allowed to come home by myself, and summarily inculcated into the (at the time) sunflower bedecked halls of mtv, which that year presented *The Real World San Francisco* and a universe of twenty-somethings whose middle-diction presentations of melodramatic events perfectly matched in content, tone, and stakes, the body of mtv's musical programming (Pearl Jam, "Better Man"; Lisa Loeb, "Stay (I Missed You)"). The symmetry there was not necessarily different from a present-day *Real World* hot tub molestation scored by Katy Perry, except for a reasonable-human-adult quality that you could get behind. The media's soundtracks, myths and fabrics reinforced one another to such an extent that an interaction with any one of them secured an entry into the larger narrative. *Pete and Pete*'s house band and left of the dial guests populated the pantheon of its New Weird universe; the lyrical meanderings and persona of Gavin Rossdale were indistinct from Jordan Catalano's illiterate subplot on *My So-Called Life*; Juliana Hatfield was an umbrella over everything, appearing spectrally on both shows to confer the ideal of early-Nineties femininity through breathy mumblings and bunched up sweater sleeves.

The parents on *My So-Called Life*—remarkable among TV parents in being allowed to have inner lives—were banner members of the larger intergenerational love-fest of 1994. They made a second Woodstock in August of 1994, and seemed to be making a second Woodstock in general throughout the year. Shannon Hoon wandered the scene as if to prove it. Bellbottoms, John Lennon sunglasses and British rock were back, and consumer fashion tried to cut mod London looks of the late Sixties into slippery rayon. Baby boomers by now had more than just a "Touch of Gray"; they had the *Big Chill* in its own anniversary editions. Boomers passed a baton to the youth with Woodstock '94, sponsored by Pepsi, and they passed the great kidney stone of their midlife crises in *Forrest Gump*, also released that year. 1994 would be among the first system-wide swells of nostalgia we engaged in culturally, and by now we have reiterated this pattern for every discernable unit of thetwentieth century. The need to frantically recycle past decades became more and more piquant as the late Nineties ushered out any semblance of temporal identity on a cloud of html code, but by '94 the urge was already there. The alternative music peak of 1994 that brought Beck's *Mellow Gold* and Weezer's blue album also initiated the genre's decline. Afterwards, white people would lose any market share they once held in the realm of articulating authenticity, parceling it out into smaller and smaller shares until the indie cred contingent of the early 00s studied its taxidermied remains like beleaguered academics.

As a sixth grader entering into the cultural landscape of 1994, the terrain ahead looked promising. The bratty chords that tumble into "When I Come Around" and the melancholic swell of "Found Out About You" defined the terms of the contract I thought I was making with music. I saw before me a landscape of teenagers in motley subcultures that could be decoded in a language of sneakers. Their Vedder-via-Beavis and Butthead ethos seemed awfully swell from within the first buds of my alienation, and I reasoned that "alternative" would offer a helpful canopy to park under, given the guaranteed shunting I would receive from the Mariah Carey set. Having no sturdy archive of the past, I wouldn't have known to think of 1994 as a unique moment of cultural jibe: I welcomed the future, and felt confident that culture would sustain that year's variegated and faintly delicious offerings for the long run.

You wouldn't have noticed 1995-1996 as distinctly different from 1994, but as the years age, you can see evidence of the first stitchings-in of the following era. By the time *Clueless* came out in 1995, Paul Rudd's socially conscious slacker already seemed anachronistic, and when Brittany Murphy shed her flannel in favor of the newly ubiquitous baby tee, girls all over America were inclined to take her cue. The apocalyptic horses that foretold the end of days for the mid-Nineties weren't Trojan; Scary Spice plainly zigazigged alternative and its ilk right out of existence. But it wasn't bubble gum that initiated the glum autumn of my relationship with culture; rather something in the eighth or ninth month of the "Mo Money, Mo Problems" juggernaut. By now I see the song's message ironically embedded in the dot-com/credit nonsense banquet that laid the groundwork for the Reagan-Eighties Aughts, but something about that song's chrome-smooth sheen and hybrid appeal seemed impenetrable and portentously pregnant even then. It was a watertight feat of industry cross-pollination to cast off all previous cultural amalgams as sheer juvenilia, to lend them an air of the naïve or ridiculous. It made it clear that nothing would be not-it ever again.

In conversations with people three or four years older or younger than me, it strikes me that those of us who were, say, ages 9–13 in 1994 remain on a little boat together, having glimpsed a period that pre-consciously knew itself to be the twentieth century's wake. Maybe what sets us apart from those who came before and after is that we were partially but not fully formed before being passed through the analog-digital converter of 1997. Anyone who ever made a mix tape off the radio in the early Nineties, pirating in the vogue of the day, knows the sensation of clipping culture like coupons in the moment of pressing "stop" too late and catching an errant commercial or a DJ's vociferous outro. If you listened to the tape enough, the ad or phrase could become so interlinked with the song that it would prompt it in any associated hearing. There is something of that temporality and physicality left in our non-generation, and it strikes me that that's probably the place where we will be stored in the archives: not quite an entry on the mix tape of that century, but as a sticky remnant clipped into the end-static, our presence always a cue to rewind.

SOURCES

NO SUCH THING?

F. A. Hayek, *The Road to Serfdom*
Albert O. Hirschmann, *The Passions and the Interests*
Plato, *Republic*
Adam Smith, *The Wealth of Nations*
R. H. Tawney, *Religion and the Rise of Capitalism*

ON NOT KNOWING WHAT YOU'RE DOING

George Lakoff & Mark Johnson, *Metaphors We Live By*
Naomi Quinn, "'Commitment' in American Marriage: A Cultural Analysis"
Mark Johnson, *Moral Imagination*

PERILOUS AESTHETICS

Tom Junod, "The Falling Man"
Susan Sontag, *Regarding the Pain of Others*

JOINERS AND QUITTERS

Gustav Landauer, "On Marriage"
Erich Mühsam, "Women's Rights"

THE LONELY INTELLECTUAL

Theodor Adorno, *Minima Moralia* and "The Essay as Form"
David Shields, *Reality Hunger* and *How Literature Saved My Life*

NATURAL LAWS

Aristotle, *Nicomachean Ethics*
Aldous Huxley, *Brave New World*
Friedrich Nietzsche, *Beyond Good and Evil*

LOOKING BACK

Christopher Lasch, *The Culture of Narcissism* and *The New Radicalism in America* and *The True and Only Heaven*

OUTRAGE

Samuel Moyn, "Torture and Taboo"
Zero Dark Thirty (2012)

PREY

Harold Brodkey, "A Guest in the Universe"
Annie Dillard, *Holy the Firm*
Janet Malcolm, *The Journalist and the Murderer*

ENLIGHTENED

Immanuel Kant, "An Answer to the Question: What is Enlightenment?"
Ralph Waldo Emerson, "Experience"
Henry David Thoreau, *Walden*

CONTRIBUTORS

Timothy Aubry *is a professor of English at Baruch College. His most recent book is* Reading as Therapy: What Contemporary Fiction Does for Middle-Class Americans *(2011). His essay "Sizing Up Oprah" appeared in Issue 4 of* The Point.

Antón Barba-Kay *teaches philosophy at Catholic University in Washington, D.C.*

Jeremy Bell *is a Ph.D. student in the University of Chicago's Committee on Social Thought.*

Sam Brody *is Visiting Assistant Professor in the Department of Judaic Studies at the University of Cincinnati. His research involves the relationship of religion, politics and philosophy in the Abrahamic traditions.*

Cole Carter *is a student at Harvard Law School.*

Cammi Climaco *is a visual artist and humorist based in New York City.*

Charles Comey *is a Ph.D. student in the University of Chicago's Committee on Social Thought. His article "A Plea for Human Food" appeared in Issue 6 of* The Point.

Justin Evans *is a writer living in Los Angeles. His article on J. M. Coetzee ("Problems with Authority") appeared in Issue 4 of* The Point.

Michael J. Kramer *teaches history, American studies and digital humanities at Northwestern University. He is the author of* The Republic of Rock: Music and Citizenship in the Sixties Counterculture *(2013).*

Mark Hopwood *is a Ph.D. student in the Philosophy Department at the University of Chicago. He is writing a dissertation on the relationship between love and moral agency.*

Katharine Smyth *is a writer living in New York. She recently completed her first book, a memoir about her father.*

Barrett Swanson *has written essays and short fiction for* Avery Anthology, The Millions, In These Times, Salt Hill *and* American Short Fiction. *He is at work on a novel and a book about aesthetics.*

Clarisse Thorn *is a feminist sex writer. She is the author of* Confessions of a Pickup Artist Chaser *(2012) and a collection of essays entitled* The S&M Feminist *(2012). Her review of* Burning Man *appeared in Issue 6 of* The Point.

Megan Walsh *is a writer living in Brooklyn.*

Alex Worsnip *is a Ph.D. candidate and Teaching Fellow in the Philosophy Department at Yale University. He has written features and reviews for numerous publications including* Prospect.

THE POINT

COMING IN ISSUE EIGHT:

Rousseau and the Ethics of Eating

•

What is the Media for?

•

Experience as Art

•

Norman Rush

SUBSCRIBE AT

WWW.THEPOINTMAG.COM

$18 FOR ONE YEAR (2 ISSUES)
$32 FOR TWO YEARS (4 ISSUES)

BACK ISSUES AVAILABLE

LOVE IN THE AGE OF THE PICKUP ARTIST	THE CONSOLATIONS OF SELF-HELP	HARD FEELINGS	PREDATORY HABITS
"i first turned to the pickup artists after losing in love"	"it was my life coach who first introduced me to eckhart tolle"	"michel houellebecq has published four novels, all of them bitter and miserable"	"amidst nature's unreasonable scarcity, wall street often seems like a refuge of reason"

WHAT IS *THE POINT* FOR?

- *The Point is for anybody who is frustrated with the intellectual poverty of the majority of today's journalism and public discourse.*

- *The Point is for serious, and seriously entertaining, essays on contemporary subjects like video games, steroids, self-help and Wall Street.*

- *The Point is for helping you think about your everyday life—how to parent, how to love, how to protest, how to read Marx.*

- *The Point is for reviews of new art, theater, literature and events— the kind you want to read long after you've seen or read the reviewed thing.*

We love publishing *The Point*, and we thank you for buying this issue and helping us keep going. However, we are a small print magazine operating in an environment that is not always hospitable to our brand of long-form writing. Editors, copy editors, artists—we all work for free. With that in mind, please consider donating to *The Point*. We promise to use your money wisely to improve the quality of our magazine and to compensate our great writers.

If you have any questions, please don't hesitate to contact us by email at **admin@thepointmag.com**. Thanks again for buying *The Point*!

The Editors

Jon Baskin
Jonny Thakkar
Etay Zwick

Thank you!

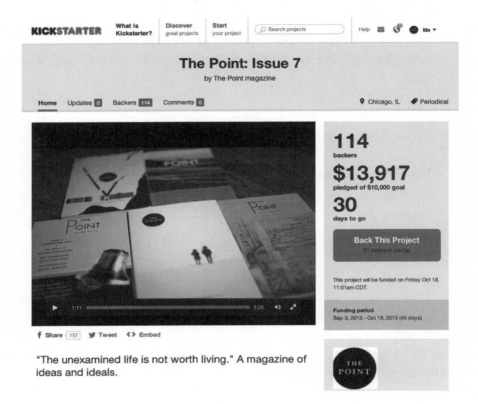

The Editors

Jon Baskin
Jonny Thakkar
Etay Zwick